The Wired City

THE WIRED CITY

REIMAGINING JOURNALISM
AND CIVIC LIFE
IN THE
POST-NEWSPAPER AGE

DAN KENNEDY

University of Massachusetts Press
Amherst & Boston

ISBN 978-1-62534-005-4 (paper); 004-7 (hardcover)

Designed by Jack Harrison
Set in Adobe Garamond Pro
Printed and bound by Thomson Shore, Inc.

Library of Congress Cataloging-in-Publication Data
Kennedy, Dan, 1956–
The wired city : reimagining journalism and civic life in the post-newspaper age /
Dan Kennedy.
pages cm
Includes bibliographical references and index.
ISBN 978-1-62534-005-4 (pbk. : alk. paper) — ISBN 978-1-62534-004-7 (hardcover : alk. paper)
1. Online journalism—United States. 2. Electronic newspapers—United States.
3. Journalism, Regional—Connecticut—New Haven. 4. New Haven independent.
I. Title.
PN4784.O62K48 2013
071'.468—dc23
2013001341

British Library Cataloguing-in-Publication Data
A catalogue record for this book is available from the British Library.

For Barbara

CONTENTS

The Wired City

INTRODUCTION

Apocalypse or Something Like It

As the first decade of the twenty-first century drew to a close, it looked like the collapse of the newspaper business that media observers had been predicting for years was finally coming true. Three mighty forces came together in a wave that threatened to sweep away an industry whose pillars had long been rotting beneath it. Corporate debt and a profit-driven, bottom-line mentality led newspaper companies to lay off reporters, slash coverage, and alienate readers. The rise of the Internet cut deeply into advertising revenues, as retailers, restaurateurs, and other business owners discovered they no longer had to rely on the local newspaper in order to reach their customers. Finally, the financial collapse of 2008 and the deep economic recession that followed it transformed what was already a serious downturn into an existential crisis. Newspapers and the companies that owned them could not postpone the inevitable, as they had for so long, with more cutting and more borrowing. The day of reckoning had arrived.

In the spring of 2009, when I began researching this book, the end of the newspaper business as we had known it appeared to be at hand. More than 40,000 newspaper jobs would be eliminated that year, bringing total newspaper employment in the United States to 284,220, down from 424,500 ten years earlier. Paid daily-newspaper circulation fell from a high-water mark of 63.1 million, reached in 1973, to 45.7 million in

2009. Advertising revenue from newspaper print editions fell from $47.4 billion in 2005 to $22.8 billion in 2010. And though newspaper owners had followed their readers onto the Web, online advertising had proved an enormous disappointment. In 2010, for instance, the newspaper industry reported just $3 billion in online advertising revenues—barely a rounding error compared to what had been lost on the print side. Thus it should be no surprise that 142 daily and weekly newspapers ceased publication in subsequent years, including such well-known titles as the *Rocky Mountain News* of Denver and the *Seattle Post-Intelligencer.* (The latter has continued as an online-only enterprise with minimal staffing.)[1]

Never mind the oft-cited, oft-scorned, and generally misunderstood notion that "information wants to be free."[2] Since the rise of the commercial Web in the mid-1990s, the question for professional journalism has been: Who shall pay? Online advertising has proved to be an unpromising route, as its very ubiquity has rendered it far less lucrative than its print counterpart. Various experiments in persuading readers to pay have been and are being tried, but it is not clear whether those will add up to more than a minor, supplemental source of revenue. Which brings us to a third possibility—namely, neither advertisers nor readers but someone else: community leaders and foundation executives who care about journalism and its role in a democratic society, and who are willing to subsidize it for the benefit of themselves and others.

My interest in learning more about the "someone else" model of funding journalism drew me to New Haven, Connecticut, home of the *New Haven Independent,* a robust example of how philanthropy and journalism could come together to create a vital source of news and information. Launched in 2005, the *Independent,* a nonprofit online-only news site, covers city politics, crime, and especially neighborhood news in the sort of depth and detail that is missing from other news sources—including the region's dominant daily newspaper, the *New Haven Register.* The *Independent's* small cadre of journalists goes about its mission with energy and panache. The circumstances that make the *Independent's* existence possible are in some ways unique to New Haven. It is not *the* answer to the question of where we will find quality local journalism in the post-newspaper age; but it is *an* answer—and one that offers hope and guidance for communities that are not well served by their existing corporate media.

The founder, editor, and publisher of the *Independent* is a remarkable journalist named Paul Bass, who came to New Haven to attend Yale University and has been covering his adopted city since the 1980s. We met for the first time in June 2009 outside New Haven's Wexler/Grant Community School, where he pulled up on his bicycle. Housed in an institutional, low-slung building, the school served nearly five hundred students from preschool through eighth grade. Congresswoman Rosa DeLauro was supposed to speak there, and Bass wanted to interview her.

Bass checked in with the principal only to learn that DeLauro was not scheduled to come until the following week. Another staff member asked Bass if he didn't used to work for the *Advocate* and what he was doing these days. As Bass no doubt had done hundreds of times over the previous three-plus years, he patiently explained that he was running an online newspaper, the *New Haven Independent.* He handed the man a business card, headed outside, and pointed his bike in the direction of downtown New Haven, where he and his staff worked out of a tiny spare office at *La Voz Hispana de Connecticut,* a Spanish-language newspaper. I followed by car.

Nearly four years earlier Bass had left his job at the *New Haven Advocate,* an alternative weekly, to launch the *Independent.* With the newspaper business coming apart, I wanted to see whether his site was a viable alternative to the traditional, for-profit print model. The *Independent's* numbers would not have impressed an observer looking for a formula to reinvent journalism. At the time, the staff consisted of Bass and two full-time reporters, supplemented by a few freelancers. But with big-city papers cutting their budgets and lowering their standards, a handful of nonprofit online-only news organizations—the *Independent, Voice of San Diego,* and Minnesota's *MinnPost* were among the most prominent—had drawn national attention for the excellence of their journalism and the scope of their ambitions. These nonprofit sites, small though they were, had already established themselves as alternatives to traditional corporate newspapers, many of which were teetering on the brink. In 2009, few were teetering more precariously than the *New Haven Register.*

Later on the day I met Bass, I visited the *Register* and interviewed the managing editor, Mark Brackenbury. Several months earlier the paper's Pennsylvania-based owner, the Journal Register Company, had declared bankruptcy. The fate of New Haven's daily paper hung in the balance, as did Journal Register's national chain of seventeen other dailies and more than 350 non-daily publications and websites. I asked Brackenbury what it was like to work in such a troubled environment. "Day to day, we don't come in here feeling like, jeez, we're in bankruptcy, what are we going to do now?" he told me. "You just go about your job every day."[3]

The *Register* was a shadow of its former self. What was once a newsroom staff of about 150 had been cut to around seventy over the previous two decades. Among other measures, the owners had eliminated the paper's reporters in the Connecticut state capital, Hartford, and in Washington, D.C. "We've just sort of pulled in the borders a little bit and tried to focus on New Haven and the areas around New Haven and do the best with what we have," Brackenbury said.

The Journal Register Company was not the only newspaper corporation in trouble. When I got back to my car, my cell phone rang. It was a reporter who wanted to commiserate about the fate of my hometown paper, the *Boston Globe*. The New York Times Company, which had owned the *Globe* since 1993, was threatening to shut it down if it could not extract $20 million in concessions from the paper's unions. The largest of these, the Newspaper Guild, was balking. There was a real possibility that Boston would soon become the biggest city in the country to lose its leading newspaper.[4]

As these examples suggest, it is impossible to exaggerate the sense of panic and crisis that pervaded the newspaper business when I set out in the spring of 2009 to learn about fledgling alternatives. I interviewed passionate journalists experimenting with new ways of doing their jobs. Everywhere I traveled, though, I found trouble.

In Hartford, I met Christine Stuart, who ran a one-woman statehouse news site called *CT News Junkie*. Having realized that her goal of covering the state capital was being stymied by cost-cutting at Connecticut's newspapers, Stuart decided to do it herself; she had acquired the site several years earlier from its founder. *News Junkie*, an online, for-profit venture, was barely scraping by, and most of Stuart's income came from an unrelated part-time job. But she had found a niche, created by hard times at the state's dominant daily, the *Hartford Courant*. A once-respected paper that had fallen into the clutches of the Chicago-based Tribune Company, which had declared bankruptcy in 2008, the *Courant* had cut back sharply on its coverage of state politics and government. "The *Hartford Courant* had more than a dozen people roaming the statehouse only a few years ago, and all those people are gone," Colin Poitras, himself a former *Courant* reporter, told me.[5] Not entirely gone—when I interviewed Poitras, the *Courant* had just reduced its capitol bureau from four reporters to three. But the days when the *Courant* enjoyed a national reputation for the quality of its journalism were over. And a competitive, hard-working young reporter running her own website was making the most of the opportunity that had created.

In Montclair, New Jersey, I met Debbie Galant, the cofounder of *Baristanet*, a for-profit community news site that was among the first of its kind. Galant launched the venture after losing her perch as a local columnist for the *New York Times.* The towns served by *Baristanet* were also covered by the *Newark Star-Ledger,* a large daily. In a business that had been besieged by massive budget cuts, the *Star-Ledger* stood out. In late 2008 the paper eliminated 151 positions from its newsroom staff of about 330 people, a reduction of 40 percent. "It's an apocalypse," one reporter, George Jordan, was quoted as saying. "I've been in the business for twenty-eight years and have seen nothing like it. The wheels fell off with a blink of the eye. Throw your notebooks in the air and run the other way."[6]

And in Batavia, New York, I met Howard Owens, whom I had gotten to know when he was a top executive at GateHouse Media, a national chain that owned several hundred community newspapers. While at GateHouse, he launched a for-profit local website, the *Batavian.* Shortly thereafter, GateHouse eliminated his job and agreed to Owens's request to take the site with him. The very week I was in town, Owens's competition, the *Batavia Daily News,* announced that it had lost its lucrative, twenty-five-year-old contract to print the regional edition of *USA Today.* "We're really disappointed," *Daily News* publisher Tom Turnbull told me. "It hurts our bottom line, and a lot of people are going to lose jobs out of the deal, because they were strictly *USA Today.* We'll survive it, but we're going to be a much different newspaper corporation."[7]

Several years later, when I sat down to think about what I had learned and to start writing, the crisis that threatened the newspaper business had abated somewhat. But it had certainly not gone away. The Journal Register Company exited bankruptcy several months after my meeting with Mark Brackenbury. The Times Company got its $20 million in concessions, and the *Globe* remains the dominant news organization in eastern Massachusetts. In the long run, though, professional journalism faces profound challenges. And if things have turned out to be not quite as bad as they appeared in 2009, they are still bad enough. Newspapers have clearly become less capable of providing their communities with the coverage they need. But newspapers are no longer the only source of local journalism.

Every week, it seems, another study comes out on the future of newspapers and what might be done to save them. What I have found is that journalism, if not newspapers, is already being saved—not everywhere, and not perfectly. But in city after city, region by region, dedicated visionaries are moving beyond the traditional model of print newspapers supported mainly by advertising.

It would be one thing if newspapers were just another business—if what they had once done *was* obsolete, and if we were no longer in need of them any more than we needed horse-drawn carriages. But professional journalism plays a unique and vital role in our society as an independent watchdog over government and large institutions. And newspapers have been the source of most of that public-interest journalism—as much as 85 percent, writes the media scholar Alex Jones.[8] The problem is that newspapers as we have known them are fading away.

As economists would put it, the cyclical downturn—the Great Recession—that created such a sense of crisis in 2009 may have eased somewhat, but the secular changes that are transforming newspapers are grinding away inexorably. The Internet has eliminated the monopoly that newspapers once had on local advertising. The newspaper itself, offering an amalgam of international, national, and local news, sports and obituaries, the comics and the school-lunch menus, the crossword puzzle and Wednesday grocery-store ads, makes no logical sense as a unitary entity. Rather, it is an artifact of the industrial age, destined to fragment into dozens of online niche services—which, to a large extent, it already has. As the media futurist Clay Shirky has written, "Society doesn't need newspapers. What we need is journalism." Expanding on that thought during an appearance at Harvard University, Shirky said he hoped that a variety of ventures—some for-profit, some nonprofit, and some volunteer-driven—would be able to offset at least a portion of what newspapers were no longer able to do.[9]

I did not set out to write a book about the *New Haven Independent.* Rather, I decided to cast as wide a net as possible. My journey took me from conference calls with the editors of *NewsTrust,* a social network whose members evaluate journalism for depth, sourcing, and fairness, to Almaty, Kazakhstan, where I interviewed Adil Nurmakov, the Central Asia editor for *Global Voices Online,* which compiles digests of citizen media from around the world.[10]

Impressive as those projects were, though, I found that my attention kept returning to the challenges facing community journalism, an essential force in building strong cities, towns, and neighborhoods, and in empowering people to take charge of their lives and their communities. I had long worried about the demise of local newspapers as they were gobbled up by chain owners that cut their budgets and eliminated reporters—at first to drive up profits, later to pay off the unsustainable debts they had accumulated in assembling their empires. After a spring and summer of research, interviews, and travel, I realized that I wanted to write a book that was largely about Paul Bass and the *Independent.*

There were several reasons for this: the excellence of the journalism; the way in which Bass used reader comments to build a sense of community and advance the site's reporting; and the financial model, which was built on foundation grants, institutional sponsorships, and reader donations rather than on the traditional advertising base. There was no guarantee that the nonprofit model would prove stable enough to keep the *Independent* in business for another five or ten years. But there was no guarantee that the *New Haven Register* would be around that long, either. What mattered was that Bass had hit upon one way of providing some of the public-interest journalism that a community needs in a self-governing society.

During my frequent visits to New Haven in 2009, 2010, and 2011, I learned that the city is a fascinating place—a geographically compact community where African Americans and Latinos outnumber whites, and where the presence of Yale University provides a cultural and economic anchor that is missing in other Connecticut cities such as Hartford, Bridgeport, and Waterbury. New Haven also has astonishingly good pizza—the best in the world, the locals will tell you, and I can't say I've had better.

Laid low by a well-intentioned but misguided urban-renewal effort in the 1950s, 1960s, and 1970s, and by drugs and crime in the 1980s and 1990s, New Haven since the turn of the century had been on a roll. A newly vibrant downtown, the rise of medical and research centers affiliated with Yale, and a nationally recognized education-reform effort presided over by the progressive administration of Mayor John DeStefano had made New Haven a desirable city in which to live and work. At the same time, the murder rate, after falling during the middle part of the 2000s, had began to rise again. By some measures New Haven was among the most dangerous cities in the country.[11] Although it would be an exaggeration to say that the city was riven by racial resentment, in 2009 its white firefighters were unhappy enough with its affirmative-action policies to file a lawsuit, and they won their case before the U.S. Supreme Court.[12] Minority neighborhoods did not share in New Haven's economic growth and prosperity. In other words, it was a place desperately in need of accountability journalism of precisely the sort that the *Independent* provides.

This book is not entirely about New Haven and the *Independent,* however. I also write about several other local and regional news sites—especially three small for-profits, *CT News Junkie,* the *Batavian,* and *Baristanet,* as well as two large nonprofits, the *Connecticut Mirror* and *Voice of San Diego,* the former of which focuses on state politics and government, the latter on quality-of-life issues in Greater San Diego. All have been doing good work, as have others that receive briefer consideration here. The *Independent* is the centerpiece of this book, but it is not the sole subject.

What unites all of these ventures is a willingness to experiment, a passion for community, and a commitment to serious journalism.

As you will learn in the following pages, what I discovered in the course of researching this book left me profoundly optimistic about the future of journalism. It will not be the same as it was when newspapers dominated the local news landscape. It will not be better. It will not be worse. It will be different.

CHAPTER ONE

Annie Le Is Missing

PAUL BASS FELT UNEASY. It was a Friday—September 11, 2009. He was getting ready to leave the office for Shabbat, the Jewish sabbath. And he was beginning to wonder if he had blown a big story.[1]

Two days before, Bass had received an e-mail from someone at Yale University telling him that a twenty-four-year-old graduate student named Annie Le was missing. Could Bass post something on his community website, the *New Haven Independent*? Sure thing, Bass replied. So he wrote a one-sentence item with a link to a *Yale Daily News* account.[2] As he recalled later, he didn't think much about it after that.

Now Bass was facing a dilemma. Annie Le was still missing, and the media were starting to swarm. He was off until Saturday night; as an observant Jew, he does not work on Saturdays until after sundown. On top of this, his managing editor, Melissa Bailey, was leaving town for a few days. Bass remembered reading somewhere that Le had once written a story about students and crime for a magazine affiliated with Yale.[3] He found it, linked to it, and wrote an article beginning: "A graduate pharmacology student asked Yale's police chief a question: 'What can one do to avoid becoming another unnamed victim?' Seven months after she printed the answer in a campus publication, the student may have become a crime victim herself."[4] It was a start—nothing special, but enough to get the *Independent* into the chase. Then Bass went home.

As it turned out, the Annie Le saga—soon to become a murder story—developed into one of the most heavily publicized news events to hit New Haven in many years. Her body was discovered inside a laboratory wall at Yale Medical School on Sunday, September 13, the day she was to be married.[5] The grisly fate of the beautiful young Yale student proved irresistible to the national media. From the *New York Times* to the *New York Post,* from the *Today* show to *Nancy Grace,* reporters, producers, and photographers besieged city and university officials.

The story proved significant to the *New Haven Independent* as well. The Le case was exactly the sort of story Bass would normally have been reluctant to pursue. The *Independent*'s focus was on the city's neighborhoods and quality-of-life issues, not Yale, which Bass believed got plenty of coverage elsewhere. "I was an idiot about the whole thing," Bass told me at *La Voz Hispana de Connecticut,* the Spanish-language newspaper in downtown New Haven where the *Independent* rents a cramped office. "We don't want to overdo Yale. That's not our community. You don't want to say one life is more important than another. But by Friday it's hitting me. 'Cause now it's been a bunch of days, and it's feeling creepy. People were writing about it, and we were resisting writing about it. And then I said, you know what? I might be really missing it here."

Once Bass overcame his misgivings, the *Independent*'s dogged coverage earned the site national attention. Readership, which Bass said was generally around 70,000 unique visitors a month at the time, more than doubled in September to about 197,000.[6] But the Le case was more than a way to garner attention and build an audience. It also became an opportunity for an online-only news outlet with a tiny staff to prove that it could keep up with—and, in a few instances, surpass—far larger and better-established media organizations. Among other developments, the *Independent* broke the news that the police had identified a possible suspect. And it was the first to report on what the suspect's fiancée and a former girlfriend who claimed that he had sexually assaulted her had written about him on social-networking sites.

The Annie Le story brought new readers to the *Independent,* but those who stayed soon learned that its day-to-day mission had little to do with covering high-profile murder cases. Since 2005 the *Independent,* a nonprofit online-only news organization supported by local and national foundation grants, corporate sponsorships, and reader donations, had been building its reputation by paying close attention to more quotidian matters: efforts to reform New Haven's troubled public schools; development proposals large and small; retail-level politics; traffic; and issues involving the city's police department, ranging from a "Cop of the Week" feature that highlighted the good work being performed by New Haven police officers to multiple stories looking into why citizens were being harassed and arrested for video-recording officers doing their jobs. No one else was covering those issues—certainly not in the detail and comprehensiveness offered by the *Independent*. Through close attention to the daily life of New Haven and its people, and through a commitment to an ongoing conversation with its readers aimed at sparking civic engagement, the *Independent* had placed itself in the vanguard of a new wave of online news organizations.

The *Independent* is one of about a half-dozen local and regional nonprofit online-only news sites that are large enough and ambitious enough to have established themselves as a significant new journalistic genre. With the newspaper business having shrunk dramatically in recent years, it is fair to wonder whether anything will arise in its stead. The likely answer is that a wide variety of projects will be tried. Some will be better than others, and many cities and regions will be underserved.

Thus, it matters to the future of journalism whether the *Independent* can survive and thrive. And so, too, in the case of large nonprofit projects such as *Voice of San Diego,* which covers that city as well as surrounding communities; Minnesota's *MinnPost;* the *St. Louis Beacon;* the *Texas Tribune* and the *Connecticut Mirror,* both of which cover state government and politics; and a handful of others. These local and regional nonprofits have emerged as examples of how technology and a move away from the traditional advertising-based model of paying for newspaper journalism can provide vital watchdog coverage of government and local issues.

On the face of it, the nonprofit route might sound unpromising. Under some circumstances, though, it has emerged as a more reliable method of funding journalism than depending on the advertising priorities of commercial interests. At the national level, nonprofits such as *ProPublica* and the Center for Public Integrity have become respected sources of investigative reporting. At the regional and local levels, too, nonprofits are distinguishing themselves. In fact, it is the operators of for-profit online news sites who have had difficulty gaining traction. In Connecticut, *CT News Junkie,* a for-profit operation that also serves as the *Independent*'s capitol bureau, has been operating for several years longer than the *Connecticut Mirror,* covering state politics from the press-room annex at the statehouse, in Hartford. But *News Junkie* was quickly surpassed in staff size by its well-funded nonprofit competitor.

Well-known for-profits such as the *Batavian* in western New York, *Baristanet* in the affluent New Jersey suburbs just beyond New York City, and *West Seattle Blog* are making money. But in contrast to nonprofit sites, their staffs are tiny. Though the for-profits have become essential resources in their communities, they are rarely able to provide the sort of in-depth reporting that the *Independent* and its five full-time journalists are able to carry out in New Haven. At this historical moment in the technological and cultural revolution that has turned the news business upside down, there is more money for local start-up ventures in nonprofits than in for-profits.

The rapidity with which the newspaper advertising model collapsed is startling. From the 1830s, when the modern daily-newspaper industry got under way with the launch of "penny press" papers such as the *New York Sun* and the *New York Herald,* to around 2005, when the long, slow decline of the newspaper industry turned into a rout, advertisers paid most of the bills. It was often said that readers paid for printing and distribution, but the news itself was free, supported entirely by advertising. And suddenly that revenue source was in free fall. Advertising revenue from newspaper print editions dropped from $47.4 billion in 2005 to $22.8 billion in 2010, a decline that $3 billion in online advertising revenues did not come close to offsetting.[7] Classified advertising melted away as users turned to free and mostly free services such as Craigslist and Monster.com for selling a car, finding a job, or doing any of the other things that newspaper classifieds had once helped them do. Vibrant downtowns gave way to big-box stores on the outskirts of town whose advertising priorities often did not include local newspapers. As the New York University professor Clay Shirky, a well-known Internet analyst, has said, "Best Buy was not willing to support the Baghdad bureau because Best Buy cared about news from Baghdad. They just didn't have any other good choices."[8] Now they do, since the Internet provides businesses with any number of ways to reach their customers directly.

In that new world, professional news organizations are exploring a variety of ways to lessen their dependence on advertising. In 2011, general-interest newspapers such as the *New York Times* and the *Boston Globe* began asking readers to pay for at least some of their online content, joining specialty business publications that had long charged their readers for Internet access, most prominently the *Wall Street Journal* and the *Financial Times.*[9] Whether those and other newspapers will be able to make enough money from readers to offset their advertising losses remains to be seen.

Meanwhile, the nonprofit model is already working. Public radio and its crown jewel, NPR, are among our most comprehensive and reliable news sources. Nonprofit community news sites should, at least in theory, be able to follow a similar path. But though the *New Haven Independent* is far cheaper to run than a radio station (its 2011 budget of $450,000 covered not just New Haven but a satellite site in the nearby suburbs employing three more full-time journalists), it is also reaching a much smaller—and poorer—audience. Like virtually all community news sites, for-profit and nonprofit, the *Independent* does not charge for access, though it does ask its readers for voluntary contributions.

The nonprofit community-news movement remains small. The sites I've mentioned were all founded within roughly the same time period, from 2004 to 2009. In the years immediately following, the rise of nonprofit journalism slowed—perhaps because the sense of crisis in for-profit journalism that peaked in 2009 had eased somewhat, perhaps because there was a finite quantity of nonprofit money available to be tapped for media ventures. In addition, the government made it more difficult to launch a nonprofit news organization than ought to be the case, a problem that may require federal legislation to solve. "There was an initial bubble of nonprofit start-ups, but you haven't seen that great wave spreading across the country," *Voice of San Diego*'s editor, Andrew Donohue, told me.[10] Donohue saw that as a good thing. What was needed, in his view, was "more diversity of business models, so we're not so dependent on one should one collapse." Still, *Voice,* like the *Independent,* was doing better than some of its for-profit competitors. Even though Donohue had to shrink his staff at the end of 2011 after the site received less funding than he had hoped for, he still had more reporting resources available than the smaller of the city's two for-profit alternative weeklies, *San Diego CityBeat.* (The city's larger alt-weekly, the *San Diego Reader,* is written mainly by freelancers. For those unfamiliar with the term, alternative weeklies are usually liberal, youth-oriented, arts-heavy newspapers modeled after such venerable publications as the *Village Voice* and the *Boston Phoenix.*) The same was true in New Haven, where the *Advocate* had been stripped to the bone by corporate chain ownership. If the nonprofit model has not proved to be the salvation of journalism, it nevertheless is a vital part of the mix at a time when for-profit news organizations continue to struggle.

Nonprofit online news should be seen not as the overarching model for the future of professional journalism but as one model that is working reasonably well in a few places. And it should not be viewed as a replacement for traditional newspapers but as a complement to them. In New Haven, for instance, the *Independent* has operated from its first day in the shadow of the *New Haven Register,* a large, middling-quality daily long run by cost-cutting chain owners. When I began visiting New Haven in 2009, the *Register*'s owner, the Journal Register Company (JRC), was in bankruptcy. But by 2011 the company was being run by a forward-looking, widely admired chief executive, and the *Register* itself had been turned over to a young editor determined to reach out to the community.

Thus even in New Haven, where Paul Bass, through several career incarnations, has functioned since the 1980s as the city's principal alternative to the *Register,* the media scene can change very quickly. It is not likely that a reinvigorated *Register* would make the *Independent* obsolete. But New Haveners who gave up on the *Register* in favor of the *Independent* may find themselves reading two daily news sources instead of just one. Still, given the *Register*'s related goals of reaching affluent readers in the suburbs and turning a profit, the *Independent*'s relentless focus on the city and its neighborhoods will almost certainly remain unmatched by any other news organization. All Bass has to figure out is how to keep his news site alive.

Bass is something of a legend in Connecticut media, and the *Independent*'s tiny office is festooned with awards he has won. Born in White Plains, New York, he came to New Haven as a Yale freshman and has spent his entire adult life reporting on his adopted city: as the cofounder of a weekly newspaper in the 1980s named, not coincidentally, the *New Haven Independent;* as a reporter and editor for the *New Haven Advocate* in the 1990s and 2000s; and as the coauthor of *Murder in the Model City* (2006), a book about the redemption of a New Haven member of the Black Panthers who had been convicted of murder.

It was in 2004 and 2005, while finishing his book on the Black Panthers, that Bass started to ponder the idea of entering the nascent world of online community journalism. The thought of returning to the *Advocate* didn't appeal to him. Under the ownership of Tribune Company—a Chicago-based national conglomerate that also owns Connecticut's largest daily newspaper, the *Hartford Courant*—the *Advocate,* he said, had become increasingly corporate, with a shrinking staff and diminished ambitions. At the same time, he had been looking at the nascent blogosphere with a mixture of contempt and fascination. "I was probably unfairly disdainful of blogs. I didn't like that they didn't do reporting. But I was excited at the way that they were engaging with the readers in new ways and telling stories in new ways," he told me.[11]

In June 2009, when Bass and I first met, he was forty-nine, speaking in a rapid-fire manner, and bubbling over with enthusiasm as he spread peanut butter on a bagel in a downtown coffee shop, Brū Café, which doubles as an auxiliary newsroom—it is at Brū, a short walk from *La Voz* and city hall, that he holds staff meetings, puts together televised panel discussions, and conducts interviews. Atop his short-cropped red hair he wore a yarmulke. He had a red beard, wire-rimmed glasses, and on this particular day was wearing a loud-but-not-too-loud buttoned shirt, jeans, and sandals with socks. Youthful in appearance, he looked more like a graduate engineering student—earnest, intense, geeky—than someone who was helping to redefine local news coverage.

After a few inquiries convinced him that it would be too difficult to support himself and his family with a for-profit venture, Bass started investigating the possibility of a nonprofit site, inspired by NPR and by a discussion he had read on the New York University journalism professor Jay Rosen's blog, *PressThink*. He received a $50,000 grant from the Universal Health Care Foundation of Connecticut and dove in, raising another $35,000 before the actual launch.[12]

On Tuesday, September 6, 2005, the day after Labor Day, the *New Haven Independent* slipped into view when Bass posted two stories about Kenny Hill, a retired National Football League cornerback turned New Haven developer.[13] Hill was suing the city over a subcontractor whom he claimed he had been pressured to hire in order to remove lead paint from an apartment building he was renovating. Hill said the subcontractor had not done the work. The city said he had. It was a story about one building in one neighborhood, but Bass used it to make a larger point. He wrote: "The saga of 235 Winchester Ave. is more than a spat between a builder and a bureaucrat. It jeopardizes both economic and neighborhood development in New Haven's Dixwell neighborhood. Decent affordable housing is hard to find in a gentrifying city. This decrepit building stands across the street from 25 Science Park, a refurbished cornerstone of a crucial high-tech project. Also across the street are new homes built for working families."[14]

The Hill stories served as a pretty good blueprint for what the *Independent* would become: a voice of the city's neighborhoods and an advocate for the idea that New Haven should be a livable city for all of its residents—not just those few who were fortunate enough to be white, well-educated, and affluent.

Late on a Wednesday morning in October 2009, the staff of the *New Haven Independent* convened at Brū for its weekly editorial meeting. Bass and Len Honeyman, a veteran reporter who was an occasional contributor, were sitting on a couch. Gathered in chairs, forming a semicircle, were the managing editor, Melissa Bailey, staff reporter Allan Appel, and, arriving a few minutes late, the then newest full-timer, Thomas MacMillan. Also taking part was Marcia Chambers, a retired *New York Times* reporter whose own online community newspaper, the *Branford Eagle,* was published on the *Independent*'s website.[15]

Bailey kicked off a discussion about ethics by pointing to a story in that morning's *New Haven Register.* An elected official in a nearby community had been accused of giving a raise to an aide because they were supposedly involved in a lesbian relationship. The story never actually used the L word, though the implication was reasonably clear. To compound matters, the official was married—to a man.

"If she's having a lesbian relationship, eventually that's going to come out," said Chambers. "The entry of lesbianism, does that make it a whole different animal?" asked Honeyman. "What if she were having an affair with someone's husband?" "I hate doing any stories about gender and sex in general," Appel interjected. To which Bass replied, "You just did one on Sunday about that church," referring to a story Appel had written about a church that welcomed gay, lesbian, bisexual, and transgender people.[16] "That's different," Appel responded.

Bass and Appel went back and forth before Bass declared, "I think it's okay to say we're not going to go overboard in covering people's sex lives." Bailey reminded everyone: "We're not going to write about it. Unless she moves to New Haven and runs for mayor."

From there matters moved on to a discussion about social media, and how the *Independent* could make better use of Twitter and Facebook; some postmortems regarding the Annie Le coverage; and the revelation that Appel did not own a cell phone. "I'm holding out," he said, surprising several of his colleagues.

Although Bass is clearly the dominant personality at the *New Haven Independent,* he has assembled a staff of interesting, strong-willed people who have bought into his vision of small-bore, community-based journalism. By 2011, he had a full-time staff of five, including himself. Their names will come up here and there throughout this book. What follows are some brief introductions.

Melissa Bailey, twenty-seven years old when we first met in 2009, was a math major at Yale who decided she preferred journalism. "I was thinking of going to graduate school in math at the very end of college, and I was confronted with this big lifestyle choice," she told me. "Do I sit in this room and do this incredibly intellectually challenging thing, but alone for hours, and work on a proof for ten years that maybe won't help anyone? Or do you do this incredibly interactive line of work where you see every day that your stories are affecting people and has meaning to the people around you?"[17]

After interning for Bass at the *New Haven Advocate* and spending a year in Italy (she was born in London and has European Union citizenship), she took a job as a reporter for the daily *Middletown Press*. Discouraged by the downsizing and cost-cutting taking place around her, she contacted Bass—who had by then launched the *Independent*—and asked if he would consider starting a similar site in Middletown and hiring her. Instead, he offered her a job in New Haven. Like Bass, MacMillan, and Appel, Bailey tools around the city on her bicycle, even in the dark, an efficient if risky mode of transportation. As managing editor, Bailey also assigns and edits stories, helps run the organization, and represents the *Independent* at national conferences.

I have accompanied Bailey on several stories. The quirkiest involved a visit to the home of a candidate for the city's board of aldermen. We had come to see if the candidate's mother intended to vote for her daughter or for the incumbent, who, oddly enough, had publicly identified her as a supporter. With me behind the wheel, we headed to a neighborhood on the outskirts of the city, near Interstate 95. We found the house we were looking for. Kathleen O'Sullivan answered Bailey's knock and told us that her daughter, Maureen O'Sullivan-Best, was out campaigning. Bailey reminded her that alderman Robert Lee had bragged she had told him she would vote for him rather than her daughter and asked if it was true.

O'Sullivan wouldn't answer. "I don't want to read in the paper who I'm voting for," she said, though she added that she had made up her mind, and that she had indeed voted for Lee in the past. Bailey asked a few more questions and took a photo of her with her grandchildren before we left.[18] On the way back, we speculated. It sounded to me like Kathleen O'Sullivan was planning to vote for Robert Lee, but there was no way of knowing for sure. In any event, O'Sullivan-Best beat Lee that November, with or without her mother's vote.[19]

At a news organization where multimedia and multitasking are part of the job, Thomas MacMillan stands out. I met MacMillan at New Haven City Hall on a May evening in 2010. MacMillan had come to cover a meeting of the finance committee, a subcommittee of the board of aldermen. I watched as he pulled out a notebook, a laptop, and a camera, propping open in front of him a copy of the proposed city budget. He live-blogged the meeting and then used his running coverage as notes from which he later wrote his article. He read and approved comments to the live-blog. He scribbled occasionally in his notebook. At one point alderman Darnell Goldson motioned to MacMillan and whispered, "Hey, Thomas!" MacMillan looked in the direction in which Goldson was pointing and saw a middle-aged man wearing a Christmas-tree hat in protest over Mayor John DeStefano's proposal to save money by doing away with the traditional tree on New Haven Green that winter. MacMillan took a picture. He also pulled out a different camera and shot some video.[20]

A few weeks later, we sat down and talked. Thirty years old at the time, a native of Northampton, Massachusetts, MacMillan had not worked as a journalist before coming to New Haven. After graduating from Marlboro College in Vermont, he studied long-form journalism at the Salt Institute for Documentary Studies in Portland, Maine, and then attended a photography workshop farther up the coast, in Rockport. He was working at a non-journalism job in Vermont when he moved to New Haven because a friend needed a roommate. He did some interning at the *Independent,* wrote a grant proposal under Bass's guidance, and was hired as a full-time reporter in 2009.

"It's really fun for me to feel like we're on a rising star rather than a sinking ship," MacMillan told me. "There's just something exciting about feeling like you're working on the new paradigm, where you can experiment and try different things and people will occasionally take notice of what you're doing. The paper gets mentioned in the *New York Times.* I imagine that my feelings for journalism and the prospects for journalism would not be as optimistic and enthusiastic if I worked for a traditional paper. I feel really happy about what we're doing."[21]

Allan Appel is a novelist, a playwright, and a poet who had done some writing for the *Advocate* when Bass was still working there. After the staff meeting at Brū in October 2009, he and I headed out to a job fair at James Hillhouse High School in Appel's old station wagon, which had a huge crack in the front windshield. At Hillhouse, the gymnasium was jammed with people looking for jobs, nearly all of them African American.

"Are you surprised by the turnout? Isn't it extraordinary? What's your assessment of the crowd?" Appel asked Nancy Collins, the director of recruitment at Yale–New Haven Hospital. Appel patiently interviewed several job seekers and took their photos. Then it was off to a Salvation Army store, where Appel planned to gather material about down-and-out bargain hunters to supplement his reporting on joblessness. We were waylaid by a shopper who would only tell us his name was John. He had a Bluetooth earpiece on one side of his head, but it wasn't clear whether or not he had a cell phone. "I have a time limit because I have to put money in the meter out there," he informed us. It struck me as unlikely that John actually had a car parked outside, but who knows?[22]

Sixty-two at the time, Appel was the oldest member of the full-time staff—a good dozen years older than Bass, and a generation or two older than Melissa Bailey and Thomas MacMillan. Appel brought a more worldly, off-the-news perspective to his job that I found interesting. It was he who told me that New Haven Green had been measured to be just large enough so that 144,000 saved souls could be spirited away in the Rapture, a fact he had learned while doing research for one of his plays. Born in Chicago, he grew up in Los Angeles, and he and his wife raised their family in Manhattan. He moved to New Haven when his wife got a "dream job" as a curator at the Yale University Art Gallery.[23]

The newest full-time staff member, Gwyneth Shaw, had worked in the Washington bureaus of the *Orlando Sentinel* and the *Baltimore Sun,* then left the newspaper business to earn a master's degree in journalism from Arizona State University. She had come to New Haven because her husband was attending law school at Yale. Shaw was hired at the *Independent* in early 2011, where most of her time was taken up with covering nanotechnology, a beat for which Bass had received grant money. Nanotechnology, which involves working with tiny bits of matter, had a foothold in New Haven through Yale. One of Bass's ideas for achieving financial sustainability was to develop specialized areas of coverage that could attract a national audience and foundation grants.

Unlike the rest of the staff, Shaw, thirty-seven when I interviewed her in the spring of 2011, had a young child at home. "I can't work all the time. I'm sort of like the slacker of the bunch. I have to go home at six," she said with a laugh. Her background in traditional journalism gave her a different perspective on the *Independent,* especially compared to those of Bailey and MacMillan. I asked her how she had made the adjustment. "What's different, obviously, is the speed," she replied. "I've always been a pretty good deadline writer, but I have a real need to organize my thoughts and think about something for a while. I had kind of gotten spoiled. And it's hard sometimes to really push that story out—I still kind of feel like maybe I need to do a little more reporting, maybe I need to think about it more."[24]

There is no question that the pace of Internet journalism is faster than the community journalism of years past. Although Shaw's experience was in dailies, Bass himself had worked almost exclusively for weeklies. In fact, it is the pace and liveliness of the *Independent* that are among its most engaging features. The tradeoff is a certain lack of depth. The long, heavily reported news features that Bass used to write for the *New Haven Advocate* are largely absent from the *Independent*—though, in comparison with typical community journalism, it publishes articles that are fairly detailed.

What you get with the *Independent* is depth and complexity that emerge over a period of weeks or months, especially with stories that are revisited again and again, such as Bailey's school-reform coverage and an award-winning series that MacMillan wrote about the harassment of Latino business owners in the nearby city of East Haven. "What Paul says is that the long-formness comes over time, where you link to past articles," MacMillan told me. "You start to create an ongoing story out of a number of shorter stories. That's really true, and that's really satisfying to me."[25]

It creates a different experience for the reader as well. Rather than conveying the news in one neatly tied-up package each week, the *Independent* is more like an ongoing conversation. It achieves that in part through a presentation that puts a premium on multiple points of entry, interactivity, and frequent updates that keep readers coming back throughout the day.

When you visit the *New Haven Independent* website, your first impression is that there is a lot going on. The site is laid out like a blog, with stories appearing in reverse chronological order. There is only one way of differentiating between the more important and the less important: fully reported local stories appear in the main story well, whereas routine police news, lesser features, or links to stories at other sites, *Independent*-affiliated or not, appear in a dark-blue column labeled "Extra! Extra!" There's an events calendar that allows users to enter their own content; the most recent postings from *SeeClickFix,* a New Haven–based start-up that enables residents to submit news about problems in their neighborhoods; "Breaking Arts," a section of brief articles submitted by the local arts council; a crime map; links to numerous local government agencies and community resources; and various options for sorting by topic or neighborhood. Many stories are accompanied by several large photos, and some by videos as well.

Although you could make the case that the *Independent* offers something for everyone, no one would describe its look as clean and uncluttered. This is an observation that the site's designer takes in stride—at least up to a point. "My background is print. I like white space. Design is being able to focus on what's important, and everything else should be in the background," said Kyle Summer, who runs a small firm in New Haven called Smart Pill Design. As for his working relationship with Paul Bass, he said: "When he asks for something, I try to make him defend it. He wants to keep it simple. What *he* calls simple. It's not visually simple. I have to let go of certain things."

Summer may have some reservations about the way Bass has implemented his ideas. But it was also Summer who came up with the site's most attractive touch: a retro image of a man in a suit and fedora reading a newspaper and surrounded by lightning bolts. It appears in the middle of the nameplate, which has an Art Deco feel to it. Just below it is written: "It's Your Town. Read All About It."

"I call him 'The Reader.' Paul calls him 'The Flasher,'" Summer said, referring to the man in the fedora. "Paul was getting disgusted with the whole commercialization of papers. That's the reason he started this. And I thought I would try to make references visually to when newspapers were really important. So he's kind of a fifties sort of guy. He's Superman standing outside in the rain reading the newspaper. That's really where that guy came from. It started off as some stock image that I found that I converted into that graphic."

Summer told me he was also working on a mobile version of the *Independent*. It would be an important step. New Haven is a poor city, largely inhabited by minorities. According to a 2010 study by the Pew Internet & American Life Project, African Americans and Latinos were more likely than whites to access the Internet with smartphones. At the same time, African Americans and Latinos were less likely than whites to have broadband Internet access at home.[26] Mobile access was vital to the *Independent*'s goal of reaching all of New Haven's communities.

On Saturday, September 12, 2009, Shabbat having ended at sunset, Paul Bass went back to work on the Annie Le story—pulling an all-nighter, as Melissa Bailey learned at a brunch held the next morning to celebrate the *Independent*'s fourth anniversary.[27] On Saturday night Bass posted an update on the investigation.[28] Late Sunday morning he ran a piece largely reported by Christine Stuart of *CT News Junkie*.[29] According to Stuart's sources, the authorities had searched an incinerator in Hartford for Le's body—but contrary to some stories in the national media, there were no suspicions that it had deliberately been dumped there. Rather, trash from New Haven was routinely trucked to the facility, and police thought there was a chance that the body might turn up. That night, however, police

announced that Le's body had been discovered inside a wall at the laboratory where she had worked.[30]

On Monday, September 14, six days after Le had been reported missing, the *Independent* became the first to reveal that police had identified
a twenty-four-year-old laboratory technician who had worked with Le as
a "person of interest."[31] The *New Haven Register*'s website followed shortly
thereafter.[32] And so began one of the more curious side stories of the Annie Le case.

As law enforcement officials continued with their investigation on
Tuesday, neither the *Independent* nor the *Register* released the name of
Le's coworker. On Tuesday night, though, the police department held a
news conference and announced that the "person of interest" was Raymond Clark and included his name in a press release.[33] Because the news
conference was covered live by a number of television stations, Clark's
identity immediately became public. On Wednesday, the *Register* named
Clark and interviewed people who knew him. "I'm in total shock," an un-
identified high school classmate was quoted as saying. "He was the nicest
kid—very quiet, but everyone liked him. I can't believe he could do this.
I'm sick to my stomach."[34] But the *Independent* continued to withhold
Clark's name.

Melissa Bailey was at the news conference too. She took notes and shot
some video of New Haven police chief James Lewis speaking to reporters. But neither her story nor her video used Clark's name. Bailey wrote,
somewhat cryptically, "Police named the target of the search, calling him a
'person of interest.'"[35] Nor did the *Independent* identify Clark on Wednesday—and not even in a story posted early on Thursday morning reporting
that police had staked out a motel where Clark was staying the night before, although it did link to a *Register* story that identified Clark in its lead
paragraph.[36] It wasn't until later on Thursday morning that the *Independent*
finally named Raymond Clark as the person police believed had murdered
Annie Le. The reason: by then Clark had been arrested and charged, and
was being taken into court for a formal arraignment.[37]

The *Independent*'s refusal to name Clark until he had been formally
charged was an admirable exercise in journalistic restraint. The decision
derived in part from Bass's institutional memory. In 1998, police had mis-
takenly identified a Yale professor as a "person of interest" in the murder
of a student named Suzanne Jovin. No evidence against the professor was
ever made public, and the murder was never solved.[38] Essentially, though,
this restraint was a statement of Bass's sense of how a news organization
ought to serve the community.

Judging by comments posted to the *Independent,* many readers appreciated Bass's decision. "Thank you for the good sense to not publish his name at this time," wrote "ASDF" on Tuesday evening, after Clark's name had begun to leak out but before the police had named him. The commenter added: "I really don't understand what there is to gain by releasing his name—if you don't have enough evidence to arrest him, then you don't have enough evidence to smear him in the media." Then there was this, from "LOOLY," posted on Wednesday morning, after Clark's name had been widely reported: "It should really be very simple. Unless he is being charged his name should not be used."[39]

Bass also had to make several other difficult decisions about identifying people connected to the Annie Le story. On September 14, as Clark's name was leaking out, the media converged on his apartment in Middletown, northeast of New Haven. Christine Stuart noticed the name of a woman along with that of Raymond Clark. She passed it along, and Melissa Bailey started plugging it into various social-networking sites. It didn't take long before she found a public MySpace page for the woman, who turned out to be Clark's twenty-three-year-old fiancée. Bailey captured a screen image before the page could be taken down—which it soon was.[40]

Bailey wrote a story that began, "The target in the slaying of Yale graduate student Annie Le had something in common with the victim—he, too, was engaged." And she quoted the young woman as writing of Clark: "He has a big heart and tries to see the best in people ALL THE TIME! even when everyone else is telling him that the person is a psycho or that the person can't be trusted. he [*sic*] thinks everyone deserves a second chance."[41] The woman's name and photograph wound up being published by other news outlets, but it never appeared in the *Independent.*

That was not the *Independent*'s only social-networking scoop. In nearby Branford, Marcia Chambers of the *Branford Eagle* was working her sources. Somehow she obtained a 2003 police report about an ex-girlfriend of Raymond Clark who claimed he had forced her to have sex when they were both students at Branford High School.[42] As a condition of receiving the report, Chambers promised not to publish it until after an arrest had been made. But that didn't meant there were not other uses to which the report could be put. Bailey typed the woman's name into Facebook, discovered that she had an account, and friended her, letting her know she was a reporter covering the murder.[43] After Clark's arrest, Bailey and Chambers wrote a story without using the woman's name. "I can't believe this is true," they quoted the woman as writing on her Facebook page. "I feel like im 16 all over again. Its jsut [*sic*] bringing back everything."[44]

The revelation that the *Independent* had the police report created a media stampede, Bailey said later. "People were calling us, begging us for this police report," she told a researcher for Columbia University. "The *New York Times* came in and practically tried to arm-wrestle Paul."[45] The *Independent* withheld the fiancée's name, a decision Bailey wrote that she had no misgivings about even though the woman later appeared on network television and identified herself.[46]

By declining to name Raymond Clark until he had actually been charged with a crime, and by withholding the identities of the two women, Paul Bass made a statement about what kind of news organization he wanted the *Independent* to be and what kind of journalism his community could expect from the site. Protecting the two women at a time when only the *Independent* knew who they were was the more straightforward of the two decisions. Any news executive who cares about journalistic ethics—or, for that matter, basic human decency—might have made the same call. But keeping Clark's name off the site even after the New Haven police had put it in a press release, and even after the police chief had freely discussed it at a news conference—well, that was an extraordinary decision. Many journalists would argue that a news organization has an obligation to report the name of someone who might soon be charged with murder when the police have very publicly placed that name on the record. But Bass clearly has a different way of looking at such matters.

Weeks later, in a conversation at his office, Bass wondered if he had done the right thing while simultaneously defending his decision. "I still believe it's a complicated question. I still believe we could definitely be wrong," he said. Yet, as he continued, he didn't sound like someone who thought he might be wrong, even as I suggested to him that his decision to withhold Clark's name could be seen as something of an exercise in futility. "I'm in no way moving toward the idea that we should have run the name. I see no reason for putting the name out sooner. Nothing served," he said. "I agree with you that it was futile. The name was out there. But we are still a news organization with standards."[47]

Those standards, I came to realize, are rooted not just in Bass's view of journalism but in his sense of place, and even in his spiritual beliefs. The *Independent* is a news site, but it's not just a news site. It is also a gathering place, a forum for civil discussion of local issues, and a spark for civic engagement. It is a mixture that reflects Bass's interests: a multifaceted approach to community journalism—to community *and* journalism—that has been visible in his life and work from the time he began writing about New Haven.

CHAPTER TWO

The Outsider

It was the afternoon of the *New Haven Independent*'s fifth-anniversary party. Paul Bass was wondering how many people would show up. The celebration, on a Wednesday in September 2010, would be competing with parent-teacher conferences at the city's middle schools that evening. There was also a major Jewish event taking place at Yale. City Democrats had scheduled something as well. The last, Bass mused, might at least pull in some political figures who would stop by on their way.[1]

I was put to work. *Independent* staff reporter Allan Appel and freelancer Melinda Tuhus, along with Marcia Chambers, the editor of the *Branford Eagle,* an *Independent* affiliate, asked me to help them open bottles of wine, so I set aside my observer's status and started pulling corks. Next to the door was a table stacked with *New Haven Independent* bumper stickers and copies of Appel's novel *The Midland Kid: Tales of the Presidential Ghostwriter,* the latter a gift being offered to attendees who signed up to pay a voluntary monthly subscription fee. Appel was a novelist, poet, and playwright of some renown. Two years earlier Bass had published *The Midland Kid,* a parody of the George W. Bush era, under the imprint of the New Haven Independent Press, one of his multitudinous schemes to raise money for the site.

Bass's worry that few people would make their way to the party proved unwarranted. By 6 p.m. the space was packed with about a hundred and fifty people: old friends, African American leaders, activists from the city's large and politically involved bicycling community, Mayor John DeStefano and assorted local politicos, and even Linda McMahon, the professional-wrestling magnate who was running for the U.S. Senate that fall. Bass's daughter Sarah, a high school senior, greeted folks as they arrived and told her father to tuck in his shirt. She had also baked the anniversary cake. Guests ate chicken wings, rice and beans, and salad, prepared by Norma Rodriguez-Reyes, the owner of *La Voz* and the board chairwoman of the nonprofit entity Bass had established to act as publisher of the *Independent*.

Rodriguez-Reyes stood on a chair and held aloft a clear plastic cup of red wine. "At *La Voz Hispana* we're very proud to have the *New Haven Independent* here with us, and we want to wish *cien años*—one hundred years more," she said.

Next it was Bass's turn to speak. "When we started out, the news business was in decline," he said. "And a lot of big media companies had been taking advantage of local communities by creating monopolies, laying off reporters, milking it for profits, and destroying quality news coverage. And communities didn't like that. Since we started, what's happening in New Haven is happening in San Diego, it's happening in Minneapolis, it's happening in Austin, Texas, and in cities around the country. And it's a powerful idea—which is that out-of-town corporations that could care less about us no longer own our news. They no longer control our news. We the people control the news."

For Bass, it was the culmination of a three-decade career in journalism. For politically active, civically engaged New Haveners, it was a celebration of a news organization that had given voice to their issues and their neighborhoods. As Bass looked around at the people who had come to congratulate him and what the *Independent* represented, he couldn't know whether there would be a tenth-anniversary party in 2015—although by 2011 he had lined up enough funding for future years to make such a celebration a reasonably safe bet. But he had already accomplished a great deal by showing that a nonprofit online-only news organization could offer the sort of detailed local coverage that daily newspapers were unable or unwilling to provide.

In order to understand the *New Haven Independent* you need to understand Paul Bass, an outsider who came to New Haven and stayed. In addition to his work as a reporter and editor, he is also an entrepreneurial fundraiser. He cares as deeply about community as he does about journalism, a dual sensibility that has defined the *Independent* from its earliest days. And he is someone for whom family and spirituality are of paramount importance, values that in turn are reflected in his work. This much is clear: The *Independent* would not exist if Bass hadn't come to New Haven.

Paul Joseph Bass was born on June 10, 1960, in White Plains, New York, the youngest of three boys and a girl. His childhood was a difficult one. In our first conversation, he told me that as a high school student he had written stories for the local daily—then added, almost as an aside, that the experience had provided him with "probably the only happy moments of my childhood."[2] I let it go at the time, but I later learned that his mother, Gloria, had died when he was quite young.

"My mother's death had a big impact on me," Bass told me in an e-mail exchange two years later. "I'm still sad about it. She died of brain cancer. I was eight. I remember them not letting me in to see her the last few days in the hospital because they had a rule that kids under fourteen couldn't be allowed in. So I interviewed the nurses out in the lobby for a little newspaper I put out. Pop psychology theory: That's why it's always important to me to sneak into places I'm not allowed on stories, especially hospitals.

"A few years ago some guy got shot in New Haven, and I found myself sneaking into his room. He was lying there, out of it; his girlfriend was just sitting there looking bored. I realized: Why am I here? There's no real story. I apologized and left. On the other hand I've definitely gotten some superb stories by sneaking in places."

Bass attended public schools through the eighth grade, then enrolled in the prestigious Horace Mann School in the Bronx, riding with a teacher for the half-hour commute during his first few years and driving himself when he was older. Horace Mann had what Bass called a "great weekly newspaper," and after getting involved as a sophomore, he pretty much lived there during his junior and senior years.

Yale was his father's idea. Milton Bass had been accepted to Yale Law School after serving in the army. But though his tuition would have been fully paid by the government, he had stayed home and attended New York University Law School so he could help his widowed mother raise his two younger siblings. Paul said that his father always regretted having said no to Yale. "His dad was a first-generation immigrant in Brooklyn. Like a lot of Jews from New York at the time—I've never fully understood this— they saw Yale as a symbol of American success and admired the place, even though it had a quota on admitting Jews," Bass told me. "He said they actually used to listen to the Yale ball games on the radio and root for them when he was a kid."

One day early in Paul's senior year at Horace Mann, his father suggested that they take a ride to New Haven and have a look at Yale. Paul was granted an interview and won early admission on the strength of his writing. For Paul, Yale was all right—but it was the city itself that really captured his attention. "I just loved New Haven since I got here. I liked it a lot more than Yale," he told me. "I came up for an interview, and I loved that Toad's Place [a legendary rock club] was a couple of blocks from my dorm, and Meat Loaf was playing."

Although Bass's earlier forays into newspapers may have been something of a diversion for an unhappy boy, at Yale journalism became a calling, and a way to connect with a community that he found well-suited to his temperament and his sense of curiosity. He reported for the *Yale Daily News,* the *New Haven Register,* and the city's alternative weekly, the *New Haven Advocate,* getting to know his adopted hometown from the bottom up.

"I just loved the community," he said. "I was spending my time off-campus. The neighborhoods, the political groups, the journalism groups—I can't articulate it well, but the city was lively enough so it wasn't like a small town or boring like a suburb like White Plains, but it wasn't overwhelming and anonymous and a little bit inhuman like New York. It's a small enough city that you could interview the mayor right away, which I did for the *Register,* even though I wasn't on staff. I loved the Italian-American culture here, I loved the black community here."

Bass met his future wife at the *Yale Daily News* when he was a sophomore. Carole Smith, from Wilmington, Delaware, was a freshman, and she was reluctant to approach Paul. "I was very intimidated because he was a year ahead of me and wrote like twenty-seven stories a day," she told me. But what started out as a working relationship turned personal, and they were married in September 1983, a few months after her graduation.[3]

Though few readers of the *New Haven Independent* may realize it, the community website they read is not a new idea. Rather, it is a revival of a newspaper that Paul Bass cofounded when he was still in his twenties.

After graduating from Yale in 1982 and freelancing for a few years, Bass helped launch a weekly community newspaper called—yes—the *New Haven Independent.* With himself as executive editor, his wife, Carole Bass, as associate editor, and their friends Bruce Shapiro as associate editor and Cynthia Savo as publisher, they set out in 1986 on what proved to be an adventure that would last more than three years. As Shapiro recalled, the four met while writing for the *New Haven Advocate,* which they worried was moving away from its alternative identity and embracing a more mainstream, advertiser-friendly approach.

"The four of us together hatched this idea—and spent a couple of years developing it—of a different kind of weekly," said Shapiro, now executive director of the Dart Center for Journalism and Trauma, based at Columbia University's Graduate School of Journalism. "It would focus relentlessly on covering the issues and the use of power in the life of the neighborhoods in New Haven. It was the journalistic equivalent of community organizing—helping people name the issues that mattered to them."[4]

The front-page stories in the debut issue, dated September 11, 1986, combined quotidian slices of life with a dash of social justice in a way that would be entirely familiar to today's *Independent* readers: Carole Bass on a condo development in the neighborhood of Fair Haven; Bruce Shapiro on a protest against homelessness on the New Haven Green; and Paul Bass on a star basketball player turned guard at a juvenile detention center. An editorial describing the *Independent*'s mission read in part: "Behind every issue of the *New Haven Independent* will stand three watchwords: fair, high-quality and broad-based. Fairness comes from conscientious reporting and thoughtful perspective. High-quality means straight facts, a readable and attractive graphic design and the best writing possible. And finally, broad-based: we hope the *New Haven Independent* will find readers in every neighborhood, in every social and economic class, in every age group."[5]

The weekly *Independent* cost twenty-five cents an issue on newsstands, but those who signed up to have it mailed to their homes got it for free. By 1988 the paper was enough of a success that it attracted the attention of the *Columbia Journalism Review,* which observed that the *Independent*'s circulation of 25,000 was half the number of households in New Haven—an impressively high penetration rate for a new community newspaper. Bass attributed the *Independent*'s success in part to what he perceived as the failures of the *New Haven Register,* telling the *CJR,* "I thought we'd just be doing the thinking, the analysis. But we found we could scoop them with five stories a week. They were ignoring some of the biggest things in town." The *Register*'s editor, Thomas Geyer, disputed Bass's assessment of his own paper's shortcomings but praised the *Independent* for its neighborhood-level reporting.[6]

Among the stories the *Independent* broke were the local Democratic Party's refusal to support a black candidate for registrar of voters; the revelation that 114 of the city's 150 highest-paid employees worked in the education department and none of them were teachers; and a state senator's career as a real-estate developer whose projects, the paper editorialized, had resulted in "overcrowding, parking shortages, evictions, and rent increases all over town."[7] The paper survived boycotts and threats of boycotts, won awards, and sparked a national investigation of the U.S. Department of Housing and Urban Development after Paul Bass reported that the city had illegally paid $50,000 to a someone who was described as a "fixer" in order to obtain a $10.7 million federal grant.[8]

Perhaps the best-known moment in the *Independent's* brief history came on August 14, 1988, when Bass faced off against the reigning cable talkshow king of his day, Morton Downey Jr. Downey was a chain-smoking, foul-mouthed populist who regularly denounced his guests—his victims—as liberal "pablum pukers."[9] He had brought his act to the Palace Performing Arts Center in New Haven, and Bass was one of several media and political panelists who were drafted to engage with the host. Among Downey's cleaner lines that evening was: "I went out drinking with the Reverend Al Sharpton the other night, and I woke up shitfaced in a garbage bag." When Downey approached Bass, he said, incongruously, "I like your socks, sir."[10]

Downey switched from admiring Bass's hosiery to engaging in fisticuffs with him after he waved his cigarette in Bass's face and Bass told him to move it. "What's the matter, you don't like my lit cigarette? Well, you can just kiss my butt," Downey responded, bringing it even closer to Bass. What happened next was a melee: Bass spat on Downey's cigarette; Downey struck Bass and grabbed his shirt; and another panelist, Jim Motavalli, editor of the *Fairfield County Advocate*, tried to pull Downey off Bass. At that point Bass's sister, Sharon Bass, climbed onto the stage and slapped Downey, who responded by hitting her hard enough for her to wind up on the floor.[11]

"I hope that it exposes him as a dangerous bully who should not be supported," Paul Bass said the next day. "His show is dangerous. I think it gives the idea that the way you have to be is to have a mass assault on somebody." Added his sister: "I was wrong to hit him, but I should have hit him harder. I felt if I did it, I should have done it right."[12] Randall Beach, a columnist with the *New Haven Register*, saw the altercation as inevitable, writing, "Bass and Motavalli are my friends; they are gentle men not inclined to get into fights. They should never have gotten on stage with that sleazy blowhard." Paul Bass filed charges against Downey, but the district attorney decided not to pursue the case, citing the pressure of more urgent business.[13]

The *Independent* may have been a success with readers, but the Basses, Shapiro, and Savo had not found enough advertising revenue to sustain it. By 1989, their paper was running out of money. Paul Bass brought in two Massachusetts newspaper executives to help run the business side. It was a move that soured when the paper's principal financial backer, Betsy Henley-Cohn, made one of them publisher and gave her authority over the newsroom. In diplomatically worded commentaries that appeared in the *Independent,* Paul and Carole Bass resigned their positions.[14] But Paul Bass was less diplomatic in an interview with the *Register,* saying of the new publisher, "She wanted to be able to tell me what to cover, to send me out to a track meet" and "It was going to become like Beirut here." Still, he said of Henley-Cohn, "I'm leaving on good terms with Betsy, even though we got pretty angry at each other. She'll probably be seen as a villain, but she's a hero for supporting the *Independent* all these years."[15]

The paper staggered on for another eight months. Bruce Shapiro succeeded Bass as editor only to resign that fall, along with his eight-member staff. For Shapiro, the end came after an associate editor—Shapiro's future wife, Margaret Spillane—accused the sales and marketing director of assaulting her. "This was a terrible, explosive, and very damaging event," Shapiro recalled. The *Independent* finally shut down on February 27, 1990, after having spent $1.5 million. The paper was reportedly losing $12,000 a week at the time of its closing.[16]

"The recession hit. Ad sales couldn't keep up," Bass said some two decades later. "I run into Betsy sometimes and it's very warm. She's terrific. Most of that money was hers. I always tell her I feel guilty about losing her money. She always says don't worry; it was the most fun she ever had with a business investment."[17]

Shapiro, more reflective than Bass, had a somewhat different take when we talked—proud of the *Independent*'s journalistic accomplishments but pained to this day over the way it ended. "Most of us who worked there really loved it in a deep way. It was a profoundly gratifying project," he told me. "I spent quite a bit of time after the Basses left trying to save it."[18]

Shapiro still lives in New Haven, so I asked him what he thought of the revived, online *Independent.* He responded with a mostly positive though nuanced assessment. He called Melissa Bailey, whom he taught in an investigative reporting class at Yale, "one of the best students I ever had." And he praised the *Independent* for filling an unmet need in city news coverage, saying: "I think it certainly is playing a useful role in New Haven, especially given the collapse of the *Register.* I think it's a lot of people's primary news source about the city, and that's good."

But Shapiro also said he was disappointed in the *Independent*'s emphasis on breaking news over more in-depth pieces that examine and challenge the local power structure. "I don't think it reaches as high as it could given the urgent issues facing the city, the gifts of the staff, or the capacity of journalism," he said. "And this is beyond the *Independent.* I find this is true of a lot of local online projects. They settle for doing limited and conventional stuff. An awful lot of the reporting is very conventional cops reporting or city-hall reporting." He added: "I hope that doesn't come across as a harsh or negative assessment. It's just an honest journalistic view."

Shapiro's critique resonated with me. Paul Bass and I have talked several times about the virtue of running the *Independent* as a breaking-news service versus what is lost by not stepping back and offering more probing analysis. Bass's response has been to agree and disagree. The depth and analysis, he has argued, come from returning to stories again and again rather than from publishing, say, a 5,000-word takeout. As an example, he has cited (as would I) Melissa Bailey's dozens of stories on the city's nationally recognized education reform effort, which she has reported on both as a local-government issue, as a traditional newspaper would, and by regularly getting inside classrooms, which is rare for any news organization. Then, too, many of the *Independent's* breaking-news stories are longer and more detailed than is typical of other community news sites—or, for that matter, newspapers, constrained as they still are by the need to fit the news into a predetermined space. Still, I have sometimes found myself wishing for more perspective in the *Independent's* stories. With limited resources Bass has probably made the right choice. With additional resources he could do both on a more consistent basis.

When I asked Bass what lessons he had carried over from the print *Independent* to the online version, he replied: "Keep it very local. Respect your readership; don't write down to people. Do your reporting in person. I much prefer the not-for-profit/public service model this time so I'm not sweating ads and being in charge of ad people."[19] It's a much more matter-of-fact view than Shapiro offered, perhaps grounded in the reality that, for Shapiro, the *Independent* is part of the past, whereas for Bass it is a living, breathing organism that occupies most of his waking hours.

Bass didn't mention it, but he might also have cited perhaps the most powerful lesson of all—that the Internet has democratized the media by lowering the barriers to entry. No longer does someone who wants to start a community news organization need to line up investors and incur the enormous expenses of printing and distribution. Of the $450,000 Bass was on track to spend in 2011, the overwhelming majority of it was for salaries and benefits.[20]

After Bass left the print incarnation of the *Independent* in 1989, he returned to the *New Haven Advocate,* the alternative weekly where he had freelanced as a Yale student. It was there that he built upon his already growing reputation as one of the most respected journalists in his adopted city.

Joshua Mamis's eleventh-floor office at the *New Haven Advocate* overlooked the New Haven Green, a near perfect sixteen-acre square dominated by three historic churches. I sat down with the then publisher a little before six in the evening on a late October day in 2009. (Tribune Company, which owned the *Advocate* as well as the state's largest daily newspaper, the *Hartford Courant,* eliminated Mamis's position in July 2011, opting to run the paper out of its corporate office in Hartford.)[21] The sky was clearing after a torrential downpour that had flooded a section of Interstate 91 between Hartford and New Haven during my drive down from Boston. I marveled at the view, and he turned off the lights so we could get a better look.

Mamis and I had first met at a media-reform conference in San Francisco in 1996. Thirteen years later he'd gone a bit gray but was otherwise as I had remembered him, friendly and low-key. He was wearing a blue denim shirt and a red tie imprinted with Russian phrases. He was hired to be the editor of the *Advocate* in 1993, he told me, because Paul Bass didn't want the job anymore—he wanted to be a full-time reporter.[22] According to Mamis, Bass had been the stalwart of the staff, writing most of the news-section copy by himself—including a weekly political column, "Hit & Run"—and almost single-handedly holding city hall accountable with his fierce reporting. The economic revival that had taken place in the downtown was at least partly Bass's doing, Mamis said, because it was he who forced Mayor John DeStefano to clean up his ethically challenged economic development office in the early years of his administration. "The speed of the way Paul processes and manages information in his brain, I've never seen anything like it," Mamis said. "He'd actually sit there writing the story and talking to you at the same time and get it right. He used to fill 70 to 80 percent of the *Advocate's* news hole."

As an illustration of how dedicated Bass was to his job, Mamis cited the events of September 11, 2001. It was a Tuesday, as we all remember—and the day of a primary election in New Haven. The editor at the time (not Mamis) said it was too late to do anything for that week's paper and that everyone should go home. Bass was incensed. Instead, he rode around the city all day and wrote a story about how the election played out in the shadow of terrorism.

Bass wrote on a wide variety of topics during his years at the *Advocate:* for instance, about a rogue police officer who, according to a secret FBI report, may have framed an innocent man for a murder (seven years later, the convicted murderer was still fighting for his freedom);[23] a white supremacist arrested by federal authorities after he allegedly asked someone to burn down a house lest black people move into it;[24] a court battle between Tom Geyer, the aforementioned (and eventually former) editor of the *Register,* and Ralph Ingersoll II, the newspaper mogul who controlled the *Register,* over a two-million-dollar deal on which Geyer claimed Ingersoll had reneged;[25] and, always, about politics. Mark Oppenheimer, a journalist who did a stint as the *Advocate*'s editor from 2004 to 2006, remembers reading Bass's column when he was a Yale undergraduate in the late 1990s. "If he featured something in 'Hit & Run,' politicians got scared and people talked about it. Everyone knew who Paul Bass was," Oppenheimer told me.[26]

In keeping with the alternative-press ethos, Bass mixed left-leaning opinion with fact more freely at the *Advocate* than he does at the *Independent.* But his fairness and curiosity led him to want to understand conservatives as well as liberals. One example of this was his relationship with Tom Scott, a Republican activist and former state senator who cohosted a radio talk show with Bass in New Haven in the mid-1990s. The matchup, Scott said, was once described in the *Meriden Record-Journal* as "The Tommy and the Commie Show." The operations manager at the radio station was a disc jockey named Glenn Beck, who was just starting to inject right-wing politics into his own program. "We really liked each other," Bass told me, though he added that he tried to avoid joining Beck on the air—not always successfully.[27]

The first time Scott and Bass met—or, rather, didn't meet—was in early October 1980. Scott was helping out with a campaign appearance by Ronald Reagan in the Italian-American neighborhood of Wooster Square, where the future president addressed what the *New York Times* described as "hundreds of city residents and a good number of Yale students."[28] Bass was the guy in the monkey mask, carrying a placard that said "Darwin Was Right, Reagan's the Proof." Still a student at Yale, he was one of a number of people who had turned out to protest Reagan's appearance. Scott recalled that some of the protesters were hanging out of a tree, and one fell onto the roof of a truck. "And Ronald Reagan," Scott said, "without missing a beat, stopped his prepared remarks and in a very genuine way said, 'You know, you ought to be careful over there. You're going to get hurt.' I don't remember if it was Paul who fell."[29] According to Bass, it wasn't. "No. I didn't go in the tree. I can't climb a tree," he told me. As for the mask and the sign, Bass recalled, "All these nice Italian women were saying, 'Honey, you didn't come from a monkey.' "[30]

Scott and I met in the basement of Trinity Episcopal Church, one of the three historic churches on the Green, while his ten-year-old son rehearsed upstairs with the nationally renowned Trinity Boys Choir. Scott, who now makes his living as a suburban real-estate agent, said he first took notice of Bass in 1990, a decade after the monkey-mask incident, when he was running for an open congressional seat. Scott nearly beat the Democratic candidate, Rosa DeLauro, who as of 2012 was still the city's congresswoman. Despite being outspent by a considerable margin, Scott ran a competitive race by appealing to blue-collar Democrats on such issues as making English the official language of government.

"Paul got it," Scott said, explaining that Bass was one of the few journalists who understood that Scott had a chance of winning. "Paul spent a lot of time watching and observing the campaign. The long and short of it, Paul has a very inquisitive mind. He asks the right questions. He can be very liberal but still be very intellectually interested in what's happening anywhere, including on the right. And it was at that time, in that campaign, that I really began to respect Paul, as much we might disagree ideologically."[31]

Eventually, the *Advocate* began to fade, as did much of the alternative press nationally. The counterculture to which it had once given voice entered the mainstream. In 1999 the founders of the *Advocate* newspapers in New Haven and four other cities and towns in Connecticut and western Massachusetts sold out to the Times Mirror Company, whose holdings included the *Hartford Courant.* It was, at best, a leap of faith to imagine that the *Advocate* papers could keep raising hell under the watchful eye of Connecticut's dominant daily newspaper.[32] (The following year Times Mirror, whose flagship was the *Los Angeles Times,* was acquired by Tribune Company, owner of the *Chicago Tribune.*)[33]

At the time of the sale, Jonathan Harr, the author of *A Civil Action* and an alumnus of the *Advocate,* said he ran into one of the founders, Geoff Robinson, at a restaurant in Northampton, Massachusetts, and that Robinson tried to assure him that he hadn't done it for the money. "He said there were other buyers that wanted to pay more money," Harr told me in 1999. "But he sold to the *Hartford Courant* because he thinks they're the ones who are going to do the best job keeping it as an alternative voice." Harr paused before continuing, "I don't know where he gets that idea."[34]

Bass took a leave from the *Advocate* in 2004 in order to write a book about New Haven's experience with the Black Panthers, coauthored with the Yale political scientist Douglas W. Rae; and when they were finished, he didn't want to go back. "They were nice people, nice to me," he said of his new corporate bosses. "But they just destroyed the place, made it boring. Sent us to human-relations seminars about how to talk to avoid lawsuits. Like someone turns in a terrible lead you say, 'I love the way you misspelled everything, I really like where you're going with these factual errors,' that kind of crap. You learned to talk like a robot. There was just no creativity, and they were cutting back, cutting back."[35]

It was during his book leave that Bass began noticing blogs. He didn't want to write a blog, which in his mind meant offering his opinions without much in the way of reporting to back them up. And he didn't want to be a manager again. He figured he could raise enough money to pay himself a salary, and supplement his own reporting by aggregating other sources of New Haven news and information.[36]

And thus was born the idea of a revived, online-only *New Haven Independent.*

Can journalism have a theology? Perhaps the proper way to think about it is to ask what kind of theology journalism should have. According to Jay Rosen, a journalism professor at New York University, the dominant theology of journalism is the "View from Nowhere," which he defines as "viewlessness"—that is, a determination *not* to have a view. (I should note that calling the "View from Nowhere" a "theology" is my conceit, not Rosen's.) At root, the "View from Nowhere" is a parody of fair, neutral journalism.[37]

I knew that, at some point, I wanted to talk about spirituality and journalism with Paul and Carole Bass. After all, it is not every day that you meet a liberal, well-educated man—especially a journalist—who wears a yarmulke and who is strictly observant. I also knew from a mutual acquaintance that Carole had been raised a Catholic and had at some point embraced Judaism.

What eased me into the subject, and gave me the confidence to believe I understood enough at least to ask a few intelligent questions, was a wonderful chapter in a book by Mark Oppenheimer called *Thirteen and a Day: The Bar and Bat Mitzvah across America.* Oppenheimer, whose many jobs included writing an every-other-week religion column for the *New York Times,* had described the bat mitzvah of the Basses' older daughter, Annie, and of Paul and Carole's own journey from secularism to religious practice.

The Basses and the Oppenheimers, who live in the same Westville neighborhood of New Haven, belong to Temple Beth El-Keser Israel, or BEKI (pronounced "Becky"), which Oppenheimer characterizes as be-

ing a progressive, feminist-oriented Conservative congregation, "a mé-
lange of Shetland-wool intellectual and post-sixties hippie."[38] The Basses,
I learned, had been led by their daughter into a deeper embrace of religion. Paul had grown up in a secular Jewish household. Carole became
a Jew—she wanted me to understand that she did not "convert" from
Catholicism, as she had long since ceased to be a Catholic—in 1996.[39] She
learned to read Hebrew and chant Torah, as she did at Annie Bass's bat
mitzvah.[40] And in the spring of 2011 she was elected to serve as president
of the congregation.

The journalism of the *Independent* clearly is not based on the "View
from Nowhere." Rather, it is rooted in a view from somewhere and based
on a community-driven vision of conversation, cooperation, and respect.
It is a vision that sounds a lot like that of many religious communities,
and is the opposite of the top-down, we-report/you-read-watch-or-listen
model of traditional news organizations.

On one of my several visits to the Basses' home, over polenta and sweet
potatoes (Paul is a vegan, Carole a vegetarian), I asked them how religion
had helped shape the way they practiced journalism. "Journalism is a spiritual quest for me," Paul replied, "whether it's the breaking through barriers
to make connections to people—intense connections to people—to wrestling every day with what's right, and how to be a good soul. Do right—
wrestling with that a lot—and also what you're trying to accomplish with
journalism, which is to make the world a little better."[41]

Then he brought up a course he and Carole had once taught on *Lashon
hara,* which is a set of Jewish laws dealing with "evil speech." Not to be flip,
but evil speech almost serves as a working definition of journalism, or at
least of certain kinds. And as the Basses became more religious, they had to
come to terms with the idea that criticizing people, writing hurtful things
about them, was wrong.

"I had been practicing as a journalist for ten years before I knew anything about Judaism," said Carole, who, after her years as a journalist at
the original *Independent* and the *Advocate,* now works at an independent
magazine for Yale alumni. "And when I learned there was this whole set
of Jewish laws governing speech—restricting critical speech—I was like,
'Hmm. What does that mean for the way I make my living?'"

Although there may be occasional lapses, the way it plays out at the *Independent* is that people are treated with respect. When criticism is offered,
it is directed at policies, not personalities. The *Independent* rarely identifies
people who have been charged with a crime but not convicted, an unusual
journalistic practice that, for Paul, predates his move to religiosity. "But

I've definitely withheld a lot more negative stories about people when I've felt it wasn't relevant," he said. "Especially about family and sexual life."

It would be an exaggeration to suggest that the *Independent* is the journalistic embodiment of socially aware, community-oriented Judaism. The journalism in the original *Independent* of the 1980s, after all, was every bit as socially aware and community-oriented, and at that point the Basses were some years away from their spiritual awakening. Mark Oppenheimer told me he thought it more likely it was the Basses' interest in community that helped lead them to religion rather than the reverse.[42] But there is little doubt that the Basses' spiritual beliefs and their dedication to community reinforce each other.

This matters, because the *Independent* itself is a community—an online community that parallels the offline community, a place where people come together to discuss their interests, talk about local news and events, and sometimes bring expertise or new information to the table that enriches the site's coverage and leads to follow-up stories. Though there have been examples of such communities dating back to the earliest days of widespread Internet access, in the mid-1990s it was still a relatively new paradigm. And though many news organizations have attempted to create such communities, few have done it as well as Paul Bass has with the *Independent*—even given some periodic adjustments he has had to make in order to keep the conversation civil. As we shall see, Bass has accomplished all this in a city that traditionally has not been well served by its daily newspaper, the *New Haven Register*.

The *Register* may be changing for the better, but its new leaders must overcome decades of mistrust stemming from pernicious ownership and devastating reductions in news coverage. And they have taken on the difficult task of improving the paper while continuing to reduce the number of journalists who gather the news. Nonetheless, when I began my research, the *Register* was the moribund flagship of a bankrupt newspaper chain. By the time I finished, the paper and its corporate owner, the Journal Register Company, were out of bankruptcy, making money, and attracting admirers with a forward-looking philosophy that it called "Digital First." Long ignored, even despised, the *Register* was suddenly recast as a possible model for how the newspaper industry could reinvent itself.

CHAPTER THREE

Rebooting the *Register*

RANDALL BEACH walked into the coffee shop where I was waiting and stuck that day's *New Haven Register* in front of my nose. A veteran reporter and columnist for the *Register,* Beach had asked that we meet at a spot near New Haven Superior Court, where he spends much of his working day. Thin, white-haired, and tieless, Randy Beach looked like a reporter. It didn't take long for us to find each other.

What had Beach all worked up was page A3, an advertising-free sanctuary set aside for New Haven news. Or at least it had been ad-free. On this day, in the early spring of 2011, a good deal of space was taken up with ads, intruding on one of the few places in the paper where readers knew they could find a decent amount of city coverage. He also told me he had learned that the width of the paper would soon be shrunk as a cost-cutting move, making it as narrow as the *Hartford Courant.* That weekend I got out a ruler and determined that the *Register* was twelve and a half inches wide, the *Courant* eleven. Twelve and a half is fairly typical these days, though narrower than most newspapers were, say, a decade ago. The *New York Times* is twelve inches wide. Eleven is narrow indeed—and, by summer, the *Register* had in fact shrunk to that width.

Beach's career spanned the heights to which the newspaper industry had risen in the 1970s all the way down to its current precarious state. A native of Westchester County, New York, he had been with the *Register* off and on since 1977. In those days New Haven had two papers, the afternoon

Register and the morning *Journal-Courier,* both owned by the heirs of John Day Jackson. The Jacksons were notorious for their right-wing politics and authoritarian style. The *Hartford Courant* once reported that the family patriarch "was disliked by many of his readers" and "was widely criticized for publishing only those stories he wanted to see in type."[1] In Beach's telling, though, the Jacksons represented something of a golden era for New Haven newspapering. "At least the Jacksons were of the community. They cared about the community. They didn't care to spread their wealth to the reporters," he said. "But you can't replace that hometown ownership."[2]

In those days reporters at the *Register* and the *Journal-Courier* shared desks. Beach worked from 7 a.m. to 3 p.m., and would be leaving for the day as *Journal-Courier* reporters were beginning their shift. Despite the common ownership (and furniture), the two papers competed. "You'd try to cover up your notes and not talk too loud when the *Journal-Courier* people came in," he said.

What Beach remembered most fondly were the time and available resources. There was no twenty-four-hour news cycle, no Internet. Reporters wrote their stories on electric typewriters. A full-time reporter covered nothing but higher education. Another reporter covered utilities. The paper had several bureaus in the suburbs; by 2011 there was none. "In retrospect," Beach said, "it looks so relaxed."

There is little time for journalists to relax today, either at the *New Haven Register* or anywhere else. Newspaper owners are trying to hang on and find new ways of making money before technological advances, cultural and social changes, and a faltering economy sweep them away. And the *Register* has embraced an online strategy that represents what many believe may be the future of newspapering.

The *Register*—against all odds, given its long and not particularly distinguished history—found itself in 2011 at the forefront of a closely watched attempt to reinvent the newspaper business. Its corporate owner is the Journal Register Company, based in Yardley, Pennsylvania. Under John Paton, its charismatic chief executive, JRC, as the company is known, has embraced what Paton calls a "Digital First" philosophy. It's even the name of Paton's blog.

The idea behind "Digital First" is to morph as quickly as possible from a business model that is dependent mainly on print to one in which both the journalism and the revenues are focused on the Internet. It is a model that makes an old print guy like Randy Beach uneasy, and Paton himself has admitted there is no guarantee it will work.[3] But given the lack of any compelling alternatives, it is perhaps unsurprising that by the fall of 2011

Paton had emerged as a powerful and influential newspaper executive, his every move watched closely by the likes of the *Columbia Journalism Review* and Harvard's *Nieman Journalism Lab.* The newspaper tradition that Paton is trying to keep alive in New Haven is more than 250 years old. To visualize where the *Register* might be going, it is helpful to understand how it got to be what it is today.

New Haven's newspaper history extends back to 1755, when Benjamin Franklin helped to launch the *Connecticut Gazette,* an on-again–off-again journal that ceased publication in 1768. After several faltering starts, by the early nineteenth century the city had a lively newspaper scene. The *New Haven Register*—originally the *Columbian Register*—was founded in 1812 and competed with several other New Haven papers. It pursued a distinctly populist agenda, supporting President Andrew Jackson and the Democratic Party in the 1830s, while its competitors, which included the *Connecticut Journal* and the *Palladium,* backed the Whigs.[4] The *Register* also played an unfortunate role in several of the more shameful moments in New Haven's racial history.

The first of these unfolded in 1831, when plans were in the works to build "a 'college' for Negroes"—essentially, a trade school. The organizers raised money with little controversy until Nat Turner's slave rebellion in Virginia took place that August, frightening white America. Residents of New Haven and its press, including the *Register,* turned against the school, and there were outbreaks of violence in black neighborhoods at the hands of white mobs. By reflecting and amplifying rather than leading public opinion, newspaper publishers missed an opportunity to prevent, or at least ameliorate, racial hatred in New Haven. Instead, they made it worse.[5]

The city's white citizens and its newspapers had a chance to redeem themselves in 1839. Fifty-four would-be African slaves who had revolted aboard the schooner *Amistad* and killed most of the crew were put on trial in New Haven. Their cause was embraced by the press and much of the local population. The men were freed in 1842 and returned to Africa.[6] The *Amistad* incident, celebrated by the press, was a watershed moment in New Haven history, as well as the subject of veneration to this day in the form of numerous memorials.[7] A highly regarded charter school in New Haven is called the Amistad Academy.[8]

Unfortunately, soon the *Register* would once again find itself on the wrong side of racial justice. The paper became a daily in 1842. And in the 1850s, it opposed efforts to settle Nebraska so that the territory would not become part of the slaveholding states—a stance that placed the paper at odds with much of the community and its churches. Leading citizens in New Haven had organized a New Haven–Kansas Company to take part in the campaign to settle Nebraska. The *Register* denounced the mission, editorializing against "the political mountebanks, who under a religious garb, assumed to invoke the blessings of Providence on a heated partisan assemblage and to beg donations of murderous weapons."[9]

The modern *Register* came into being in 1895, when John Day Jackson acquired the paper from a prominent local newspaper family, the Osborns. A member of that family, Colonel Norris G. Osborn, continued as editor of the *Register* until 1907, after which he signed on to edit the *Journal-Courier.* Jackson bought the *Journal-Courier* in 1925, giving his family what would soon become a daily newspaper monopoly in New Haven, which lasted until his heirs sold out to chain ownership in 1986. The historian Rollin G. Osterweis describes the patriarch of the Jackson dynasty as "a vigorous journalist."[10] Vigor, of course, is no substitute for excellence or a commitment to serving the community, and by most accounts the Jackson papers fell short in both areas.

The Jackson family continued to operate the *Register* and the *Journal-Courier* for more than another half-century. But as with so many American newspapers—from the *Boston Globe* to the *Louisville Courier-Journal,* from the *Los Angeles Times* to the *Chicago Tribune*—the singular control exercised by the founder had dissipated by the third and fourth generations. In the 1970s, 1980s, and 1990s, a time when the newspaper business was a relatively easy way to earn high profits in monopoly markets, local ownership in city after city gave way to corporations that built media empires both regionally and across the country.

The story of Lionel Jackson, a son of John Day Jackson, is instructive for what it says about the demise of family-owned papers, not just in New Haven but also more generally. Lionel Jackson worked in various capacities at his father's papers, becoming national advertising manager in the 1940s. Upon their father's retirement in 1958, Lionel and his brother Richard took over. When their father died in 1961, they continued the family tradition of suppressing news they did not want reported by refusing to publish the news that John Day Jackson had left a $61.2 million estate.[11] But aside from that brief moment of family solidarity, the brothers did not get along. In 1972, the board of directors took advantage of Richard's ill health to name Lionel the sole publisher, whereupon Richard sued—one of several nasty legal actions that divided the Jackson family. As publisher, Lionel Jackson nearly destroyed his father's legacy with the disastrous 1973 purchase of the *Hartford Times,* a daily that was in the midst of losing a long battle with the *Hartford Courant.* The *Times* was shut down in 1976.[12]

Lionel's son Lionel Jackson Jr., known as Stewart, took over as publisher in 1982; but his father continued to control the papers as chairman and chief executive officer. As a sign of how poisonous family relations had become, when Stewart Jackson took the first step toward selling his family's papers in early 1986, he concealed his intentions by telling employees that an appraisal was being conducted in order to settle a lawsuit that family members had brought against both him and his father—a cover story that apparently no one found surprising or suspicious. Then, in 1988, Stewart and two of his sisters sued their father for removing paintings from their homes, selling two for nearly $1.8 million and attempting to sell a third. The children claimed that the paintings had been Christmas gifts. The father responded by saying they were still his.[13]

The end of family ownership came in 1986, when the *Register* and the *Journal-Courier* were sold to the Ingersoll chain for a reported $185 million.[14] It was a lot of money, and it would be unimaginably high a quarter-century later. By way of comparison, in 2009 the New York Times Company put the much larger and more valuable *Boston Globe* up for sale, only to pull it back when it was reportedly offered just $35 million—a fraction of the $1.1 billion it had paid for the *Globe* in 1993.[15] In the spring of 2011, another group of local investors was said to be preparing a bid of more than $200 million for the *Globe.*[16] That represented a slight recovery from the depths of the 2009 financial crisis.

Nevertheless, the days of the newspaper business being a lucrative one were over. For Ralph Ingersoll II, who headed up the purchase of the New Haven papers, the newspaper business ceased being lucrative a great deal earlier than that.

The first thing the new owners of New Haven's daily newspapers did was start slashing. The *Journal-Courier* was shut down, and the *Register* was moved from afternoon to morning publication. The full-time newsroom staff was cut from 186 to 150. Yet, at least in some quarters, Jackson ownership had been regarded as so toxic that the Ingersoll moves were seen as a breath of fresh air.

Paul Bass was among those who were charmed. Several months after Ingersoll took over, Bass wrote a full-page, largely positive profile for the original *New Haven Independent* of Thomas Geyer, the president and chief operating officer of Ingersoll Publications.[17] Geyer put down roots in New

Haven, taking a desk in the smoking section of the newsroom and even giving himself the title of editor.[18] Stewart Jackson continued to hold the publisher's title for several years under Ingersoll ownership, but Geyer was clearly the driving force.

For someone like Bass, Geyer seemed like a dream come true. Bass complained that, under Jackson ownership, the papers had editorialized that gay people should consider themselves lucky to be able to get mortgages, and that the attempted assassination of Ronald Reagan demonstrated the folly not of guns but of gun control. (That latter position has become mainstream, at least among some conservatives; but it was still considered exotically right-wing in the 1980s.) In contrast to those conservative positions, Geyer told Bass that one of his top priorities was greater diversity in the Sunday wedding announcements. "I notice we've run remarkably few black weddings, which is my ultimate test of whether a community feels like part of a paper," Geyer told Bass. "Obviously there's a problem there."[19]

Despite espousing good intentions, Geyer was never entirely trusted in the newsroom. But he fulfilled his promise to become more involved in the community, returning phone calls, taking part in local functions, and generally doing the sorts of the things for which the Jacksons had not been known. The Ingersoll era reached its pinnacle in June 1988, when the *Register* paid for the city's 350th-anniversary party on the New Haven Green—a two-day bash that began with Ingersoll and Geyer riding in the front seat of a carriage. The following year they demonstrated their journalistic ambitions by publishing a five-part series on race relations in New Haven that filled twenty pages of the paper.[20]

Not long afterward, it all fell apart.

Ralph Ingersoll II was the estranged son of Ralph Ingersoll, an admired journalist who had been the managing editor of the *New Yorker* and who in the 1940s founded *PM*, a left-wing daily newspaper in New York, long gone but not entirely forgotten.[21] (Coincidentally, Paul Bass told me that *PM* was an inspiration for the original print version of the *Independent*, and that he received his first $260,000 check to launch it on the same day that Ingersoll II's acquisition of the *Register* and the *Journal-Courier* was made public.)[22] Unable to and uninterested in competing with his father's legacy as a journalist, the younger Ingersoll set out to accomplish the one thing at which his father had failed: make money.

Ingersoll befriended Michael Milken, whose junk-bond operation, Drexel Burnham Lambert, raised nearly $600 million for Ingersoll to play with. By 1986 Ingersoll had built a chain of thirty-two daily papers and 110 weeklies, with revenues of about $300 million per year. Most of Ingersoll's papers were in smaller markets; thus, the *New Haven Register* stood as the chain's flagship.[23] In a fawning profile published by the business magazine *Forbes,* Ingersoll II was portrayed as "a smart, tough businessman," if a bit "snobbish," building a mighty newspaper empire with the help of Milken's "financial genius."[24] Within a few years Ingersoll would be broke, and Milken in prison for securities fraud.[25]

The weak advertising market of the late 1980s—the same ad market that had claimed the life of the first *New Haven Independent*—began to take a toll on Ingersoll and his newspapers, as he struggled to keep up with payments on the debt he had incurred in building his chain.[26] Ingersoll's behavior grew increasingly irresponsible. Under the terms of the complicated deal he had put together to purchase the New Haven papers, he was not the actual owner. Instead, he held them for an investor, Mark Goodson, the television impresario who had created or cocreated well-known game shows such as *The Price Is Right, Family Feud,* and *To Tell the Truth.*[27] In 1989, Ingersoll announced that he would buy out Goodson for an unheard-of $275 million. He also began devoting most of his time to a paper he had recently launched, the *St. Louis Sun,* a misconceived venture that placed a further strain on his company. The *Sun* lost $40 million in 1989.[28]

The end came in July 1990, when Ingersoll's financial backers, the New York investment firm of Warburg, Pincus, moved in and took over. The layoffs began on what came to be known as "Black Wednesday." In October 1990, nineteen *Register* employees were terminated. Shortly thereafter Tom Geyer got a call from Robert Jelenic, a onetime Ingersoll Newspapers president who was by then running the papers for Warburg, Pincus, telling him that he needed to lay off another thirty. Geyer asked for a face-to-face meeting, hoping he could talk him out of it. Jelenic responded by flying to New Haven, walking into Geyer's office, and firing him. In 1988 the *Register* employed 151 full-time newsroom staff members. By late 1990 that number had fallen to 108.[29] Ralph Ingersoll II left the country in order to manage his holdings in Europe. And by 1992 Tom Geyer, who had moved to New Jersey to become the editor of the *Parsippany Daily Record,* was suing his old friend and boss, claiming that Ingersoll had reneged on a $2 million payout.[30]

It was from the ashes of Ingersoll Newspapers that the Journal Register Company was built. The Journal Register story is not a happy one. At a time when the newspaper industry in general was slashing costs and cutting back on local coverage in order to boost profit margins, JRC was often cited as Exhibit A. In 1999 the *American Journalism Review* published a report on the state of local newspaper chains that included a long, withering assessment of JRC, which at that time owned twenty-four dailies and 185 other publications. It was an era very different from the current one. Monopoly newspapers in small and medium-size cities were a gold mine, and sharp-eyed investors realized they could enjoy profit margins of 30 to 40 percent by raising ad rates and circulation prices and by cutting staff. Jelenic was portrayed as a cross between a number-crunching wizard and the boss from hell. Gerald Ryerson, who quit as chief operating officer of the *New Haven Register* in 1992, said his duties included tracking the amount of film the photographers used, comparing odometer readings to see if they matched up with expense statements, and keeping the supplies under lock and key "because people would be stealing tape to take home for Christmas presents." And though Jelenic earned high marks for JRC's enviable cash flow, by the end of the 1990s many of his papers were losing circulation as they cut back on local news coverage.[31]

By the spring of 2008, the newspaper business was in serious trouble, and so was JRC. Jelenic had left the company because of illness; he was so despised that his subsequent death from cancer was actually celebrated by some on Internet message boards.[32] Among the challenges facing JRC was a rare miscalculation on Jelenic's part. In 2004 he had acquired a string of newspapers in Michigan, paying more than $400 million just as the automobile industry was about to nose-dive. Though JRC's profit margin was still more than 19 percent, the company was having serious trouble making payments on its debt, which was more than $628 million. Less than a year later, in 2009, JRC sought Chapter 11 bankruptcy protection.[33]

Given this dismal history, it is something of a shock that the Journal Register Company today is carrying out one of the more eagerly watched experiments in the news business. In August 2009, the company emerged from bankruptcy with new financing and a new organizational structure.[34] Then, at the beginning of 2010, the company hired John Paton as its chief executive. Paton had previously run impreMedia, a Spanish-language newspaper company with which he built a reputation for shifting the emphasis from print to online.[35]

Paton may or may not succeed, but he has proved to be a smart, savvy operator when it comes to marketing and public relations. Among other things, he put together a board of advisers comprising digital-journalism luminaries such as Jay Rosen of New York University, Jeff Jarvis of City University of New York, and Emily Bell, formerly of the *Guardian,* and since 2010 the director of the Tow Center for Digital Journalism at Columbia's Graduate School of Journalism. Perhaps JRC's best-known move was to open a "Newspaper Café" at the *Register Citizen* in Torrington, Connecticut. Anyone could walk into the café for coffee and muffins, print out free articles from the paper's archives, and, if they chose, attend the afternoon news meeting, which was also webcast. Paton's initiatives seemed to be working: JRC reported earning a profit of $41 million in 2010. Still, Paton acknowledged that the newspaper industry would likely be considerably leaner and smaller than it was at its peak. His characteristically blunt response to the likelihood that online advertising may never be as lucrative as its print counterpart was: "Stack digital dimes to match print dollars."[36]

In a profile in the *Columbia Journalism Review* Paton recalled outlining his "Digital First" vision to several hundred JRC employees. "They were like, 'Who's the fat guy in the front telling us that we're broken? Who the fuck is he?'" Paton said. His goals were ambitious. In 2011 the company was earning 85 percent of its revenue from print and 15 percent digital— the industry average, but a more favorable ratio than when Paton started, as JRC's digital properties had lagged under the Web-phobic Jelenic. By 2015, Paton aimed to push that up to 50 percent. "The sense of urgency at JRC is profound. I might run out of time. I mean, that's an honest and obvious question," Paton told the *CJR*.[37]

Paton is not afraid to reach out to the best minds in the business. In addition to bringing in the likes of Rosen, Jarvis, and Bell as advisers, he hired digital-media veteran Jim Brady, formerly of the *Washington Post* and *TBD.com* (the latter a short-lived experiment in online local journalism in Washington, D.C.), as JRC's editor-in-chief. Another *TBD.com* alumnus, Steve Buttry, joined the company and was put in charge of community engagement.[38] But there are real questions as to whether Paton's vision of community journalism—online, revitalized, and reengaged with its audience—is compatible with corporate chain ownership. As 2011 wore on, Paton found himself running an operation that was ever larger and ever more removed from, say, the newsroom of the *New Haven Register*. In July 2011, JRC was acquired by Alden Global Capital, a hedge fund that had also invested in several other newspaper companies.[39] Then, in September, Paton's portfolio expanded when he was put in charge of another property controlled by Alden—MediaNews Group, a national chain whose holdings included more than fifty daily papers in eleven states, the best known of which was the *Denver Post*. The new venture joining JRC and

MediaNews was dubbed Digital First Media.[40] Given Paton's increased responsibilities, he was going to have to delegate a great deal of authority to local editors and publishers to implement his program.

I met Matt DeRienzo, the editor of the *New Haven Register,* just before Labor Day weekend in 2011. It was not my first visit to the *Register.* I was struck, as I had been previously, by the unfortunate contrast between the *New Haven Independent*'s location and that of the *Register.* Whereas the *Independent*'s office at *La Voz* was in the heart of the downtown, providing easy access to city hall, Yale, and the surrounding neighborhoods, the *Register* occupied a former shirt factory, part of which was surrounded by a chain-link fence topped with barbed wire, amid an unattractive strip of offices and industrial buildings that ran parallel to Interstate 95.

The *Register* left the downtown in the 1980s. It was a story repeated again and again across the country. In the name of greater efficiency, newspapers moved into large plants accessible only by car in order to accommodate their huge presses and to make it easier for trucks to deliver newsprint, as newspaper-grade paper is called. But with no ready access to the people and institutions they were covering, reporters often found it more convenient, and faster, to do their work by phone rather than in person. Nor did members of the public often find their way to the offices of their local paper.

The person I had come to see, though, was promising to change all that. Just several weeks earlier, DeRienzo had been the publisher of JRC's Torrington paper, home of the "Newspaper Café." But in a midsummer shake-up, longtime *Register* editor Jack Kramer was removed, and DeRienzo was named regional editor of the *Register* as well as two other, much smaller JRC papers, the *Torrington Register Citizen* and the *Middletown Press,* and *Connecticut Magazine,* a monthly lifestyle publication.[41] In May, Kramer had turned down my request for an interview, telling me that if I wanted to speak to someone it would have to be handled "at the corporate level."[42] DeRienzo, in contrast, reached out to me after I wrote a blog post critical of the *Register*'s policy of not screening online comments, a policy that frequently resulted in racist content being posted on the *Register*'s website.[43] He said he agreed with my criticism, and told me he wanted to meet. It was a breath of fresh air, especially in light of the brush-off I had received from Kramer.

Just thirty-five when we met, DeRienzo came across as energetic and enthusiastic, bristling with ideas. "'Digital First' to me means putting journalism first, and it means putting community first, or readers first," he told me. "Readers don't need to come to us as this exclusive voice on high, like the nightly news. There are eight million sources of information out there for us, and our job is to sift through that for them and curate and aggregate and do original reporting as well, and to work with them at every step of the process to connect them with that. And we're the better for it, I think."[44]

We talked about some of the *Register*'s shortcomings, and he had an answer for every one of them. Racist comments on the website? He replied that he was going to put reporters and editors in New Haven to work screening comments before they were posted as soon as possible, as he already had in Torrington. (By the end of 2011, comment screening was in place.) A remote, pedestrian-unfriendly location? He told me he was already thinking about opening a downtown office that would include some of the innovations over which he had presided in Torrington, such as news meetings that were open to the public, coffee and muffins, and the like. (The *Register* took a big step in that direction in early 2012, when it signed an agreement with the *Hartford Courant* to print and distribute the paper. The presses were shut down, and, unfortunately, more than a hundred people lost their jobs.[45] As of June 2012, though, the *Register* staff had not yet moved out of its old headquarters.) A clunky, unattractive website, hardly befitting a company whose mantra was "Digital First"? DeRienzo agreed that it was "a horrible user experience" and added that a new design, and a new content-management system, were just months away.

But journalism is carried out by, well, journalists, and what DeRienzo couldn't promise was that there would be more of them. Quite the opposite in fact. At the time of our meeting, the *Register*'s newsroom staff comprised about seventy full-timers, fewer than half the number employed at the height of the brief Ingersoll-Geyer era. Nor was the *Register* done shrinking. One day after Kramer was let go, the paper laid off its Sunday editor and a full-time photographer.[46] What DeRienzo did say was that most staff reductions would take place in back-office operations such as circulation and production rather than in the newsroom. To the extent possible, even newsroom reductions would be focused on functions that could be centralized within JRC, such as putting together pages for national and international news. His hope, he told me, was that by engaging in a conversation with the community, the *Register* and the other publications he was running could improve even without adding costs. And he pointed out that, as regional editor, he commanded a staff of some 120 journalists who could be deployed on stories that none of the three papers could handle on its own.

In a business filed with journalism-school graduates in the newsroom and business-school graduates in the executive offices, DeRienzo has a distinctly unconventional background. He grew up in a conservative, evangelical Christian family in Gorham, Maine, a suburb of Portland. He was home-schooled, graduated from high school when he was sixteen, and went to college in Georgia with the idea of becoming a minister. He dropped out after one semester when he realized that the ministry "was clearly not for me." Following that, he worked a string of newspaper jobs, eventually becoming a top lieutenant to Bob Jelenic, where his duties included making sure JRC papers were not putting too much content on their websites. It was precisely that kind of retrograde thinking that he was trying to reverse.

I was particularly intrigued by DeRienzo's idea that the *Register* and the *Independent* could become partners. From the moment he arrived in New Haven, the *Register* began linking to some *Independent* stories, something that had rarely been done previously. Even during the Kramer era, *Register* journalists took part in community events organized by the *Independent* such as political debates. But DeRienzo told me he envisioned much more than that. He added that he had already met with Paul Bass to discuss how the two news organizations might work together.

"There seem to be opportunities where we could help him with funding while he maintains editorial control, which would be neat," DeRienzo said. "And there are all kinds of opportunity for us to expand his audience. Maybe even in print."

Could it happen? When I followed up with Bass, he responded with an e-mail that was full of ideas, including the possibility of running stories from the *Independent*'s Naugatuck Valley site, the *Valley Independent Sentinel,* in the *Register* and printing a weekly version of the *New Haven Independent* in collaboration with the *Register.* He added that he had previously had a similar conversation with John Paton, but cautioned that it was likely to be a "long long way til we get there for a variety of reasons. On both sides. But it's fun to dream about and maybe pursue at some point."[47]

One final observation. Shortly after I interviewed DeRienzo, I received a firsthand lesson in how aggressively he and Paton would defend their company's image. In early September 2011, the four candidates for New Haven mayor debated for the last time before the Democratic primary, discussing issues related to public education. The *Independent*'s Melissa Bailey covered it, took five photos, and wrote a 3,500-word story that attracted thirty-six reader comments. The *Register* did not; instead, on its website it linked to the *Independent's* story. I wrote a blog post criticizing the *Register* and expressing the hope that "Digital First" didn't mean that it would "outsource a story about an important city election to another news organization."[48] I posted a link to what I had written on Twitter and received an immediate response from Paton, who tweeted, "NHR doesn't cover one event and you think that calls into question Digital First as a strategy? Ridiculous."[49] DeRienzo posted a comment on my blog, explaining that the *Register* would have covered the event except for the fact that his editors and reporters had been led to believe it would be a "meet-and-greet social event and not a formal debate." He added that I was "off-base," writing, "To imply that we're doing less original reporting and linking to others to make up for that is just not correct."

I was taken aback, but I was also impressed. And I took it as an encouraging sign. Rather than erecting a wall of silence, both Paton and DeRienzo had showed that they really cared about what people thought of how they were performing. That pugnacity should serve them in good stead as they try to figure out how to reinvent their business and restore their newspapers so that they are once again profitable, essential resources in their communities.

Up to this point, it may seem as though the only media that matter in New Haven are the *Independent* and the *Register,* with an occasional contribution from the *Advocate.* To a large extent, that's true. As I wrote earlier, it has been estimated that as much as 85 percent of "accountability journalism"—the public-interest reporting that we depend on to govern ourselves in a democracy—comes from newspapers or, as is the case with the *Independent,* an updated, online version of a newspaper.

That is not to say that there aren't other news organizations in New Haven. The city has two commercial television stations with local newscasts, an ABC affiliate, and an NBC affiliate, but they are not considered enterprising sources of local news. Paul Bass has worked on some collaborations with the NBC affiliate—including a televised and webcast sitdown with the police chief, an alderman, and a neighborhood activist at Brū Café.[50] Connecticut also has an excellent public radio station, WNPR, the flagship of Connecticut Public Radio. But, as with most public radio stations, its mission revolves around national NPR programming such as *Morning Edition* and *All Things Considered.* Its original programming is regional and statewide rather than specific to New Haven.[51] And, as is the case with commercial radio in every part of the country, local news and talk shows have long since given way to syndicated programming. The local talk station, WELI, where Tom Scott and Paul Bass once held forth, had precisely one local weekday host, a former Glenn Beck sidekick named Vinnie Penn.[52] The rest of the lineup featured the likes of Rush Limbaugh, Sean Hannity, Michael Savage, Mark Levin, and Beck himself.[53] In such a media environment, the *Register* and the *Independent* are of paramount importance.

Back near the courthouse, Randy Beach was talking about what he saw as the differences between the two news outlets. Beach was a longtime admirer of Bass (the admiration was mutual, according to Bass)[54] and of the *Independent*—both the original print version and the website. Given what clearly came across as a skeptical attitude toward the Web (he groused about having to set up a Twitter account and to carry a Flip camera everywhere), I was amused when he listed one of the advantages that the *Independent* had over the *Register:* "They have so much more space compared to writing for the paper."[55] Well, yes.

I also asked him about a perception that went back to the original print *Independent* and was still persisting twenty-five years later—namely, that the *Independent* excelled at neighborhood coverage, while the *Register* played down city coverage and focused on the affluent suburbs. (When I asked Matt DeRienzo about that perception several months later, he did not disagree, saying, "I've heard criticism internally here that we don't cover the city as well as we cover the suburbs. My ears perked up at that.") Beach replied that he thought the *Register* did a good job of covering New Haven stories involving crime, public education, city hall, the courts, and Yale. It was an assessment I found interesting, as it had seemed to me that the *Register*'s major interests in New Haven were indeed crime and Yale. Furthermore, I told him that some African American activists I had interviewed saw the *Register*'s focus on crime as a negative reflection on their community.

Beach's response was both thoughtful and thought-provoking. If there's a murder, he said, he covers the court proceedings. And as someone who is often the only reporter there, he bears witness to the families of victims. "I do talk to the people, and of course a lot of them are African American," he said. "I'll tell the story through the survivors. Of course, we can always do better. I understand the criticism." It was a compelling media observation on Beach's part. Rather than being criticized for dwelling too much on crime in the black community, he was arguing, the *Register* deserved praise for taking the lives (and deaths) of its minority residents seriously. On the other hand, the *Independent*'s reporters are in New Haven's black neighborhoods every day, covering not just crime but also community issues, development, events, and the like. Though it is true that the *Independent* does not often venture into the courthouse, it was not difficult to see why the black residents I spoke with saw the *Independent*'s coverage of their community as more well-rounded.

I asked Beach whether he thought the *Register* had attained some stability since emerging from bankruptcy. "We haven't seen big layoffs in recent years," he replied, although he added that non-newsroom functions were still being downsized and outsourced. Then he grew more animated. "I've seen terrible layoffs," he said, citing in particular a move in 2008 to eliminate the paper's statehouse reporter.[56] He also mentioned sportswriters and photographers who had been laid off and were never able to find similar work. "They loved their jobs," he said. "It just kills you, because they were good at their jobs and it was in their blood." He told me that he was laid off during the Ingersoll meltdown of 1989. He freelanced, got hired by the *Advocate,* and in 1997 returned to the *Register.* He added: "I'm glad I was able to come back."

Beach is an accomplished journalist who cares about his craft, respects his community, and is worried about the future of his newspaper. He's seen a lot of changes over the years, and most of them have been for the worse. It's not hard to understand why he's skeptical about a shrinking news hole and about a new emphasis on the Web and social media over print.

Yet John Paton and Matt DeRienzo are almost certainly right in thinking that there's no turning back. Their efforts may not succeed. But in New Haven, at least, they've been able to establish a sense of momentum and excitement about a newspaper that just a few years earlier seemed destined to fade away.

CHAPTER FOUR

A Hotbed of Experimentation

IN A SIDE ROOM at the Mark Twain House in Hartford is a collection of artifacts related to Samuel Clemens's involvement in the printing industry. The most unusual is a hulking mass of metal and wood from the 1880s called the Paige Compositor, which could set type 60 percent faster than the Linotype machines in use at the time. Clemens sunk a fortune into James Paige's invention. But the Linotype already had a head start in the marketplace, and the Paige units proved too temperamental for heavy use. Paige died broke. And Clemens declared bankruptcy.[1]

I went to the Mark Twain House in March 2010 for the premiere of a documentary called *On Deadline: Is Time Running Out for the Press?* The film was about the near-death and uncertain rebirth of two small daily newspapers in Connecticut. Just as the Paige Compositor had been a reminder of how technology had revolutionized the newspaper business in the nineteenth century, when the rise of cheap, high-speed presses transformed it from a small-scale craft to an industrial operation serving a mass market, the story told in *On Deadline* was, at root, also one of technological change. So it was interesting that the panel discussion that followed included not just people from traditional newspapers but also from the post-newspaper age that was well under way: Christine Stuart, the editor and proprietor of *CT News Junkie,* and Keith Phaneuf, a staff reporter for the *Connecticut Mirror.*

Stuart and Phaneuf had both worked for the *Manchester Journal Inquirer,* a feisty tabloid published just outside of Hartford. Both had left for the uncertain but growing world of online journalism. *CT News Junkie* was a small, underfunded, for-profit website that churned out numerous stories, photos, and videos every day from the state capitol in Hartford. The *Connecticut Mirror* was a larger, newer enterprise, a well-funded non-profit site that covered the same state-government-and-politics beat. Early on a Tuesday afternoon in June 2011, the home pages of the two sites demonstrated both similarities and differences in content and tone. The stories in *News Junkie* tended to be short and punchy; in the *Mirror,* longer and more analytical. The two sites complemented each other, providing real competition of the sort that we used to get from print newspapers.

At *CT News Junkie,* the top story was about a federal lawsuit filed against the state's Department of Social Services on behalf of people who had been denied Medicaid benefits. (Because *News Junkie* is laid out like a blog, the top story is merely the most recently posted.) That was followed by an article from the *New Haven Independent,* with which Stuart had a content-sharing arrangement (she was also paid a monthly stipend to work as the *Independent's* statehouse reporter), on a letter sent by bicycle activists to Governor Dannel Malloy seeking state funding for bike paths. *News Junkie* had also posted a story about the Malloy administration's displeasure over a maneuver that allowed a higher-education official to collect his pension and a paycheck simultaneously.

The *Mirror* led with a feature on an innovative, faith-based health-insurance initiative that was exempt from the federal health-care law, and that was described as a possible model for those seeking to avoid government mandates. Its second story was on the double-dipping higher-education official. And the third article was about an ongoing effort to persuade state employees to accept a package of concessions approved by the Malloy administration and union leadership in order to avoid up to 7,500 layoffs over a two-year period. Such stories are standard statehouse fare, and some of them were also covered by the *Hartford Courant,* a traditional newspaper that still had a capitol bureau, although a far smaller one than in years past. Behind those stories, though, was a more intriguing one: how Connecticut emerged as a leading incubator for new forms of online journalism.

I first met Christine Stuart in April 2007, when we served together on a panel about blogging, journalism, and the law at the University of Massachusetts in Lowell. Nearly two years later we met again, on the fourth floor of the Connecticut statehouse in an underused annex to the main press room, which was itself something of a ghost town compared to earlier times.

The decline of statehouse coverage was nothing new, either in Connecticut or nationally. One of my first articles as the media columnist for the *Boston Phoenix* was about the shrinking statehouse press corps in Massachusetts. That was in the mid-1990s, a good decade before the crisis in journalism became acute. By 2009, the *American Journalism Review* found that only 355 full-time newspaper reporters were covering state capitols, down from 524 in 2003—a decrease of 32 percent. It was an across-the-board decline, with forty-four states being served by fewer full-time reporters covering state government than they had six years earlier. Overall, the *AJR* called the cuts "a staggering loss of reporting firepower at America's state capitols."[2]

Connecticut was hit especially hard. The *AJR* survey showed there were just nine full-time reporters covering the statehouse.[3] By early 2010, that number had shrunk to seven or eight, down from about twenty-five in the 1980s.[4] Financially pressed publishers may convince themselves that their readers don't care about state government. But the doings of governors and legislators, and what they mean in terms of taxes, social services, public education, and the like, are important, and reporting on those issues goes to the heart of public-interest journalism. How are voters supposed to be well-informed if journalism does not inform them?

Christine Stuart, who was in her early thirties when I first interviewed her in 2009, grew up in Illinois and attended Central Connecticut State University on a volleyball scholarship, graduating in 1999. Her first job out of college was at the *Hartford Advocate,* a sister paper to the *New Haven Advocate,* part of the chain of alternative weeklies that had just been purchased by the Times Mirror Company. A year later, when Times Mirror sold out to Tribune Company, employee stock options she had received allowed her to make a down payment on her house—a rare case of corporate newspaper ownership being good for journalists.[5]

By 2002, Stuart was at the *Journal Inquirer,* covering stories ranging from municipal government to the troubled state trash agency to a triple murder. But she wanted to cover the statehouse. When I pointed out that she might have had to wait five or ten years before a statehouse job opened up at the *Journal Inquirer,* she replied, "Right. Or kill off another reporter." She said it with an easy laugh, as she often does in conversation. Behind that laugh, though, was some real competitive fire.

In 2006 Stuart had a chance to buy *CT News Junkie* from Dan Levine, a *Hartford Advocate* alumnus who had started the site the year before. She wouldn't tell me what she paid for it; given the site's modest beginnings, it couldn't have been much. But with it came a part-time job with benefits, compiling legal cases and writing occasional stories for the Courthouse News Service.

During my first visit, *News Junkie* consisted of just Stuart and an intern. Web traffic and revenue were modest. Her audience was mainly political insiders, though her additional status as the *New Haven Independent*'s statehouse reporter broadened her readership beyond that circle. She told me that she saw herself as filling a niche left by the diminution of the traditional media's capitol coverage. And despite the luxury of not having an editor to tell her what she could or could not write, she said she worked hard to provide straight, unbiased reporting and to keep her opinion out of her stories. "I want to be a well-respected online news site that people can trust and go to for their information," she said.

As for the niche she was filling, that was pretty obvious. For example, during my visit she was the only reporter who covered the release of a national study on domestic violence conducted in part by the University of Connecticut. Stuart took notes, shot photos, and posted a PDF of the study along with her story.[6] She also frequently shoots video to accompany her stories and has experimented with live video as well. She seemed to have garnered the respect of the people she covered. State representative Gerald Fox, a Stamford Democrat, told me that Stuart's work was "consistently accurate" and "a valuable resource." Colin Poitras, a spokesman for the University of Connecticut and a former statehouse reporter for the *Hartford Courant,* called himself "a big fan of *CT News Junkie.*"[7]

Still, it was clear that Stuart, for all her hard work, was barely scraping by. She talked about various schemes she had to convert her site from a for-profit to a nonprofit. Her only real income came from her Courthouse News job. "I think that I'm pretty dedicated to trying to make this work," she said. "I would love to see it flourish and grow, and I would love to be able to pay myself a salary from it. I've turned down a few jobs in order to do that, and in order to dedicate myself to coming up with a business model that works, that actually could be replicated across the country for other people who wanted to do this."

Two years later, as we shall see, Stuart was doing considerably better. She hadn't figured it out yet. But she was a lot closer than she had been in 2009, even with a complication she didn't have to worry about back then—competition, in the form of the *Connecticut Mirror.*

The largest online-only news organization in Connecticut in 2011 was not the *New Haven Independent,* and it was certainly not *CT News Junkie.* Rather, it was the *Mirror,* which employed ten people, nine of them journalists, to cover state government, politics, and policy. You might say the decline of the *Hartford Courant* was what made the *Mirror* possible. The first editor of the *Mirror,* Michael Regan, had previously been a high-level editor at the *Courant.* The capitol-bureau chief, Mark Pazniokas, covered politics for the *Courant,* which laid him off in March 2009. Regan told the *Columbia Journalism Review* that Pazniokas's layoff was the catalyst for discussions that culminated in the creation of the *Mirror.* Several other *Mirror* journalists had also worked for the *Courant.*[8]

Also unlike the *Independent* and *News Junkie,* both of which began as one-person operations, the *Mirror* was born big, on the strength of $1.8 million in foundation grants intended to pay for its first three years. Those foundations included the John S. and James L. Knight Foundation, a major funder of journalism projects across the country, and the Community Foundation for Greater New Haven, which also provided much of the grant money for the *Independent.* Since its launch in January 2010, additional grants and sponsorships allowed the *Mirror* to boost its annual budget from $600,000 into the $800,000 range.[9]

In late March 2011, I visited the *Mirror's* offices on the fourth floor of the Hispanic Health Center in downtown Hartford, several blocks from the statehouse. The offices were nearly empty. Staff members all had laptop computers, and most of them worked at the state capitol or elsewhere—including Washington, D.C., where the *Mirror* had the only full-time reporter employed by a Connecticut news organization.[10]

I was met by James Cutie, a former *New York Times* executive and venture capitalist who was the chief executive officer of the Connecticut News Project, the nonprofit that was set up to publish the *Mirror.* A friendly, bespectacled, mild-mannered man with salt-and-pepper hair and a beard, Cutie worked out of a crowded space furnished with two battered metal desks and a conference table with a plastic top.

Large as the *Mirror* already was, Cutie said he needed $1.5 million to $2 million a year "to really perfect what we're trying to do." To get there, he was trying to build on the foundation money the *Mirror* already had by adding such revenue streams as corporate sponsorships and individual donations, similar to the funding model for public radio stations—or, for that matter, the *New Haven Independent.* Cutie's goal was to become the source of record for statehouse news in an era when newspapers could not afford that responsibility. He compared the *Mirror* to the *Texas Tribune,* another large nonprofit website that provided statewide coverage of politics and government.

Web metrics are hazardous. External measuring services such as Compete.com undercount traffic, especially that of small, local sites. Internal measurements such as those provided by Google Analytics overcount traffic.[11] But Compete.com does provide a roughly accurate apples-to-apples comparison. And it showed that the *Mirror* had a somewhat larger audience than *CT News Junkie,* both in good months—about 27,000 to 17,500 unique visitors in May 2011—and not-so-good—about 13,000 to 8,500 unique visitors the previous month. (By way of comparison, the *New Haven Independent* attracted more than 43,000 unique visitors in May and more than 38,000 in April, according to Compete.) Cutie told me his Google Analytics count for February 2011 was 65,000 uniques, approximately triple the 21,000 that Compete measured—a ratio that I have found is typical when I ask website operators about their internal traffic and compare it with Compete's data. Cutie guessed that the *Mirror* had a steady daily readership of about 5,000, which, he observed, could grow to 20,000 to 40,000 if the site reached just 1 or 2 percent of the state's two million voters. "There's got to be that many people who are attentive and civically engaged," he said.

Moreover, the Internet was not the only route by which the *Mirror* distributed its journalism. Cutie told me that ten of the state's seventeen daily papers had licensing agreements to carry *Mirror* content. Though the *Courant,* the largest paper in the state, was not one of them, it had on occasion gotten permission to republish stories as well. The cost to those newspapers—nothing, though Cutie said that could change.[12] "On any given day one of our reporters' stories can end up in a fair amount of circulation the old-fashioned way, which is still the way a lot of people read news," Cutie said. "It's part of our mission as a nonprofit to get the content out there."

The world of Connecticut journalism is a small one. So it was not surprising to see Paul Bass listed on the site as one of the Friends of the Connecticut News Project, which consisted of fourteen people who gave advice to the *Mirror,* even though Christine Stuart was his capitol reporter. (Mark Oppenheimer, who'd written about Annie Bass's bat mitzvah, was among the fourteen as well.) Marcia Chambers, the retired *New York Times* reporter whose online *Branford Eagle* is part of the *New Haven Independent's* website, was a member of the project's board of directors.[13]

I asked Cutie to define the difference between the ways in which the *Mirror* and *News Junkie* approached stories. His answer reflected my own experience in reading the two sites. "I think Christine's probably a little bit more on the immediate news coverage," he said. "We're probably more on the take-an-extra-day-and-be-a-little-bit-more-analytical. And I don't mean one's better than the other. I think they integrate."

Another difference was the *Mirror*'s use of databases and documents. The *Mirror* offered a deep "Political Guide" on the state's elected officials, including information such as their committee assignments, bills they had sponsored, and their financial-disclosure forms. The "Document Library" consisted of just about everything the staff could get its hands on—education reports, budget documents, environmental studies, and the like. As Regan, the *Mirror*'s founding editor, had explained, "That's a central part of our mission—in addition to covering the news, we want to give people access to stuff that's hard or impossible to find on the Web."[14] *News Junkie* frequently posted source documents, as does just about every online news organization. But by gathering those documents in a comprehensive archive, the *Mirror* had created a valuable resource for researchers, other news organizations, and the public.

If you scroll down the left-hand column of the *New Haven Independent* (or, for that matter, the *Connecticut Mirror*), you will find several dozen links to other websites, many of them devoted to local news in Connecticut. Some of them are produced by unpaid citizen journalists. Some are quite a bit more ambitious than that. A sampling gives you an idea of the range and depth of the Connecticut blogosphere. *My Left Nutmeg* is a political blog for liberals in the Nutmeg State. Tom Ficklin's eponymous blog covers events in New Haven's African American community. *CT GreenScene* is an environmental blog. *Design New Haven* is a remarkably detailed blog that covers "design and urban affairs in Downtown New Haven, Connecticut." *WestportNow* is an advertiser-supported community site that harks all the way back to 2003.

Several projects are large enough and interesting enough to warrant special mention.

SeeClickFix. Thanks in part to a story in the *New York Times* in early 2010, this site, which combines mapping and user participation, had become well-known both locally and nationally. Users could post complaints—from potholes on their streets to drug dealers in front of their houses—and plot them on a Google map. The idea was that local officials and the media would see those complaints and take action, either by fixing the problem or reporting on it.

The *Times* story told the tale of Doug Hardy, an editor at the *Manchester*

Journal Inquirer, who decided to use *SeeClickFix* on the paper's website as a way of restoring traffic after access to full stories was blocked by a paywall.[15] Though the story did not say so, Hardy is Christine Stuart's husband. He later left the *Journal Inquirer,* and was devoting most his energies to building up the business side of *News Junkie.* Did I say that the world of Connecticut journalism is a small one?

I met the cofounder and chief executive of *SeeClickFix,* Ben Berkowitz, then thirty-one, on a rainy day in May 2010. His second-floor office was just a few blocks from the *New Haven Independent.* He looked like a tech entrepreneur, casually dressed and in serious need of a shave. The project started, he told me, with graffiti he was trying to get removed from his neighborhood. "I thought the Web would be a good place to publicly voice my concerns to city government, and to my neighbors," he said.[16] He built the basic engine, and *SeeClickFix* started to grow. In 2009, he contacted an editor at the *Boston Globe,* complimented him on the paper's online pothole map, and said he could do it better. Soon the *Globe* was partnering with *SeeClickFix.*[17] Berkowitz said the project also won a $25,000 grant from We Media, an organization that supports media entrepreneurship.

At the time we met, *SeeClickFix* had some four hundred media partners, including the *Independent* and the *New Haven Register.* A year later, he told me that number had doubled.[18] A news organization can embed *SeeClickFix* on its site for free (users see advertising when they click through) or pay for a customized version. Berkowitz said he had not originally considered it to be a journalism project, but he realized it had become one. "I remember this guy from the Associated Press saying to me, 'This is what I used to do when I was twenty-two years old and I was starting the beat. I would go out and I would report potholes, right? And this is the thing that the local press was made to do. They were meant to hold governments accountable,' " Berkowitz said. "This is what it's all about. The local press, strapped for resources, having to think more efficiently, more like a start-up, figuring out how to use citizen resources to hold governments accountable. It all kind of fit in."[19]

The *Independent* embeds the *SeeClickFix* RSS feed for New Haven near the top of its right-hand column. As an example of how it can work as a reporting tool, consider a story written by Melissa Bailey in January 2010 about "the ugliest storefront on Chapel Street," a tattoo shop turned AT&T store with a hideous facade that looked like it was made of some sort of black foam. Bailey learned about the storefront by reading the complaints at *SeeClickFix.* She quoted from some of the forty-two complaints in her story—which in turn generated another twenty-four comments on the *Independent*'s site.[20]

It was a lesson in how technology can change the relationship between journalists and their readers for the better, helping the *Independent* build community and civic engagement, which in turn creates interest in the *Independent*'s journalism. It's not the stuff of awards. Rather, it's something more important than that: building an engaged audience. "I always say that potholes are the gateway drug to civic engagement," Berkowitz once said.[21] It may prove to be a gateway drug for connecting people with news about their communities as well.

CT Watchdog.   As with the *Connecticut Mirror*, this site got its start via the *Hartford Courant*—the proprietor, George Gombossy, was laid off from the *Courant* in August 2009. But it gets uglier. Gombossy claimed that his job was eliminated because he criticized an advertiser, the mattress company Sleepy's, in his role as the *Courant*'s consumer columnist, an accusation that management denied. Gombossy later sued the *Courant* and its owner, Tribune Company, claiming he had been wrongfully terminated for exercising his First Amendment rights. In late 2011 he withdrew the suit without explanation just as it was about to go to trial. A brief story he posted on his own site shed little light on what had happened.[22]

CT Watchdog, Gombossy's for-profit, advertiser-supported site (which was also the name of his blog at the *Courant*), may have been born from anger, but its journalism is solid. He brought in several other journalists as contributors, and they report on consumer and health issues, the economy, foreclosures, and the like. Gombossy told me that his consumer column was carried by a number of Connecticut media outlets, including the *New Haven Register*. As of the summer of 2011, he said, all revenues were being reinvested in the business. He was also preparing to launch similar sites in Massachusetts and Florida.[23]

Connecticut Health I-Team.   Yet another site founded by former *Hartford Courant* journalists, the nonprofit *C-HIT* was hosted by the *New Haven Independent*. (Technically, *C-HIT,* as well as the *Branford Eagle,* are part of the Online Journalism Project, the nonprofit organization that Paul Bass established for tax purposes and that is the *Independent*'s publisher of record.) The editor, Lynne DeLucia, and the senior writer, Lisa Chedekel, both won Pulitzer Prizes for their work at the *Courant*. Several freelance journalists work for the site as well. Journalism students at Quinnipiac University in nearby Hamden, Connecticut, help with research.[24]

The idea for the site began rather idyllically, on a beach in Nantucket in August 2009, when a national debate was unfolding over what would become the Affordable Care Act, also known as Obamacare. "Lisa was there visiting me, and we were having a conversation among friends (non-journalists, a doctor and a nurse/health consultant) about the need for good coverage of health care," DeLucia told me. "Staff cuts were ongoing in newsrooms in Connecticut. Downsizing meant less coverage in key areas: health, environment, education, and investigations, among others. And at the same time, small investigative websites were starting to crop up across the country. And we asked ourselves: Could we launch our own website?"[25]

The mission, DeLucia continued, was "to provide original, unbiased coverage of health and safety issues in Connecticut and the region." The site launched in late 2010 with $125,000 in foundation funding and, later, another $25,000 from private donations and content-sharing arrangements with other media outlets, which include the *Manchester Journal Inquirer,* the *New London Day, CT Watchdog,* and public radio station WNPR. The stories are often featured on the *New Haven Independent's* home page as well.[26]

As with the *Mirror, C-HIT* had assembled searchable databases on subjects such as school-cafeteria inspections, ambulance-company response times, and nursing homes. On an afternoon in June 2011, the site featured stories on a physician who had lost his right to practice because of his record as a sexual offender; the precipitous rise in health-care premiums; and a Memorial Day piece on the state of health care for veterans.

DeLucia's goal was to make *C-HIT* self-sustaining by selling its content, by soliciting private donations, and by putting together educational programs such as summer journalism camps. She said she hoped that *C-HIT* would become "a mini AP for other media in Connecticut," and that the project could expand into other parts of New England.[27]

CT Capitol Report. Begun in 2010 by a former state legislator named Tom Dudchik, the site was a knockoff of the *Drudge Report,* right down to the cheesy fonts and the blaring headlines. For instance, a bland headline in the *Connecticut Mirror* on the possibility that state employees would vote against union givebacks, "AFSCME Unit Rejects Concessions, Making Ratification Unlikely," became, in the *Capitol Report's* telling, "Showdown: AFSCME Votes No Toast: CEUI/SEIU Rejects SEBAC."[28] Granted, that's a lot of alphabet soup. But it sounds like it might be interesting, doesn't it?

Dudchik had attracted a devoted following among political insiders— as well as the attention of the *Wall Street Journal,* in which Paul Bass was quoted as calling Dudchik "Connecticut's paperboy."[29] Like Matt Drudge, Dudchik offers virtually no original content; rather, he has a good eye for what people might click on, and he links to it. Also like Drudge, Dudchik's provocative style has its detractors. Once he went so far as to run a photo of two gay, shirtless men in sailor hats to illustrate a story about whether Navy chaplains should be allowed to perform same-sex marriages.[30] Not exactly fair, neutral journalism, but certainly designed to attract eyeballs.

It is one thing to observe that Connecticut is the home to a number of innovative online news projects. It is quite another to explain why. Which is why I paid a visit to Lisa Williams, the founder and chief executive of a small company called Placeblogger, which tracks and studies the four thousand or so local news sites that had sprung up across the United States. I had known Williams from her days of running *H2otown,* a pioneering local blog that covered Watertown, the Boston suburb where she and her family live.[31] *H2otown* was no more, but Williams had maintained a keen interest in new ways of doing local journalism. We met at the Cambridge Innovation Center, which took up nine floors of an office building in Cambridge's Kendall Square and was home to more than two hundred start-up ventures. As she talked, she illustrated her points by writing on a wall—a built-in whiteboard, naturally—with a red sharpie.

"When I look at places that are really vital, they tend to be what I think of as second-tier media markets," she said. "Particularly if they're adjacent to a big media market. Oakland"—home to *Oakland Local*—"is better than San Francisco. New Jersey"—home to *Baristanet,* an inspiration for many local blogs, including *H2otown* and the *New Haven Independent*— "is better than New York."

And size matters. Williams had found that a number of successful local websites serve areas with a population right around 100,000. New Haven, with about 124,000 people, was thus an ideal location for a project like the *Independent.* Places with 250,000 to 400,000 people had proved to be fertile ground too, she said. Oakland's population, for instance, was just below 400,000. Other forces come into play in a city like Boston, whose population is nearly 620,000 and whose metropolitan area of 4.5 million people is larger than the entire state of Connecticut, with its population of 3.6 million.[32] "Once you get up above this number, bigger companies will come in and invest, and there's not as much opportunity for a bootstrap organization," Williams said. "I think the reason that there isn't much in Boston is that you're outgunned."

Williams's findings, combined with my own sense of what had happened in Connecticut, should inspire optimism among anyone concerned about the future of journalism. Simply put, where there's a vacuum, someone will try to fill it. The *New Haven Register's* decline paved the way for the *New Haven Independent*. The shrinking of the *Hartford Courant* gave birth to *CT News Junkie*, the *Connecticut Mirror*, *CT Watchdog*, and *C-HIT*. These projects may not fully replace what was there before. But journalists are finding ways to provide the information we need.

In May 2011, a little more than two years after my first visit to the Connecticut statehouse, I returned to the pressroom annex to catch up with Christine Stuart and *CT News Junkie*. What I found was that both the site and the business were growing.

As I have already mentioned, Stuart's husband, Doug Hardy, had quit his job at the *Manchester Journal Inquirer* and was devoting most of his time to building what had become a *News Junkie* network.[33] The couple had brought in a freelancer to write a daily "Morning Coffee & Politics" e-mail, a free, advertiser-supported venture that Stuart said had become a must-read among capitol insiders. They had brought in another freelancer to take some of the reporting load off Stuart. Other freelancers and interns were contributing as well. They had started a new site, *CT Tech Junkie*, to cover the state's burgeoning technology economy and launched yet another site, *CT Photo Junkie*, to give the freelance photographers who were shooting for them a chance to resell their work.

They told me that 2010 had been an especially good year, with the site making some $47,000 in advertising revenue. In large measure, that was a reflection of several high-profile races, including hotly contested campaigns for the governor's office and for the U.S. Senate. So much political advertising came in, Hardy said, that he and a business partner started a network in order to steer some of it to smaller independent sites. Revenues were split on a fifty-fifty basis. In 2011, a non-election year, the site continued to grow, pulling in nearly $64,000 in ad revenue and turning a slight profit.[34]

Still, Stuart and Hardy were not getting rich. Stuart continued to work part-time for the Courthouse News Service, and Hardy had a similar job with Westlaw. I asked Stuart whether she had explored the idea of working for the *Mirror*. She said she had, but ultimately decided not to because she and Hardy believed it could mean the demise of *News Junkie* without any guarantee of long-term job security.

He: "We thought that the brand would be gone. It was a very hard discussion."

She: "I was about to say yes, and he was the one who stopped me. We fought for days."

Stuart also couldn't contain her competitive edge when I asked her to define the difference between her coverage and the *Mirror*'s, saying: "I think that they have a different mission than I have. Their mission is to give this in-depth analysis of public policy that's fairly dry and boring." She laughed, and added, "I got an eighty-five-year-old woman to say 'penis.' And I got ahold of the union agreement before anybody else did." The first was a reference to state senator Edith Prague, who had said of a notorious murder suspect, "They should bypass the trial and take that . . . animal and hang him by his penis from a tree out in the middle of Main Street." The second concerned the state's budget negotiations, which involved a proposal for public-employee unions to make concessions in return for a no-layoff agreement.[35]

Hardy was visibly pained by Stuart's criticism of the *Mirror*, and before I left she had softened it. "The *Mirror* does have great coverage, and the coverage that they do comes from the experience they have at the capitol," she said, referring to the site's veteran reporters. "I mean, they've been around here for a long time. They've got a lot of sources. They have a lot of knowledge about things."

Competitiveness aside, Stuart and Hardy also offered a more noteworthy criticism. When I interviewed Stuart in 2009, she said one of the ways she hoped to make money was to syndicate her work to newspapers in Connecticut.[36] Two years later, she and her husband said the *Mirror*'s practice of giving away its content to for-profit news organizations had killed off that opportunity.

"Newspapers recently have actually been coming to me, and they're like, 'Oh, can we take your content for free like we do the *Mirror*'s?'" Stuart said. "And I was like, 'No, you can't.' So they completely undercut us in that market, where we could have had a little bit more income coming in—a few hundred bucks from newspapers to take our copy." Added Hardy: "By giving away their newspaper-of-record-level coverage of the capitol, they are providing for-profit newspapers with coverage that would otherwise be a job. They could be creating the impetus to undercut the marketplace."

There is no good answer to Stuart and Hardy's lament. One of the ways in which newspapers are providing coverage that they no longer can pay for themselves is by running free content from nonprofit organizations. In Boston, for instance, journalism students at Northeastern University, where I work, produce free stories for the *Boston Globe,* including front-page investigative pieces under the direction of Walter Robinson, a Pulitzer Prize–winning former top editor at the *Globe*. At Boston University, the New England Center for Investigative Reporting employs several full-time journalists and works with students to put together high-profile reports that have run in the *Globe* and other local media outlets. In 2009, a landmark report titled "The Reconstruction of American Journalism," by retired *Washington Post* executive editor Leonard Downie Jr. and Columbia Journalism School professor Michael Schudson, highlighted those and other such collaborations across the country, and called on universities and nonprofit institutions to do more.[37] In that context, the *Mirror*'s service is just a small example of that growing practice. To most observers, it seems like a good idea—unless you are being harmed by it, as Stuart and Hardy clearly were. (A year after we talked, the *New Haven Register* and other Journal Register papers in Connecticut were paying for some content from *CT News Junkie* in what Hardy called "an experiment.")[38]

By 2011, Stuart was no longer thinking about pursuing nonprofit status for *News Junkie*. She and Hardy believed the business was progressing strongly enough to stick with it as a for-profit venture. Their preferred metric was not unique visitors but page views, and in May 2011, a big month for political news in Connecticut, Stuart said users looked at some 247,000 webpages at *News Junkie*—which was, for her, a new record. Another record, nearly 340,000 page views, was set in June, as a state budget deal was rejected by the largest union, leading to fiscal chaos. (Eventually a new deal was reached.)[39]

The story of *CT News Junkie* is encouraging. There is, after all, a limit to how much journalism nonprofit organizations can support. In that regard, the continued survival and growth of a for-profit site is good news. But you cannot help but note the contrast in resources and money available to a commercial site like *News Junkie* and a nonprofit like the *Mirror*. The hard work of journalism is expensive. The question of who—if anyone—will pay for that journalism remains an open one.

CHAPTER FIVE

Print Dollars and Digital Pennies

THE IDEA THAT a nonprofit organization can be more financially viable than a for-profit business may seem counterintuitive. Yet as the experience of *CT News Junkie* and the *Connecticut Mirror* suggests, technology—at least in these early years of online news—has turned the economics of journalism upside down. At *News Junkie,* Christine Stuart and Doug Hardy struggle to build a for-profit business. At the *Mirror,* Jim Cutie is able to pay a relatively large staff of experienced reporters, provided he can continue to persuade foundations, corporate underwriters, and readers to give him money.

The disparity came up the first time I met Paul Bass. He told me that when he started thinking about resurrecting the old *New Haven Independent* as a website, he first looked into establishing it as a for-profit venture, as the original *Independent* had been. He soon realized, though, that he could raise more money more quickly by simply asking foundations for grants than he could through the laborious process of trying to attract advertisers. In describing his decision to take the nonprofit route, Bass wrote: "In my mid-forties, with two kids and a mortgage, I couldn't afford to dive in without a guaranteed living. I would launch a daily online New Haven news site only if I had guaranteed funding for at least the first year. So I read some more, called up venture capitalists and editors and publishers in the new field, and decided the for-profit model wouldn't work. Too much time chasing too few ads that clutter up the site and require constant tending."[1]

Starting with an initial grant of $50,000 in 2005, by 2010 Bass had an annual budget of $450,000 to pay full-time salaries for five journalists (including himself) at the *New Haven Independent* and three more at the *Valley Independent Sentinel*, in the nearby Naugatuck Valley. As Bass told me, "The thing I don't like is that I continually have to raise money. The problem is I'm not bad at it."[2]

But if Paul Bass, Jim Cutie, and others have found that the nonprofit route enables them to pay for online journalism more readily than a commercial venture would, why is that the case? There are a variety of reasons, all related to the idea of what happens to the economics of news once the newspaper as a discrete product no longer exists.

On the Internet, there is no logical reason for international and local news, sports, comics, the school lunch menu, and the horoscope to appear as part of the same package. So they don't, which means the businesses that wanted to be seen in the sports section, and thus indirectly helped subsidize the capitol bureau, have gone elsewhere. Online advertising on newspaper websites nationally grew by $716 million between 2005 and 2009, but that figure was more than offset by the loss of $22.6 billion in print advertising over the same period.[3]

Those businesses that do advertise on news websites pay far less than they would in print, partly because Internet advertising can be measured so precisely (before news moved online, no one knew whether readers had actually looked at an ad or not), partly because there are so many websites—not just news sites—competing for those ad dollars. The result, as the Federal Communications Commission found in a study of local journalism, is that "each print dollar was being replaced by four digital pennies."[4]

Charging users for online access, another possible revenue source, has met with mixed success—and, in any event, is something Paul Bass refuses to do except on a voluntary basis, as he believes such a policy would drive away many of his less affluent readers.[5] In 2011, the *Wall Street Journal* and the *New York Times* were enjoying modest success by charging for online content, and a number of local and regional papers unveiled paid websites as well. Perhaps at some point the topic can be revisited. In the early part of the 2010s, though, user resistance to paying for online news was well established. At the local level, competition from free online sources such as the websites of television and radio stations would appear to rule out any sort of comprehensive attempt at charging for online news. Indeed, the *Boston Globe,* which unveiled a paid site in late 2011, continued with its free *Boston.com* site, which included most of its sports coverage and some of its news stories, as well as quite a bit of online-only content.[6] To do otherwise would have risked losing readers to local competitors. Similarly, in New Haven, the *Register* probably can't charge because the *Independent* won't. Though few cities host a free news site as robust as the *Independent,* competitive pressures exist virtually everywhere.

So is this the end of the for-profit model? Not necessarily. Nor should it be. There are certain advantages to a for-profit that a nonprofit can't readily replicate. For one thing, most nonprofit news sites depend on just a few funders, giving those philanthropists a disproportionate voice—if they choose to use it—on which issues should be covered and which issues should not. For another, a nonprofit is forbidden under federal tax laws from endorsing political candidates. Thus it is essential that for-profit journalism survive and remain a part of the mix of news-and-information services in the post-newspaper age.

On a hot Monday afternoon leading up to the Fourth of July in 2009, Howard Owens and I were driving through the tiny farm town of Stafford, New York, in his less-than-mint-condition Scion hatchback. "If you find out that I've joined the Stafford Country Club," he said, gesturing toward a well-manicured golf course, "then I've been successful."[7]

Stafford is part of Genesee County, a rural outpost of about 60,000 people, bisected by Interstate 90. Buffalo is about forty miles to the west along I-90, and Rochester is the same distance to the northeast. In the middle of the county is the small (population 15,000) blue-collar city of Batavia, where Owens published the *Batavian,* an online-only, for-profit news site that had been covering the county since 2008.[8]

Two years later, I telephoned Owens and asked him about the status of his country club aspirations. "I have not joined. Not even close," he said, laughing. "We're supporting ourselves, and I have a part-time employee sitting next to me. But I think it will be a long time before I have that kind of money, because any time we have some extra money we reinvest. I'd love to join the Stafford Country Club and have time to enjoy the privileges thereof, but we're probably years away from doing that."[9]

Batavia was not necessarily the most promising place to start a local news site, and the founding of the *Batavian* can be traced in part to an accident of geography, in part to a touch of arrogance. In 2008 Owens was the director of digital publishing for GateHouse Media, a national chain of more than 300 community newspapers, most of them weeklies. The corporate office was located in Fairport, New York, a suburb of Rochester. Owens took notice of a community news site in nearby Watertown called *Newzjunky.com,* a near-psychedelic hodgepodge of local news and headlines that had attracted a devoted following despite operating in the shadow of an established daily newspaper, the *Watertown Daily Times.* He had been looking for a place to launch an online-only news site as a pilot project for GateHouse, and he settled on Batavia. For one thing, it was relatively near the home office; for another, the local newspaper, the *Batavia Daily News,* owned by the same regional chain as the *Watertown Daily Times,* did not have a website.

The *Batavian* launched in May 2008 with two staff reporters and Owens acting as publisher, personally selling many of the ads. But GateHouse, struggling with a $1.2 billion debt it had taken on to assemble its chain, was looking to cut costs. In February 2009, the company laid off Owens. He asked if he could take the *Batavian* with him and was granted his wish. Owens and his wife, Billie Owens, moved to Batavia, downsized their lives, and began the slow process of building a business, with Howard as the only full-time employee and Billie as a part-time reporter. They did have a bit of a head start. The $5,000 a month GateHouse had been spending on promotions, ranging from ads on the local radio station, WBTA, to refrigerator magnets that read "The *Batavian.* Online News. Community Views," had already given the site some visibility.[10]

Owens had grown up in San Diego, yet when I visited him, he was obviously reveling in having found a new hometown to adopt. We met for an agreeably artery-clogging breakfast at the Pok-A-Dot, a diner where we may well have been the only customers who could not trace their roots in Genesee County back at least several generations. From there it was on to his office, a large, second-floor space overlooking Main Street. Downtown Batavia is an unlovely place, dominated by the aftermath of an ill-conceived urban-renewal project that Bill Kauffman, a prodigal son and an author of some note, has described as "a ghastly mall, a dull gray sprawling oasis in a desert of unused parking spaces."[11] But even though national chain stores had invaded Batavia, the city still had a reasonably strong base of locally owned auto dealerships, restaurants, real-estate offices, funeral homes, and the like, which was what Owens needed to try out his ideas for an advertiser-supported news site.

The *Batavian* had received a fair amount of national attention, largely on the strength of Owens's background as a pioneer in digital journal-ism (before his stint at GateHouse he had won awards for his work in California with the *Ventura County Star* and the *Bakersfield Californian*) and his blunt, outspoken manner.[12] Yet, at first glance, there was noth-ing about the *Batavian* that seemed particularly innovative. The design was a spare, three-column format with a blog containing news items in the middle. Stories did not jump off the home page; instead, you scrolled down to read the content. The site was loaded with small ads—more than a hundred of them, at the top of the page and in the left- and right-hand columns, touting a myriad of goods and services: ice-cream and pizza shops, insurance agencies, tattoo parlors, music stores, HIV testing, and much more.

Unlike the detailed, often enterprising stories published in the *New Ha-ven Independent,* the journalistic fare in the *Batavian* consisted of updates, often brief, on life in a small city and county. On an early evening in July 2011, the most fully developed story was about a woman who might have tried to get herself run over by a car and later shot herself to death. Other posts included a press release from the local state assemblyman; a press release and photos of a dachshund named Rudy touting an upcom-ing "wiener race" at the local track; "Deal of the Day," a regular advertorial featuring discounts offered by local merchants; a reader poll on the federal debt crisis; an upcoming house auction; several examples of Owens's first-rate landscape photography (prints were for sale on the site); and a video interview with a player for the Batavia Muckdogs, the city's community-owned minor-league baseball team. Such modest fare reflected Owens's belief that online community journalism should not be the same as news-paper journalism—it should be quicker, shorter, and more geared toward the everyday lives of readers. "We cover a lot of things the *Daily* doesn't," he said, referring to the *Batavia Daily News.* "If the siren goes off, people want to know what's going on. I'll put something up even if it's a false alarm, which the *Daily* won't do."

The content and design were based on ideas that Owens had developed during the course of his career in online journalism. Unlike the practice at most websites, ads did not slip in and out of view on the *Batavian* or appear on some pages but not others. The reason was that Owens had come to believe that advertisers and readers preferred that nearly all of the content—and ads—appear on the home page. Businesses were charged a flat rate for advertisements, a significant deviation from the standard prac-tice of charging more for each page view and for each click-through. The practice brought in more money for the *Batavian* while still keeping rates well below those of the *Daily News*. By not jumping longer stories off the home page, as was done on many sites, readers were encouraged to scroll down. Ads were rotated from top to bottom so that everyone got a turn at the top of the site.[13]

Just a few weeks before my arrival in Batavia, Owens formed a partnership with the local radio station, WBTA, an AM outlet that played forgettable pop music from decades past but also provided news coverage of the sort that, in larger markets, had long since given way to virtually news-free programming at stations owned by massive national radio chains. WBTA's offices were almost next door to the *Batavian*. When I walked in, Dan Fischer, who co-owned the station with his wife, Debrah, was talking on the phone with one of his reporters. It seemed he had had trouble getting ambient sound for a piece on farming: he couldn't persuade a cow to moo.

Fischer told me he had been suspicious of Owens when the *Batavian* first launched, mainly because Owens would link to some of the news stories posted on WBTA's website. "When I saw that, I couldn't believe what I was looking at," he said. "Here's my stuff, yes, attributed to me, but my product. Showing up on this website—an obviously for-profit website. What the hell is this?"[14] Owens eventually convinced him that what he was doing was legal, and Fischer said he came to respect his capacity for hard work. Their conversations, in turn, led to a more formal content-sharing relationship.

There is no question that Owens sees himself as a businessman first. But he's also a journalist, and he takes news seriously. He has published his share of tough stories, done some investigative reporting, and is a regular presence at local government meetings, civic events, and the courthouse. In fact, I tagged along with him to a few of those events, including the arraignment of two young men who had been arrested after an unusually brazen armed bank robbery. The uncle of one of the defendants told Owens he wanted to talk about his nephew after the hearing, but reneged after the defense lawyer nixed it. Owens hung around for a bit, bantered with a *Daily News* reporter, and then told me on the way out that he was kicking himself for not having pulled the uncle away from the lawyer and the *Daily* reporter. It was just one moment in a long day of covering the news, selling ads, and promoting the *Batavian*.[15]

In business terms, the *Batavian* appeared to be succeeding. In 2009, Owens was scrambling. By 2011, he said his situation had improved substantially, with an annual income for the site of about $150,000. "Our expenses are right in line with what we're making. We're making a living. We never have too much of a sense of struggle. It's not like a hand-to-mouth existence," he said, although he added, "I'm making a hell of a lot less than I was as a newspaper executive."

Owens had ideas to make more money. One was to raise enough from a voluntary subscription program to bump his advertising salesperson from part time to full time. (Those who signed up would get discounts at local businesses.) Another was to supplement the free classified ads he posted with paid video ads. Yet another was to charge local merchants to put together websites for their businesses. An accomplished photographer, he began actively soliciting commercial clients in 2012. And he had become a dedicated localist, telling me that he wouldn't take ads from national chains even if they came knocking. From all appearances he was enjoying what he was doing, despite working long hours. "Last Tuesday I had a doctor's appointment in Pittsford, and so I left the office at noon," he told me in 2009. "And it felt strangely like a vacation. Entrepreneurship isn't for everybody. It takes that personality. Entrepreneurship is probably a gene you're born with. You go around to just about any of these business owners, I mean, they're putting in the same kind of hours. They have no sympathy for me." By all indications, his workload had not eased in the intervening two years.

Although the *Batavia Daily News* remained the dominant news organization in the Genesee County area, the *Batavian* had clearly carved out a niche for itself. The *Daily*'s main source of readership and advertising revenue, of course, was its print edition, the circulation of which, publisher Tom Turnbull said in early 2011, was 10,500 on weekdays and 12,000 for its weekend edition, published on Saturdays.[16] Online, the *Batavian* and the *Daily News*—which started a website several months after Owens came to town—were competitive. Fortuitously, both organizations had placed code on their sites that allow them to be tracked by Quantcast, which provides more accurate numbers than Compete.com. In rough terms, Quantcast showed that the *Daily News* attracted between 65,000 and 75,000 unique visitors per month during the first half of 2011, whereas the *Batavian* attracted between 45,000 and 55,000. But the *Batavian* covered only Genesee County and its 60,000 residents; the *Daily News* also covered Orleans County, to the north, and Wyoming County, to the south, for a total circulation-area population of about 145,000.[17] In June 2012 the *Batavian* was also leading the *Daily News* in Facebook fans by a margin of nearly 5,400 to about 4,000.

Again, it must be emphasized that, for the *Daily News,* print is the main course and online is dessert. Still, there was no question that the *Batavian* had found a home in the shadow of its larger competitor.

When I met Tom Turnbull, the publisher of the *Daily News,* in 2009, he was still getting used to the idea of competing with Howard Owens. Moreover, the day of my visit was not a good one for the *Daily* or its parent company, Johnson Newspapers, a small regional chain. Turnbull had just learned that Gannett would end its arrangement to print some 40,000 regional copies of *USA Today* at the *Daily* and would instead save itself some money by moving the job to the underused presses at the nearby *Rochester Democrat and Chronicle,* a Gannett paper. "It's a big portion of our work. We did the job for twenty-five years, from the early days of *USA Today.* We're really disappointed," Turnbull told me. "It hurts our bottom line, and a lot of people are going to lose jobs out of the deal, because they were strictly *USA Today.* We'll survive it, but we're going to be a much different newspaper corporation." The *Daily*'s managing editor, Mark Graczyk, added, "We stand on our own. The *Daily News* is profitable on its own. We'll still be very viable."[18]

Turnbull and Owens struck me as a good match—two competitive, outspoken news executives, Turnbull wiry and intense, Owens more solidly built but no less intense. A few weeks earlier, Mark Brackenbury, the managing editor of the *New Haven Register,* had spoken respectfully about the *New Haven Independent* and Paul Bass. By contrast, in Batavia there was a war going on—or at least a skirmish. Turnbull was dismissive of Owens, and wanted me to know that the *Daily*'s website had been in the works long before the *Batavian*'s launch. He expressed incredulity over the national attention Owens had received from trade publications such as *Editor & Publisher* and *Presstime,* as well as the fact that I had driven all the way from Boston so that I could include the *Batavian* in a book.

"Quite frankly, as a business model it's been a failure. It's already failed once. That's why GateHouse got rid of it," Turnbull told me. "If you want to work twenty-four/seven, and you want to be the blogger, you want to be the editor, you want to be the ad salesman, and you want to go out and collect that money for ads, and do everything—yeah, you can eke out a living at it. But if this is the hope for new media and journalism in the future, we've got a bleak future." At the same time, both Turnbull and Graczyk said they considered the *Batavian* to be a serious competitor on news stories, and that they had stepped up their coverage in response.

Turnbull's pique persisted. Early in 2011, the Inland Press Association, a trade group, interviewed Owens about hyperlocal journalism. Owens volunteered some critical remarks about the *Daily*'s website and said the size of his readership was approaching that of the *Daily*. This prompted Turnbull to post several comments in which he called Owens "a hard-working, enterprising self-promoter" whose claims did not always match reality. Owens responded by bringing up a long-standing complaint—the fact that the *Daily* had declined to profile the annual Genesee County Chamber of Commerce award winners in 2010 after the *Batavian* had won one of those awards, "causing hard feelings all over the community." Turnbull replied that the awards "had been cheapened by allowing them to become a self-promotion tool where businesses could nominate themselves for the award, as you did."[19]

It was quite a combative display, and it demonstrated the hard feelings that can be stirred up when a newspaper's long-standing monopoly is threatened. Owens told me that Turnbull had subsequently spoken more kindly about him at a public event in Batavia, and said of Turnbull that "there might as well be détente." He added that his own combativeness toward the *Daily News* was, in part, a business tactic—he knew that any community news site could benefit by rallying readers who have built up resentments against the local newspaper, a dynamic that was hardly unique to Genesee County. "Unfairly or not," Owens said puckishly, "Tom was kind of a substitute for some of the asshole publishers I've worked for over the years."[20]

During my visit to Batavia in 2009, I also checked in with several civic leaders to see what they thought of the *Batavian* and its effect on the local media scene. What I found were some mixed opinions, along with some befuddlement.[21] For example, Jason Molino, the twenty-nine-year-old city manager, told me he preferred WBTA to the *Daily* and ranked the *Batavian* somewhere in between. He said at first he hadn't taken it all that seriously, but thought it had improved since Owens had acquired it from GateHouse. But, he added, "I don't think a lot of people are reading it." Nancy Balbick, the district director of Catholic Charities of Buffalo, told me that she had visited the *Batavian* just two or three times, explaining, "When it first came out, I heard it was a blog. And when I think of blogs, I think of nonsense. I'm sorry, I do."

On the other hand, Lynn Freeman, president of the Genesee County Chamber of Commerce, described himself as something of a news aficionado—a regular reader of the *New York Times,* the *Washington Post,* the *Christian Science Monitor,* and the *Economist,* as well as the *Daily News* and the *Batavian*. Freeman told me he liked both and said that, although the *Batavian* had not penetrated the consciousness of many ordinary folks in Genesee County, his conversations with fellow civic leaders led him to believe it had a devoted following among the local elite.

Like Freeman, Patrick Weissand, the director of the Holland Land Office Museum in Batavia, pronounced himself to be a fan of both the *Daily* and the *Batavian*. But also like Freeman, Weissand told me he didn't think many people had heard of it. "He's never going to get William Randolph Hearst money out of it. Not out of this community," Weissand said of Owens. "If you want to get anything out of Batavia, you've got to put a hell of a lot into it."

Howard Owens has proved it is possible to start a for-profit local news site in a small community and make a decent living, as long as you don't mind working long hours and wearing multiple hats. What remains to be seen is whether a for-profit site can bring as much journalistic firepower to bear as a nonprofit website—or, for that matter, a for-profit newspaper. Owens argues that we need to give it time, writing, "If it took newspapers more than 100 years to build the business and content models that we all now cherish, why do we expect a fully formed online model to emerge in just 10 years?" It's a good question.[22]

The *Batavian* functions well as an alternative and supplement to the *Daily News,* and as an additional engine of civic engagement. If I lived in Genesee County, I would find it indispensable. But, in contrast to the *New Haven Independent,* I wouldn't rely on it as my primary source of local news and information.

It is hard to think of a development more corrosive of local journalism than the rise of corporate chain ownership. Local quirks disappeared as chains adopted a cookie-cutter approach, standardizing their papers' design and content while moving around reporters and editors as though they were pieces on a checkerboard. As the media scholar Howard Ziff observed, journalists were no longer valued because they were rooted in their communities. Rather, they were "interchangeable," able to "put themselves behind the word processor in whatever city to which they are called by their corporate employers."[23]

Online local journalism is not immune from this trend. In fact, national corporations entered the fray not long after the development of the commercial Internet in the mid-1990s, when Microsoft launched *Sidewalk,* an ill-fated local entertainment guide that for a time struck fear into the hearts of alternative-weekly publishers.[24] Over the years, we have seen the rise and fall of *Backfence,* a group of community sites built around the hope that readers themselves would contribute much of the content, and *TBD.com,* a site based in Washington, D.C., that was launched amid great promise only to be shrunk and folded into a local television station's website within a matter of months.[25] None of those projects, though, matched the ambition of *Patch,* an effort by AOL to operate about a thousand hyperlocal sites in communities across the country.

There are things to like about *Patch.* The sites are well designed and include some slick tools for uploading user content. Of necessity, AOL went on a hiring binge, providing jobs to more community journalists than any other company and paying them between $40,000 and $50,000 a year.[26] In most markets, that's on the high side for community journalists, although some who have held those positions describe it as an unrelenting grind. "I've worked in journalism for more than twenty years as a newspaper reporter, online editor, magazine editor, and I've never worked so much in my life," a *Patch* local editor wrote.[27]

Several analysts who have tried to puzzle out the numbers doubt that *Patch* can survive, and I find their logic compelling. The project was costing AOL an estimated $120 million a year, and advertising at the sites I have looked at was sparse—especially compared to an ad-rich site like the *Batavian.* In addition, the *Los Angeles Times* found ad rates for *Patch* were so low that "it's hard to see how even a regional or national quilt of *Patches* . . . will succeed where many other local news start-ups have failed."[28]

Patch's trajectory was altered considerably in February 2011, when AOL bought the *Huffington Post* for $315 million and put Arianna Huffington in charge of all its content.[29] In a move reminiscent of the way she built her eponymous site, *Patch* editors were ordered to recruit unpaid community bloggers—five to ten per site—in order to supplement the paid content. Perhaps *Patch* will become a success. As of 2012, that seemed unlikely.[30] (I should note that in late 2011 I started writing unpaid commentaries for the *Huffington Post.*)

As long as *Patch* is around, though, it could drain advertising dollars away from the independents that are trying to make a go of it. So I was intrigued when, in May 2011, a group of forty-five independent sites rose up under the banner of Authentically Local (slogan: "Local Doesn't Scale") to assert their bona fides as the anti-*Patches.* The leader of the effort was Debbie Galant, a cofounder and editor of *Baristanet.* Among the forty-five were the *New Haven Independent* and the *Batavian.* In a statement posted on the Authentically Local website, Galant said: "The Authentically Local campaign seeks to illuminate the difference between authentic *local* businesses and those that are just cashing in—before every town in America becomes one giant strip mall. This is not just about us, the owned-and-operated sites that write about place. It's about place."[31]

Baristanet, founded in May 2004, was among the first successful hyperlocal sites. It was an inspiration for Paul Bass, who keeps a frisbee from a *Baristanet* anniversary party on the wall of his office at the *New Haven Independent.* Centered in the New York City suburb of Montclair, New Jersey, *Baristanet* in 2011 covered seven communities—six of which had their own *Patch* sites. AOL reportedly chooses communities based on an algorithm comprising fifty-nine factors, including advertising potential, voter turnout, and household income.[32] Clearly the affluent, well-educated suburbs served by *Baristanet* were exactly what AOL was looking for.

Despite the threat posed by *Patch, Baristanet* continued to do well, according to Galant. When I interviewed her in 2009, she told me that revenues for the site were between $100,000 and $200,000 per year. Two years later, she said revenues were "a bit higher than $200,000, but our expenses have gone way higher too." She did not specify what those expenses were. Unlike Howard Owens at the *Batavian,* Galant and her business partner, Liz George, had always treated *Baristanet* as a sideline, doing much of the work themselves but hiring part-time editors and designers as needed to accommodate their other projects—which, in Galant's case, includes having written several published novels.[33]

I met Galant on a rainy day in June 2009 at a Panera—a then new advertiser—just outside Montclair's downtown. At the time, it was covering only three communities, and had just recently incorporated a parenting site that was renamed *Barista Kids.* Galant said she got the inspiration for starting *Baristanet* after losing her freelance position as a local columnist for the *New York Times* and then meeting Jeff Jarvis, an online-news expert and the author of the blog *BuzzMachine.* "He was talking a mile a minute about this idea of hyperlocal blogging and hyperlocal journalism. And the idea just really clicked in my head," Galant said. "I thought it would be a fun thing to do. I'd been freelancing for years and years, and I saw that you could be vulnerable as a freelancer. I'd rather be a publisher." The name of the site was based on the idea of "a virtual coffee shop," she said, explaining, "In the old days you used to go to your bartender and talk to your bartender. These days, everybody's at the coffeeshop, so you talk to your barista."

The tone of *Baristanet* is conversational, fun, and a bit snarky, and Galant is adept at involving readers. For instance, during an outbreak of swine flu just a few days before our meeting, she quoted from a news release issued by the Montclair public schools promising that students would not be punished if they were absent because of illness. "Does the usual policy for staying home sick from school include reprisals and punishment?" Galant asked. The brief item attracted thirty-seven comments. "A traditional journalist would have taken the same tip, would have gone to the schools, interviewed the superintendent, interviewed the high school principal, and attempted somehow to find a whole bunch of representative parents and students to get their input," she told me. "But they wouldn't have actually gotten it nearly as efficiently or with as widespread a response from parents as from just having put it on the website."[34]

Baristanet is tracked by Quantcast, which found that the site attracted between 27,000 and 35,000 unique visitors a month for the first half of 2011. Galant told me her internal count was about double that, between 50,000 and 70,000 uniques per month.

As with the *Batavian* and the *Batavia Daily News, Baristanet* could not compete head-to-head with the weekly *Montclair Times* or other newspapers in its seven communities, even though Galant said she had sometimes beaten the *Times* on breaking news. *Times* editor Mark Porter told me he had twelve full-time and one part-time editorial employees working for him, a startlingly high number for a weekly newspaper. Porter was dismissive of his online competition, saying, "*Baristanet*'s skill is getting press releases and people throughout the community who e-mail or text-message breaking news to people who sit in front of computers." Despite his rather caustic assessment of the competition, there was no doubting his dedication or sincerity as he described the hours he and his staff put in and the local meetings and events they covered.[35]

When I asked Galant in 2009 how long she wanted to keep doing *Baristanet,* she replied, "I really don't know." She surprised me by saying that she wished the *Newark Star-Ledger*'s parent company, New Jersey Media, had tried to acquire *Baristanet* before its own business problems became so acute that they precluded such a move. "I think that's every start-up business's dream—somebody coming in and offering a whole big pot of money," she said. "It would have made tremendous sense. Of course, no newspapers have any money anymore, so that's not going to happen." Two years later, when I asked about her battle with *Patch,* she replied, "Competition is no fun, but we're hanging in there." (In the summer of 2012 Galant left *Baristanet* in order to accept a position at Montclair State University, with Liz George continuing as the editor.)[36]

My conversations with Howard Owens and Debbie Galant helped to clarify what I already suspected. At least at this early stage of online local journalism, there was more money available to pay for reporting in the nonprofit world than in the for-profit world. The *Batavian* and *Baristanet* were as sophisticated and ambitious as any independent for-profit community news site in the country, yet they were dwarfed by well-funded nonprofits such as the *New Haven Independent, Voice of San Diego,* and *MinnPost.* And many of them faced the additional challenge of competing with *Patch* and AOL's deep pockets.

Technology has lowered the cost barriers that had made it nearly impossible to compete with established local newspapers. With no printing bills and no distribution to deal with, entrepreneurs can launch lively local websites and make enough money to keep them going. What they lack is a business model robust enough to fund the sort of in-depth reporting that we associate with newspapers. Then again, newspapers themselves are able to afford less and less of such reporting. And as Howard Owens has pointed out, we are still in the early stages of online journalism. Better business models may emerge as technology improves.

I realize that I am engaging in some oversimplification here. New Haven is a poor, largely minority city with a sophisticated nonprofit funding base whose leaders already knew and respected Paul Bass. Thus it was logical for Bass to conclude that the nonprofit route was the right one for him. In contrast, it is possible that no amount of effort could have brought in sufficient nonprofit funding for Debbie Galant to operate *Baristanet,* or for Howard Owens to build up the *Batavian* once he acquired it from GateHouse. Then, too, as we shall see, the Internal Revenue Service has made it more difficult than it ought to be for nonprofit news organizations to establish themselves. By 2012, only a handful of nonprofit news sites were up and running, not counting the websites of public radio and television stations. The for-profit route may be difficult, but it is an opportunity open for anyone to try.

At this point, though, a well-funded nonprofit site would appear to be the best way of paying for journalism that consistently holds local government and other institutions to account. That proposition, in turn, leads to some serious questions. Can small nonprofit news organizations truly replace the well-staffed newspapers of years gone by? Can they stake out ground that is independent of the groups that give them money? And can they find a way to sustain themselves once the grant money runs out?

CHAPTER SIX

From Here
to Sustainability

WILLIAM GINSBERG is a Very Important Person in New Haven journalism. In the old days, that might have meant he was in charge of buying newspaper advertising for a major department store or a venture capitalist backing media businesses that he hoped would bring a nice return for his investors. But Ginsberg is neither of those things. Rather, he is the president and chief executive officer of the Community Foundation for Greater New Haven, which in 2010 awarded some $18 million to finance programs for the elderly, the poor, and the sick, as well as provide funds for scholarships, museums, and the New Haven Symphony Orchestra.[1]

The foundation has also been a major backer of the *New Haven Independent.* In 2005, the organization helped launch the *Independent* by giving Paul Bass $10,000, one of several grants he received from foundations and philanthropists that provided him with about $85,000 in start-up money. In 2009 Ginsberg and his board, working with the Valley Community Foundation, their affiliate in the nearby suburbs of the Naugatuck Valley, won a two-year, $490,000 grant from the Knight Foundation to start the *Valley Independent Sentinel;* the site is closely tied to the *New Haven Independent,* with Bass acting as publisher. The Greater New Haven group also awarded a three-year, $190,000 grant through mid-2013 to fund education reporting in both New Haven and the Valley.[2]

I visited Will Ginsberg on a beautiful afternoon in late October 2009. He met me in his fifth-floor office in New Haven's Audubon Arts District, which provided us with a spectacular view of the fall foliage. Ginsberg cut a striking figure with his bushy mustache, wire-rimmed glasses, white shirt, tie, and suspenders. Before his arrival at the foundation in 2000, he had been, among other things, a city official, running the development office for Mayor Biagio DiLieto in the 1980s. He worked in Washington, D.C., for the Clinton administration in the 1990s.[3] He told me that he'd known Paul Bass for some twenty-five years, and though they didn't see eye-to-eye on every issue (indeed, I later found a scorching opinion piece by Ginsberg in the old *Independent* blasting a story that he claimed contained "a string of factual errors, unsupported accusations, and glib generalizations"), he respected Bass's journalism and his understanding of the community.[4]

The foundation expanded its initial modest contribution to the *Independent,* Ginsberg said, as the crisis affecting journalism, and in particular the *New Haven Register,* became more acute. "As the whole for-profit journalism industry has come apart," he said, "the importance of this, I think, has been increasingly evident." Ginsberg was dismissive of the *Register,* telling me: "I hate to say this, but there's not much to it at this point. There's very little news, there's very little local news. The *Register* is still fulfilling an important function as a community newspaper, but I would say—barely."[5] (Ginsberg and I spoke just as the *Register*'s parent company, the Journal Register Company, was emerging from bankruptcy. Nearly three years later, with the "Digital First" era well under way, Ginsberg offered a more positive assessment, praising the *Register*'s "different and very promising direction"—although, he added, "I cannot say that this new direction is yet manifested in a dramatically different reading experience.")[6]

Our conversation turned to civic engagement, and the role of the *Independent* in bringing together disparate communities. I found it interesting that Ginsberg cited—and expressed a different emphasis from—the philosophy of the Knight Foundation, whose money had launched the *Valley Independent Sentinel.* The John S. and James L. Knight Foundation is the philanthropic arm of the Knight Ridder newspaper chain, a corporation that no longer exists. Between 2007 and 2011 it invested more than $100 million in various journalism experiments, including more than two hundred community news and information sites.[7] The Knight Foundation's president, Alberto Ibargüen, has talked about the importance of working with community foundations such as Ginsberg's, telling one interviewer, "For me, the issue of information has always been at the center of democracy. . . . We thought that if information really is a critical need for democracy and foundations are trying to satisfy critical needs for their communities, they should be addressing the information needs of those communities."[8]

Yet journalism was not the sole or even the most important reason Ginsberg mentioned for supporting the New Haven and Valley projects. "It isn't to say I don't believe in the importance of a free press to a functioning democracy," he told me. "But our business here is community—specifically, *this* community. One of the things community means is that there's some thing or things that connect people and institutions in Greater New Haven. What connects us? We're connected by our history, we're connected by our traditions, we're connected by our sense of a shared future, we're connected by our charitable causes and the institutions that are important to us. We're connected by pizza on Wooster Street. This is all pretty inchoate. But my view is that one of the things that connects people is a common base of information about what's going on in this place. That it's actually a very powerful connector. And it's therefore a very powerful ingredient in creating a sense of community." He added, not insignificantly given his role in funding social services in New Haven: "When people feel like they're part of the community, they act on that, and that's what our business is. They give money."

So which comes first—the sort of neighborhood-based local journalism practiced by the *New Haven Independent?* Or public engagement in the civic life of the community? Traditionally, news organizations have acted as though the purpose of local journalism is to cover those aspects of the community that civically engaged residents are interested in: municipal government, public education, development, police news, and the like. The flaw in that way of thinking about civic engagement is that when the public exhibits a lack of interest in such matters, the people who are running the local newspaper are tempted to cut down on such news and load up on celebrities, gossip, and "news you can use," such as personal finance or gardening advice. In the model described by Ginsberg, the news organization doesn't just *cover* civic life but also helps to *foster* civic life. Rather than losing readers because of a lack of civic engagement, such a news organization could gain readers by creating a sense of interest and excitement about the community.

Of course, a for-profit news organization can do these things too. But the practice of journalism as a form of civic engagement is particularly well-suited to nonprofits because they can cover news that engages their readers without having to be concerned about whether advertisers will be willing to support it. The question, as always, is How are we to pay for such journalism? With newspapers in decline and community after community in need of good local journalism, it is not at all clear that there will be enough resources to go around.

If the rise of nonprofit community news sites is a heartening development, it is also a very small one—especially in comparison to the resources that have vanished from traditional, for-profit journalism. Between 2006 and 2009, newspapers cut their newsroom budgets by an estimated $1.6 billion each year, for a total of a quarter of their spending on journalism. The number of full-time journalists at daily newspapers fell from 56,900 in 1989 to 41,600 in 2010. Meanwhile, foundations donated about $180 million over a five-year period to help launch various online news organizations. This disparity between the enormity of what has been lost and the paucity of what has been gained is well illustrated by a sobering statistic: in 2010, a dozen of the top nonprofit local news sites reported that they employed just eighty-eight staff reporters among them.[9]

The Naugatuck Valley, as the suburbs northwest of New Haven are known, is a good example of how strong daily newspaper coverage has given way to much lighter coverage by a nonprofit news site. I traveled to the Valley in July 2010. One of my stops was in an office park in the city of Shelton, where I met James Cohen, the president of the Valley Community Foundation. Along with Will Ginsberg, Jamie Cohen was the driving force in obtaining the Knight $490,000 grant that launched the *Valley Independent Sentinel.*

Cohen, who grew up in the valley town of Derby, told me the story of the *Evening Sentinel,* a family-owned paper based in nearby Ansonia that covered the Valley starting in 1876. "It was part of the fabric of the community," he said. "It was an afternoon paper, right next to city hall. It would come out about one o'clock. If you were a candidate for office, you stood on Main Street in Ansonia right outside the building and waited. It had the largest per capita circulation of any newspaper in the United States for a number of years. Everybody bought it."[10]

In the 1980s, the *Sentinel* was sold to the Thomson chain, which already owned the two daily papers in the nearby city of Bridgeport, the *Post* and the *Telegram.* Thomson executives promised to keep the *Sentinel* alive—a promise that turned out to have an expiration date. "Basically they eviscerated the whole thing," Cohen said. "And then, on Christmas Eve 1992, they just killed it. They fired everybody. And that was the end. Just said, 'Don't come in tomorrow.' Merry Christmas, and a happy New Year." This, of course, was well before journalism's financial crisis and took place at a time when newspapers chains were seeking to maximize profits rather than merely survive.

The Bridgeport papers (eventually to become one morning paper) kept changing hands and were eventually acquired by Hearst, which renamed its property the *Connecticut Post*. The *Post* today provides some coverage of the Valley, as does the *New Haven Register*—although it closed its Valley bureau a few years before my visit—and the *Waterbury Republican-American*. No longer was there a newspaper whose sole mission was to cover the Naugatuck Valley. And there still isn't. There is, however, the *Valley Independent Sentinel*, named to evoke the old *Evening Sentinel*. The *Valley Indy* covers five communities with a combined population of about 100,000.[11]

Cohen pronounced himself pleased with the *Valley Independent Sentinel* and his foundation's role in creating it. Yet the site was thinly staffed, with only a full-time editor-reporter and one full-time reporter at the time of my visit. Readership was modest, running about 35,000 unique visitors per month in the middle part of 2011, according to Google Analytics.[12] That could grow over time, of course. But the sense of community a newspaper can enhance was greatly diminished, replaced by the generic process of suburbanization.

Cohen gave an example—one he had heard about secondhand, but telling nevertheless—of a woman who lived in the Huntington section of Shelton and who was surprised when a fire engine showed up in her neighborhood with "Shelton" painted on the side rather than "Huntington." "Someone who doesn't know that they live in the city of Shelton is someone who may very well not want to read anything called the *Valley* anything," Cohen said. "She has no connection to the community. She gets in her car and gets on the parkway and goes to the Trumbull Mall, and shops somewhere else and does something else and doesn't come this way."

Yet he also conceded that old-timers who do care about the community were not necessarily checking out the *Valley Indy* on their computers, either. "Most of the people who fondly remember the *Sentinel* from twenty years ago I'm sure have no idea," he said, though he was optimistic about the site: "They cover things that haven't otherwise been covered. So if you're interested, I think you go to it. It's like what people used to appreciate about having a local newspaper."

As for whether the *Valley Indy* could sustain itself beyond the life of the Knight grant (although it was only for two years, Paul Bass had stretched it over three), Cohen said he hoped so, but wasn't sure the community would respond by supporting it with their donations. "There are people who don't have any experience with philanthropy," he said. "The idea of putting your hand in your pocket and writing a check on a regular basis to somebody other than the electric company or your mortgage, if you didn't derive personal benefit from it, you didn't do it."

Several weeks before my meeting with Jamie Cohen, I stopped by the *Valley Indy*'s spacious second-floor office in downtown Ansonia to meet Eugene Driscoll, the editor, and Jodie Mozdzer, at the time the only staff reporter. (A second staff reporter started in January 2011.) Mozdzer, twenty-six when we met, had come directly from the *Hartford Courant,* where she covered education.[13] Driscoll, thirty-six, had worked at the *Courant* as well, but was at the *Danbury News-Times* when Bass hired him. Driscoll described Ansonia and Derby, where he and his family lived, as "economically challenged," saying, "I mean, a reporter can afford to buy a house there. So that tells you—people work for a living there." Mozdzer described Ansonia and Derby as former factory towns that were slowly making the transition to bedroom communities. The other three communities, she and Driscoll said, were more affluent and typically suburban.[14]

The demise of the *Evening Sentinel* was very much on their minds because, they had learned, it was still fresh in the minds of longtime residents even though it had closed its doors nearly eighteen years earlier. "When I first moved up here, I said, 'What is the *Sentinel?*' I had no idea," said Driscoll. Added Mozdzer: "If you drive through the neighborhoods, they still have the boxes out from fifteen years ago. You still have your *Sentinel* box."

In both coverage and approach, the *Valley Indy* differs from the *New Haven Independent.* For one thing, the *Valley* reports on local sports, especially high school football, which Driscoll said was one of the few areas of coverage Jamie Cohen specifically asked for. (Cohen told me that, although he was not a sports fan, he believed the popularity of high school football, and especially certain key rivalries, made it an important story and had brought readers to the *Valley Indy* who might otherwise not have sought it out.) For another, Driscoll and Mozdzer make more extensive use of digital tools than do Bass and company. Driscoll pumps out tidbits on the *Valley*'s Twitter feed at a prodigious rate, and the feed is embedded on the site's home page. As of June 2012, the *Valley* also had more Facebook fans than New Haven—about 4,300 to 2,400. And whereas the *New Haven Independent* runs lots of large photos with its stories, the *Valley* offloads many of them to its page on Flickr, a social network for photo sharing, which makes for a cleaner layout and creates yet another avenue for people to discover the site. In addition, reader contributions are separated out better than in the *New Haven Independent,* running in a "News by You" section.

The *Valley Indy* has also been more adventurous than the *New Haven Independent* in the way it covers certain types of live events. For instance, in August 2009 Mozdzer used a tool called Cover It Live to report from the scene of a hostage taking, responding to questions from Driscoll as well as from a couple of readers. She also uses Qik to post live video from her cell phone from time to time. An example is an annual *paczki*-eating contest at an Ansonia bakery. (A *paczek* is a deep-fried Polish pastry served just before Lent.) In August 2011 Driscoll covered an intense summer storm using Storify, a tool that makes it easy to combine Twitter posts, video, photos, and text.[15] It's not that the New Haven folks don't try such things too. But it seems to come more naturally at the *Valley.*

The *Valley Indy's* strength, Driscoll said, is that, unlike its daily-newspaper competitors, its sole focus is on the Naugatuck Valley. "We're of the Valley, and we're only the Valley," Driscoll said. "It doesn't have to be a shooting to get you on the front of our website. It's all Valley. I think people have more ownership of it."

Yet with just three full-timers and a few freelancers to cover five communities with almost as many residents as New Haven, Driscoll and company cannot hope to offer anything approaching comprehensive coverage. On a late afternoon in July 2011, the site featured, among other things, items on a fire and a controversial housing proposal in Ansonia; a dog mauling and a new sub shop in Oxford; a courthouse escapee in Derby; and a quirky story about Republicans in Shelton who pledged allegiance to the mayor's lapel pin when an American flag could not be located. A regional story reported the results on standardized tests in the five communities. The *Valley Indy* also does more aggregating than the *New Haven Independent,* linking to stories published in local newspapers.

Two years post-launch, the *Valley Independent Sentinel* had succeeded in establishing itself as an interesting and useful supplement to newspaper coverage of the Naugatuck Valley—a place to go for stories too small for the papers to cover, for breaking news, and for occasional enterprise pieces. Its long-term survival was uncertain. But that is true of any news organization in the early years of the twenty-first century, nonprofit or otherwise.

On April 26, 2010, the Knight Foundation brought together people from a dozen nonprofit news organizations in Austin, Texas, to discuss the most important issue facing them: how to move from relying on a few major donors and foundations toward a broader financial base that included contributions from readers and advertising. Among those attending was Paul Bass, who told those gathered there that the *New Haven Independent* had achieved some success in charging sponsors a $15,000-per-year flat fee, which brought in considerably more money than typical online ads based on page views or clicks. Bass referred to such sponsorships as "branding," and the right-hand column of the *Independent's* site includes ads from a local community college, a real-estate company, a hospital, and the like.[16]

Bass's was just one of many ideas bandied about. Particularly active in the discussion was John Thornton, chairman of the *Texas Tribune,* a large nonprofit site that is similar to the *Connecticut Mirror* in its coverage of state politics and government. The *Tribune* launched in November 2009 with an annual budget of $2.3 million, with about two-thirds of that coming from large pledges of more than $5,000, Thornton said. The site had also signed up some 1,600 paying members (that is, contributors) at $50 apiece, or $10 for students, with a goal of 10,000 members paying $100 apiece each year. Sponsorship ads, special events supported by corporations but free to the public, and specialty publications covering issues such as environmental policy, law, or politics were among the other ideas Thornton put forth as ways of generating revenue that did not depend on major foundation gifts.[17]

These multifaceted efforts paid off. At the end of 2010, the *Texas Tribune* reported having received nearly $7.8 million in actual revenues or in pledges through 2012. Of the $1.8 million the *Tribune* received in 2010, just 51 percent was in the form of major gifts and grants, with another 11 percent coming from membership fees, 17 percent from corporate sponsorships, and 21 percent from events and specialty publications.[18]

The success of the *Texas Tribune* suggests that there may be a path to sustainability for nonprofit news organizations. What the *Tribune* had accomplished during its short life was similar in some respects to the success of public radio stations, which in 2009 received about 34 percent of their funds in the form of listener contributions and another 20 percent from corporate underwriting. (Less than 6 percent came from direct government funding.) Then again, what works for a statewide site such as the *Texas Tribune* may not work for a city news site like the *New Haven Independent.* In early 2010 some 58 percent of *Tribune* readers reported a household income of $100,000 or more, and 90 percent said they had college degrees. The *Independent,* in contrast, covers a poor city in a rich state. The median household income in New Haven from 2006 through 2010 was $38,963, with about 25 percent below the poverty line. By comparison, the median income for Connecticut as a whole was $67,740, well above the national average of $51,914, and just 9 percent were living in poverty.[19] Thus the *Tribune* may have more in common with *ProPublica,* a large, well-known national site dedicated to investigative reporting, than it does with the *Independent.*

Another nonprofit site whose leaders have figured out at least some answers to the sustainability question is *Voice of San Diego.* Founded in 2004, which makes it among the oldest of the nonprofits, *Voice* had a 2011 budget of $1.2 million and a staff of fifteen, eleven of whom were full-time editorial employees. On the face of it, that sounds richer and deeper than what the *Independent* can muster, but a few comparisons are in order. About 1.3 million people live in the city of San Diego, and *Voice* sometimes covers stories outside the city too; the population of San Diego County is nearly 3.1 million.[20] Since all of the *Independent's* $450,000 budget and eight editorial employees were devoted to covering the 230,000 people who live in New Haven and the Valley, the *Independent* actually had more reportorial resources per capita than *Voice.* That may be why *Voice* editor Andrew Donohue told me that his staff picks its spots, covering quality-of-life stories that other media do not, whereas the *Independent* offers fairly comprehensive coverage of New Haven.[21]

Voice of San Diego's story may be the most frequently told of any nonprofit news site, and Donohue and Scott Lewis, *Voice's* publisher and chief executive officer, are frequently sought out for their views on the future of journalism. Donohue, thirty-three when we met in July 2011, exuding California calm, had an amusing theory as to why that's the case. "It's not because we're so great," he said, "but because reporters all want a reason to fly to San Diego."

Voice was launched as an alternative to the *San Diego Union-Tribune,* not because of the dire straits in which the news business found itself, but because of what critics perceived as the latter's shortcomings. Donohue likes to emphasize that *Voice* preceded the journalistic apocalypse that was to come. "I think that's an important detail that gets written up incorrectly in almost every story I read about us," Donohue said. "We were not a reaction to the financial collapse. We were a reaction to a newspaper that was out of step with its community and that had individual reporters and editors doing good work but did not have the DNA of a strong news organization or culture."

Within a few years, though, the *U-T,* as it is known, was laid low by budget cuts. In a particularly notorious move, in 2008 the then owners eliminated the paper's Washington, D.C., bureau just two years after reporters there had won the *U-T's* only Pulitzer Prize, for their coverage of a bribery scandal involving the soon-to-be-former congressman Randall "Duke" Cunningham.[22] The following year the *U-T* was sold to Platinum

Equity, a privately held company based in Beverly Hills.[23] "They have a new owner, they have a new editor, they have half of the reporters that they used to," Donohue told me. "It's not really an us-versus-them sort of mentality or anything like that. They have a new culture, a new mission."

As is the case with most nonprofits, grants comprise the bulk of *Voice*'s funding. R. B. "Buzz" Woolley, a retired venture capitalist, is chairman of the board and has contributed a considerable amount of money over the years, including $101,000 in 2010. Woolley is also a director of the La Jolla Community Foundation, an affiliate of the San Diego Foundation, which provided $313,000. On a year-to-year basis, Donohue said, Woolley gives *Voice* about one-fifth of its funding, which makes the site heavily reliant on just one person. Of greater concern to Donohue, though, was the expiration of national grants from the likes of the Open Society Institute Foundation ($100,000 in 2010) and the Ethics and Excellence in Journalism Fund ($50,000).[24] (That concern turned out to be well founded: by the end of the year, *Voice* had to trim its staff.)

Voice's offices are located amid an enormous former naval training academy, a pleasant grassy area near the harbor dotted by low-slung brown buildings—a nine-minute drive from the downtown, according to Donohue. The offices are part of space rented by the San Diego Foundation, though Donohue said the site was not getting any special breaks. *Voice* commanded an attractive, sunny corner of the building, with reporters working in modern cubicles and Donohue ensconced in a glass office. A small, open television studio was in another part of the office, which is one of the ways that the site makes money. For several years, Donohue said, *Voice* had partnered with KNSD-TV, a majority of which is controlled by NBC. That partnership received a boost when the station was bought by the Comcast Corporation, which agreed to help fund nonprofit news ventures in cities with NBC-owned stations as a condition of its acquisition.[25] At first, Donohue said, he and Lewis were happy just to get free publicity on KNSD. But the station wanted to do more, and *Voice* needed money. By 2011, *Voice* was producing three segments a week for the station. "That's been awesome for revenue and just for exposure," Donohue said.

Voice also sells articles and photographs to *San Diego Magazine* and *SanDiego.com*. It has other revenue streams as well, including more than 1,300 members who pay anywhere from $35 to $15,000, with perks ranging from get-togethers over coffee to advertising. Businesses can also advertise without becoming members.[26]

During my visit to San Diego I also dropped by *San Diego CityBeat,* one of the city's two alternative weeklies, and met with David Rolland, the editor, and David Maas, the staff reporter. The contrast with *Voice of San Diego* was stark. Our conversation took place in Rolland's un-air-conditioned office; it was sometimes difficult to hear as trucks rumbled past his open window. Rolland and Maas offered their assessment of *Voice,* with Rolland somewhat more positive about the site than Maas. What really struck me, though, was the difference in resources available to the two news organizations. *Voice's* staff was approximately double the size of *CityBeat's,* which severely limited the kind of reporting that the latter could do. Rolland was diplomatic, but his tone took on a real edge as we were about to part.

"We have to put out basically a special issue every single month to stay alive. And most alt-weeklies are like that," said Rolland, who was in the midst of personally updating a massive database of bars-and-clubs listings. "How that relates to *Voice* is that they don't have to worry about any of that crap. And frankly, I am envious. It's why I wish they were more aggressive than they are. Because maybe they don't realize how good they have it. They have nothing but time and space on their website to do great journalism. And while I think they're good, they could be great. They could be better."[27]

Given its resources, should *Voice of San Diego* be better? I'm in no position to judge. On the face of it, the site is attractive and filled with interesting content. Its reporting has won awards. If I lived in San Diego, I'd be glad to have a resource like *Voice.* I'd be a *CityBeat* reader, too. But regardless of the specific merits of Rolland's lament, I think it speaks to something significant. We are at a historical moment when nonprofit media—supported by foundations, donations, and, indirectly, taxpayers, since contributions are tax-deductible—are, in many cases, more stable than for-profit media. It is not unusual for public radio and television stations to own the nicest broadcast facilities in town. Paul Bass spends most of his time on journalism while Howard Owens and Debbie Galant fight for advertising. David Rolland edits bar listings. And Andrew Donohue focuses on quality-of-life stories.

Donohue told me he'd like to see *Voice* find a way to raise $5 million a year, which is what he estimated it would take to fulfill his vision for what the site ought to be. And I have no doubt that a larger *Voice* would be an even greater asset to San Diego than what was being published in 2011. But as it turned out, 2011 was a high-water mark for *Voice of San Diego.* At the end of the year, Donohue and Scott Lewis announced they had been forced to cut their budget from $1.2 million to $1 million and lay off four full-time staff members, three of them journalists.[28] "There's no one cause for the change," they wrote. "No major donor has dropped out. Our sponsorships are consistent and our membership is growing rapidly. But in the past we've relied on grants from national foundations to make up a large part of our funding and we can't be sure they'll be there for us again." They also announced continued efforts to raise more money from readers and to reduce their dependence on national foundations—the very concern Donohue had identified when I interviewed him six months earlier.

Nor was that the only (or even the most) significant change in the San Diego media landscape in 2011. Several weeks before *Voice* announced lay-offs, the *Union-Tribune* was sold to a local hotel magnate named Doug Manchester, who reportedly paid in excess of $110 million—more than double what Platinum Equity had bought it for just two years earlier. Manchester was described by *Voice* as a conservative opponent of same-sex marriage and a developer heavily involved in projects that the *U-T* and other news organizations report on—"a minor-league Donald Trump," in the words of Tony Perry, the San Diego bureau chief for the *Los Angeles Times*.[29] A few months later, David Carr of the *New York Times* wrote a blistering assessment of *U-T San Diego,* as the paper was renamed, and of Manchester's unapologetic practice of promoting his business interests in the paper's news pages.[30]

Like David Rolland at *San Diego CityBeat,* Andrew Donohue and *Voice of San Diego* were faced with the prospect of trying to do more with less—and at a time when changes at the city's dominant media institution, the *Union-Tribune,* made the existence of a strong, independent alternative more important than ever.

The *New Haven Register,* through its now extinct *Journal-Courier* branch, traces its origins to 1755. The *Hartford Courant,* which began as the *Connecticut Courant* in 1764, touts itself as the oldest continuously published newspaper in the United States. But when Paul Bass, John Thornton, Andrew Donohue, and others talk about sustainability, they are not talking about building news organizations that will last 250 years. At a time of rapid, technology-fueled creation and destruction, it may well be that projects such as the *New Haven Independent* and *Voice of San Diego* already represent some new definition of sustainability. Perhaps they could be considered venerable news organizations if their life spans are measured in Internet years.

Bass and I have talked several times about how to move the *Independent* to a more sustainable financial footing. In 2010 and 2011 the site depended on grants for 75 percent of its money, and on contributions and other forms of income for the other 25 percent. Bass said he would like to turn that ratio around in order to make the *Independent* less reliant on grants, which are generally time-limited. Getting there was the challenge. Successful as he had been at keeping the *Independent* thriving since 2005 (the print version, you may remember, lasted only a little more than three years), his journey had also been marked by some odd detours and dead ends.[31]

For instance, at one point he got grant money to start a nanotechnology beat, hoping to provide some national coverage of a story with strong ties to Yale. But it had been an odd fit, and the reporter he hired to do it, Gwyneth Shaw, was by early 2011 doing more and more non-nano stories. Bass covered the 2010 election campaign in Connecticut for the *New York Times*. But as the *Times* regards the state as part of its metro area and has its own correspondent assigned there, he was unable to parlay that into the sort of formal arrangement the *Times* maintained with other nonprofits, most durably the *Texas Tribune*. (The *Times* also partnered with the Chicago News Cooperative, a venture that suspended operations in February 2012, partly because of its inability to win nonprofit tax status from the Internal Revenue Service. Two months later, the *Times* ended its relationship with the *Bay Citizen* in San Francisco after that site merged with the Center for Investigative Reporting.)[32]

In addition to grants from the Community Foundation and a few smaller foundations, the *New Haven Independent* had several other sources of funding. One of those was the sponsorships Bass discussed at the Austin summit of nonprofit news entrepreneurs. The site also solicits individual contributions, from "Ultra Angel" ($1,000 or more) to "Basic Angel" ($250). "Friends" pay $10 or $18 a month in the form of voluntary contributions; and every so often noncontributing readers encounter a screen asking for money courtesy of Press Plus, a company founded by the media entrepreneur Steven Brill (he founded Court TV and the *American Lawyer*) that provides news sites with easy-to-manage payment systems. Wealthy individuals gave nearly $80,000 in 2011. Small ads brought in another $5,000 to $6,000. Legal notices accounted for another $8,000 to $10,000.

Where did the money go? The vast majority of it—nearly 90 percent— paid the salaries and benefits of the *Independent*'s eight full-time journalists in New Haven and the Valley, as well as for the services of Christine Stuart of *CT News Junkie*, Kyle Summer of Smartpill Design, and freelance writers. The rest was spent on such things as rent, libel insurance, equipment, accounting, and the like. The top salary in 2011 was paid to Bass, who made $62,000. The other salaries ranged from $30,000 to $47,000, depending on experience and responsibilities. The *Independent* also covered 100 percent of its employees' health benefits, an unusually generous perk. In the decidedly nonlucrative world of community journalism, the *Independent*'s salaries might best be described as middle-of-the-road. That is, no one was getting rich, but neither was anyone making a sacrifice by working for the *Independent* rather than for a small- to medium-sized for-profit newspaper.

Even though Bass himself has doubts as to whether the *Independent* is sustainable in the long run, he has succeeded in making it sustainable for the time being. The *Independent*'s finances are an ever-shifting picture, but in July 2011 Bass told me that both the New Haven and Valley sites were fully funded through 2012, with modest raises and no layoffs built into the budget. Twenty percent of the funding that the sites needed was in place for 2013, and 15 percent for each of the three years after that. The Valley was a bigger challenge than New Haven, he admitted, but he said he had some thoughts on how to continue raising "Valley-specific money" beyond 2012.

Bass is a font of ideas. At one point he was talking about pursuing a partnership with Comcast's NBC station in New Haven, much as *Voice of San Diego* has done, though that proved to be a deal that he could not bring off.[33] He would like to sell *Independent* content to a print publication. He has sought grant money to fund a closer relationship with *La Voz.* More than anything, though, Bass wanted to find a way to shift the burden of financing the *Independent* from foundations to high-net-worth individuals. An endowment of $12 million, he said, would fund the *Independent* and the *Valley Indy* at their current level in perpetuity. He certainly wasn't counting on it; but when he brought it up in conversation, it was apparent that he didn't consider it impossible either.

By the spring of 2012, the last time we talked about funding, Bass had made progress on several fronts. Perhaps most significant, he said that an increasing share of the money was coming from wealthy patrons and less from foundations. "I'm always worried I'm not going to be employed in a year," he said. "I'm scared I'm not going to be able to make it to retirement."[34] Yet the *Independent* was continuing to prove its sustainability a little bit at a time.

For the foreseeable future, though, money from foundations was almost certainly going to provide a substantial share of the *Independent*'s financing. Nearly two years after Will Ginsberg and I first met, I followed up with him and asked whether he thought his organization would continue to support the *Independent*—and if he saw community journalism as a service that deserved ongoing support along with meeting the social and cultural needs of the region. Though Ginsberg cautioned that he could not speak for the board or for what the foundation's funding priorities might be in 2013, when its current grant to the *Independent* was to expire, he said that he believed such projects do need ongoing philanthropic support. "The *Independent* is a central part of our strategy to give New Haveners the knowledge and the information they need to engage in the life of their community," he said. "It does seem clear that community news sites are taking their place in the philanthropic pantheon alongside other important contributors to the public good that are not 100 percent able to be sustained in the for-profit marketplace."[35]

I found Ginsberg's invocation of "public good" interesting, even if he meant it in the more generic sense of the term. In economic terms, a public good is something that benefits everyone, whether each of us pays for it or not—which, perversely, creates incentives for us *not* to pay. That is why we must pay taxes rather than make voluntary contributions to fund national defense. "Public good" is a phrase that also comes up a lot in discussions of why it is so difficult to fix the news business. For example, the local newspaper reports that members of the school committee are taking bribes from a bus company with a record of safety violations. As a result of that reporting, those committee members are removed and prosecuted. Schoolchildren are safer. Yet people who don't buy or even read the paper benefit just as much as those who do. Thus, there needs to be a way to pay for such journalism outside the for-profit, advertiser-based context that worked reasonably well until a few years ago.[36]

Seen in this light, community journalism is a public good that deserves funding beyond what the market is willing to pay. It can be a tough sell, pitting journalism against real human need. But as Ginsberg has said, an engaged, active community is also one that is more likely to give money to pay for the kind of work that foundations support; which means that, properly understood, nonprofit journalism can be regarded, not just as a cost, but as an investment.

CHAPTER SEVEN

How to Win Readers and Influence Government

Paul bass walked into his office at *La Voz* on the afternoon of Thursday, March 3, 2011, called up the *New Haven Register*'s website on his iMac, and, after a few moments of reading, matter-of-factly announced: "We got fucked."[1] The reason for Bass's displeasure was an article the *Register* had posted about the findings of an internal investigation at the police department. The probe focused on officers who, during a raid at a downtown nightclub the previous fall, had illegally ordered partygoers to put away their cellphones so they couldn't video-record actions by the police. There were a number of Yale students at the party, and five of them were arrested; the raid made national headlines. It was a story the *New Haven Independent* had begun covering in October 2010, following reports in the *Yale Daily News*. For months, the *Independent* posted numerous follow-ups about that and a similar incident in which police had confiscated an iPhone from a man who had recorded them making a sidewalk arrest. They erased the video and charged him with interfering with police. Now, with the denouement at hand, the *Independent* had been beaten by its larger competitor.[2]

Thomas MacMillan, a staff reporter for the *Independent*, returned to the office, and Bass explained to him what had happened. "I was on the phone to Adam Joseph all morning. You'd think he could have told me," said MacMillan, referring to the spokesman for Mayor John DeStefano. "I know," Bass replied. "That's why I'm pissed."

Bass picked up his cellphone and called Joseph. "We just really felt screwed on this, big-time," Bass told him. "I know some things are a little deal, but this is our story." There was a pause as Joseph responded, then: "Is there just a way to get a heads-up if something's coming?" After Bass hung up, he turned to me and said, "He's a great guy, but he fucked up on this one." (Bass later realized that Joseph had sent him the press release at the same time the *Register* got it, but that no one at the *Independent* had been online to receive it.)[3]

Bass and MacMillan made a quick recovery. They learned there was actually a second report, on the sidewalk incident, something the *Register* did not mention in its initial online article. That gave the *Independent* an angle of its own. A few minutes before 4 p.m., MacMillan and I drove to police headquarters, where police chief Frank Limon served up some mea culpas, taking "full responsibility" while making sure to point out that the real culprit in both cases was an assistant chief who had since retired. By late afternoon, the *Independent* had uploaded two stories, several photos, and two videos, one an oft-posted clip by a partygoer that was also used by the *Register*. (I should disclose that I was drafted into proofreading duty.) The next day Bass ran an account of a police training session on how officers should respond to video-recording by members of the public. Bass and I had attended that session, which was held just before Adam Joseph's press release went out and all hell broke loose. The training had come about because of the controversy stirred up by the *Independent's* reporting.[4]

Anyone who has ever worked for a small news organization—especially in the shadow of a large daily newspaper—knows how difficult and frustrating it can be to break a story only to have few people take notice. Even before he learned that the *Register* had beaten the *Independent* on the internal investigator's report, Bass was expressing his frustration regarding the *Register's* failure to cover the controversy over citizens who were harassed, or worse, for video-recording police officers. According to a search of the *Register's* archives in NewsBank, a commercial database, and on the open Internet via Google, the *Register* never mentioned Luis Luna, the man arrested in the sidewalk incident, until the internal-affairs reports came out on March 3. The *Register* also stopped covering the fallout from the nightclub incident within several weeks of its occurrence. The *Independent*, meanwhile, gave heavy coverage to both incidents, paying special attention to the retirement of the assistant chief mentioned by Limon, Ariel Melendez, who left the department while under investigation, taking with him a $124,000-a-year annual pension.[5]

But if few city residents beyond the *Independent*'s regular readership knew about the video-recording controversy before March 3, Bass's work nevertheless resonated and reached a larger constituency. Both Mayor DeStefano and Chief Limon took notice, and made it clear that officers were not to interfere with citizens who were video-recording them so long as they weren't preventing them from doing their jobs. In the Connecticut state legislature, Martin Looney, a Democrat from New Haven and the Senate majority leader, introduced a bill making it easier for citizens to bring civil suits against police officers for interfering with their right to video-record. (At his statehouse office in Hartford a few weeks later, Looney was full of praise for the *Independent,* telling me it had "filled in a gap" created by the *Register*'s cutting back on routine coverage of city government, neighborhood news, and union issues.)[6] The *Independent*'s coverage also helped spark the internal investigation and led to a new policy issued by Limon, as well as to the training session for officers at the city's police academy. In other words, the *Independent,* despite its relatively small number of readers, was successful in performing the civic functions of a news organization—not only by covering the news, but by calling attention to problems and prodding government officials into action.

To the extent that the *Independent* has succeeded at influencing city events, it may be a matter of *who* its readers are rather than how many. That may sound elitist, but not everyone can be a government official or has the interest in being a community leader. Nor is everyone an involved citizen. Ideally, Bass would have statistics from each neighborhood in New Haven showing how many people are reading the *Independent*. Such numbers are unavailable. But my conversations with people in local government, from affluent white neighborhoods, and from the African American community have led me to conclude, anecdotally at least, that the *Independent* is common currency among those who make it their business to know what is going on in the city.

"Virtually all the right people are reading it," said Michael Morand, an associate vice president at Yale and, among other things, a former New Haven alderman. (To be fair, I should note that I used the phrase "right people" first. He winced, calling the term "loaded.") Morand characterized *Independent* readers as "active voters, elected and appointed officials, opinion makers, civic activists as measured by people who are on boards, leaders of block watches and other neighborhood organizations. In the grassroots and grasstops circles I travel in, everybody knows it, most people read it regularly, and/or if there's an item of importance or usefulness to them, somebody else has shared it with them."[7]

Relying on such anecdotal evidence is problematic but necessary. As I have written previously, measuring online audience is not just an uncertain process; it is a complete mess. Without becoming overly bogged down in the details, it is time to take a closer look at why this is so—and how news organizations can find other ways to establish their relevance and exert their influence in the post-newspaper age.

In 2010, Columbia University published the results of a study on the state of Web metrics. The title, *Confusion Online,* was an accurate summary of the findings. Among other things, the authors looked at the differences between panel-based services such as Nielsen NetRatings and comScore, which derive their numbers by counting the sites that members of a panel of users are viewing, and server-based services, mainly Google Analytics, which measure incoming traffic directly. The divergence was stark. For instance, *Talking Points Memo,* a well-known site that covers national politics from a liberal point of view, reported that Google Analytics found it had received 1.8 million unique visitors during the same month that comScore only counted 300,000. Nor was the problem restricted to panel-based versus server-based services. Even though comScore and Nielsen theoretically use similar methodologies (their actual formulas are a trade secret), comScore reported that the *Washington Post*'s website received 17 million unique visitors during the same month that Nielsen reported fewer than 10 million.[8]

The problems with panel-based services are several. They depend on users to install code on their computers, something that is generally prohibited in the workplace, where a lot of people use downtime to catch up on the news. And the panels themselves are small, which can lead to considerable distortions when attempting to measure the audience for hyperlocal sites. For instance, the panel for Compete.com, the only free panel-based service (it also charges for a premium version), and one not mentioned in the Columbia study, had two million members in 2011—but even that covered only 1 percent of U.S. Internet users. That might be enough for measuring a large site with national reach. But if you think about trying to use Compete to measure traffic at—say—the *Batavian,* whose entire target audience comprises the 60,000 residents of Genesee County, New York, then the difficulty becomes clear.[9]

By contrast, Google Analytics is completely accurate but dumb—that is, it measures incoming traffic in every way imaginable, but it leaves out some important information about the provenance of that traffic. Essentially, Google Analytics overcounts in a variety of ways. If someone uses multiple computers—say, at home and at work—then each of those computers counts as a unique visitor. If a security-conscious user clears cookies at the end of every online session, then she is counted as a unique visitor every time she accesses a particular site. Search engines and various types of bots—generally defined as programs that perform automated routines online—send out feelers across the Internet, registering still more false positives. When you look at a site's Google Analytics (which you can do only if you have been granted access, as Paul Bass did for me), you find an extraordinary number of visits are for ten seconds or less. For the first five months of 2011, for instance, nearly 62 percent of visits to the *New Haven Independent* fell into that category. Maybe some of those were from compulsive readers who were checking back to see if anything new had been posted since their last visit. But a good number of those visits had to be bot-generated noise of one sort or another. Thus even though Web publishers generally believe that comScore and Nielsen—the industry standards for large sites in terms of setting advertising rates—undercount their traffic, they also concede that Google Analytics overcounts it.[10]

One promising alternative to these services is Quantcast. With both Google Analytics and Quantcast, publishers must install code on their sites in order for it to work. Unlike Google Analytics, though, once the code is installed, the numbers are made public, which means that anyone can access the data simply by using Quantcast's website. And though it is a server-based service like Google Analytics, Quantcast claims to have developed statistical models that eliminate, or at least reduce, some of the false positives, theoretically producing a more accurate count than either Google Analytics or a panel-based service. Howard Owens, who uses Quantcast at the *Batavian,* told me that Google Analytics put his site at 85,000 unique visitors for July 2011,[11] whereas Quantcast counted 65,000. Bass started using Quantcast at the *Independent* in July 2011 as well, and the ratio seemed to be roughly similar. For instance, Quantcast reported that the *Independent* received 7,800 unique visits on August 2, 2011, a day on which Google Analytics put that number at 12,382. Ten months later I checked again, and those numbers were substantially the same.

Uncertain though online metrics may be, they are perhaps no more imprecise than audience measurements for other types of media. Trying to figure out how many people watch a particular television show or listen to a radio station has always been more art than science. Newspaper circulation figures do not take into account how many people actually opened a particular section or read a particular story—or, for that matter, how many papers went directly from the front porch to the recycling bin at the end of a busy week at work. Newspaper publishers invariably claim that their readership is larger than their circulation (the National Newspaper Association says that you should multiply circulation by 2.1 to get the true readership figure), but such pass-along ratios have long been criticized as fanciful or worse.[12]

Despite these caveats, it is worth taking a closer look at the *New Haven Independent*'s audience numbers in order to get a rough sense of its influence, especially in comparison to the *New Haven Register*. The *Register*'s influence, of course, is measured mainly in terms of paid print circulation, which in early 2011 was about 75,000 on weekdays and 98,000 on Sundays.[13] That alone gave the *Register* breadth and reach that the *Independent* couldn't match. Online, the *Register* was accessed by roughly four times as many unique visitors a month as the *Independent*, according to Compete .com, whose numbers are thought by some publishers I have talked with to be reasonably accurate when making comparisons between sites—certainly more so than its actual count of visitors to any given site. Many of the *Register*'s online readers would presumably be from the suburbs that it covers. The *Independent*'s visitors would include residents of the five communities of the Naugatuck Valley; the town of Branford, as the *Branford Eagle* site is hosted by the *Independent;* and statewide, through the *Connecticut Health Investigative Team,* or *C-HIT.* But visitors from New Haven would far outnumber everyone else. (I am referring to the bulk of these sites' traffic, which would come from their target audiences. Obviously some small amount of traffic would also come from across the country and around the world as well.)

According to Google Analytics, the *Independent* in May 2011 received 329,891 visits from 176,521 unique visitors. Those accounted for a total of 684,478 page views for the month. The average length of a visit was two minutes and twenty seconds. A little more than 34 percent of *Independent* readers arrived by directly accessing the home page. More than 35 percent came from "referring sites," such as blogs that had linked to *Independent* stories or from social networks such as Facebook and Twitter. Another 30 percent came from search engines.

These ratios are typical for online news sites and show that social media are an increasingly important source of referrals. The *Independent* staff takes those findings seriously. The New Haven and Valley sites, as well as *C-HIT,* all make extensive use of Facebook and Twitter—not only through site-branded feeds but also by the individual journalists, who use their social-media presence at least in part to promote their work and that of their colleagues. In addition, Melissa Bailey, the *New Haven Independent's* managing editor, writes a weekly e-mail compiling and linking to recent top stories. The e-mail was sent to more than 1,900 people as of July 2011. Between 350 and 450 recipients typically opened the e-mail, and between 120 and 220 of them clicked through and read at least some of the stories.[14] The effect of these various efforts was to provide a sense of connection and conversation with the community that went beyond site-based comments, as well as to offer multiple points of entry for the *Independent's* journalism.

These numbers do not add up to the mass audience that the *New Haven Register* enjoys through its print circulation. But they do show how the *Independent* stays connected with the "right people"—the government officials and community activists, the influencers and opinion leaders who comprise its narrow but deep group of readers.

I introduced Mark Oppenheimer earlier as the chronicler of the Bass family's journey toward spirituality. I learned that Oppenheimer has a fascinating take on media sociology as well. And his explanation of why people of his social and cultural class (mainly white, well-educated, highly mobile, most likely affluent but not necessarily so) read the *Independent* resonated as one of the more interesting I have heard of why the site had managed to become influential beyond its raw numbers. It starts with his opinion of why daily newspapers lost their hold on the public in the first place.

Oppenheimer's view is that his generation (he was thirty-six when we met) differs from earlier ones in that, when he and his classmates finished college, they tended to head off to just a handful of places—New York, Washington, San Francisco, or the Silicon Valley. Oppenheimer is a graduate of Yale, the director of the Yale Journalism Initiative, and an editor of the *New Haven Review,* as well as a prolific freelancer. He told me he caught a glimpse of an older, more rooted world than the one he grew up in when he worked as a bartender at alumni events. There he talked with people who had returned to their hometowns after graduation and became part of their communities. Oppenheimer himself is an anomaly—he grew up in Springfield, Massachusetts, and, like Paul Bass, stayed in New Haven after college. A person for whom place is important, Oppenheimer once wrote a lyrical homage to his neighborhood for the *New York Times Magazine* headlined "It's a Wonderful Block."[15]

The rootlessness that Oppenheimer described helps us to understand why local news consumption has dropped. And it plays out not just in large metropolises but in smaller places, too—like New Haven, which has a substantial population of residents who moved to the city to take jobs in higher education, medicine, or a similar field, and were thus not rooted in the civic life of the city when they arrived. In addition, as has been well documented, many people at some point lost the newspaper habit. Oppenheimer said he saw very few households in his neighborhood taking home delivery of the *New Haven Register,* and only a few more taking the *New York Times.* As a substitute, they listened to WNPR, Connecticut's leading public radio station, where they found excellent national and international reporting as well as some statewide news, but little in the way of coverage specific to New Haven. "There was a time, when I was growing up, that educated people thought it was important to get their daily paper," Oppenheimer said. "It's not that educated people have ceased thinking it's important to get news. It's that now they feel that NPR fills that vision."[16]

Enter the *New Haven Independent,* which reaches this class of people where they are—at work. In Oppenheimer's view, the fact that the *Independent* is free is less important than its being online. Even a free, home-delivered paper wouldn't succeed, he told me, because people simply haven't built any time into their day to sit down and read it. In contrast, while they're at the office they can check out the *Independent* to find out what's going on in their city. And because the *Independent* is conveniently just a click away, it sparks an interest in local news and civic life that these nomads might not have previously had. "If you're going to get people interested, you have to create a product that meets them where they are," Oppenheimer said. "And I think that's what Paul has done."

But if Oppenheimer's analysis rings true for well-educated, mostly white residents of New Haven, what about the rest of the community? Who, exactly, are the folks who read the *New Haven Independent*? I have asked Bass whether he has any statistics showing which sections of the city his readers are logging in from, and he does not. Oppenheimer's sense of the readership base is similar to my own assessment: Yale professors, doctors and other professionals, white ethnic union members, and African American and Latino community leaders and activists. (I am, of course, referring to Latinos who can read English. Those who can't are served by *La Voz,* which has a content-sharing relationship with the *Independent.*) City employees, including teachers, comprise another racially and ethnically diverse group whose members are *Independent* readers. Simply in terms of whom stories are aimed at and what types of people turn up as commenters, I would also add what I might imprecisely define as an alternative-left community that exists more or less apart from Yale: car-less folks, mostly young, who ride their bicycles around town and consider it at least partly a political statement, local-food activists, and musicians. "I think it is the most socioeconomically diverse audience of any news outlet—of any print news outlet, word-related news outlet—in the country," Oppenheimer said. That may be an overstatement. But there is no question that people from a variety of different backgrounds talk to each other through the *Independent*.

In terms of assessing the *Independent,* there are few topics more important than its coverage of the African American community. And as I have already said, evidence of how deeply and broadly the site reaches black readers is necessarily anecdotal. But a large proportion of the content in the *Independent* consists of stories and photographs about the black community—the neighborhoods, the public schools, the churches, and, yes, the crime.

Among the better-known African American residents of New Haven is Shafiq Abdussabur, a city police officer and the author of *A Black Man's Guide to Law Enforcement in America* (2010), which aims to teach black men approached by police in "driving while black" and similar incidents how to prevent such encounters from escalating into confrontations. He is seemingly involved in every aspect of community life—from working with young people through his CTRIBAT (Children and Teens Retreat) program to founding a construction company that builds affordable housing. His wife, Mubarakah Ibrahim, an activist in her own right, runs a fitness program for Muslim women that she brought to Saudi Arabia during a visit to that country.

Abdussabur, forty-three when we talked in July 2010, was a force of nature, juggling two cellphones, making it absolutely clear that *he* was buying *me* coffee, and virtually eliminating the need for any questions from me during the course of our conversation. He was wearing a black T-shirt that said "Stetson Stars," a kids' program at the Stetson branch of the New Haven Free Public Library. Abdussabur and Paul Bass have enjoyed a friendly relationship for a long time, and in 2006 Abdussabur was named the *Independent*'s "Man of the Year." We talked about everything from the problems he was having with a housing development he was hoping to build to the state of black–Jewish relations in New Haven. Mostly, though, we talked about the *Independent*.[17]

Abdussabur hit upon two themes I heard from a number of people in the African American community: appreciation for the *Independent*'s day-in, day-out commitment to covering the full range of black life in New Haven rather than focusing on crime; and for the civil tone of its online comments, at least in comparison to those at the *New Haven Register*'s website. Abdussabur called some of the comments in the *Register* "just horrifying," specifically citing one that was written in what he called "Ebonics"—that is, in a degrading dialect that the commenter claimed was the way black people talked. Abdussabur contrasted this with Bass's practice of screening all comments before posting any of them. (A year and a half after we spoke, the *Register* began screening comments as well.) "He tailors the comments," he said of Bass. "He just doesn't allow people to say anything and post anything. And I think that really speaks volumes to his character. And in return it speaks volumes to the reputation and character of the newspaper. Because let me tell you, one bad racial comment that you stick in a paper like that, you can lose your whole urban readership."[18]

Abdussabur continued: "What has made this online newspaper so infectious amongst the urban population is because they're in it in a positive light. When they go in there, they can live and die in that newspaper. They see when their baby is born. They see when their kid graduated from school. They see the accident in front of their house. They see when there was a big parade. They can see if there's issues down at the city hall. They can see when the new police chief is coming in, what he's got to say. He's informing them about the day-to-day things that go on in their community from their perspective. And not only did they get the black community to buy in, but the Hispanic community has bought in, the Jewish community has bought in, the Muslim community, the Christian community, conservatives, your liberals, your haves have bought into it, your have-nots have bought into it. The politicians have been drawn into it. You know what I'm saying?"

But Abdussabur also told me that in working with young people in poor black neighborhoods such as Newhallville and Dixwell he had noticed that, though computer ownership was widespread, in many cases the computers were not up-to-date, and broadband penetration was limited. Residents of those communities were also inexperienced at using technology to find local news, he said. I once asked Bass about the "digital divide"—the idea that poor people have less access to information technology than others—and he came back with a provocative retort: "That's a bogus line by liberals to get grants." And he pointed to gang violence that had broken out over taunts posted on MySpace as evidence that the digital divide is "liberal tripe."[19] Abdussabur's experience, though, suggests that it may not be quite that simple.

Telling people how to vote is a time-honored tradition at newspapers. Though editorial writers universally harbor the suspicion that many of their readers either ignore their sage advice or deliberately vote for someone else, endorsing candidates for public office is one of the ways in which newspapers have traditionally sought to exert influence within their community.

But not at the *New Haven Independent,* or at other nonprofit news organizations, which are sometimes referred to as 501(c)(3)s. The name comes from the federal tax code, which governs what sorts of activities nonprofit organizations may or may not engage in if they want to keep their tax-exempt status. And one of those prohibited activities is political advocacy.

Paul Bass professes not to mind. During the *Independent's* first couple of years Bass used to do an opinionated weekly video commentary called "Compost Heap," but he stopped because he felt uncomfortable imposing his views on his audience. And he said he has never minded the no-endorsements rule governing nonprofits. "I've written endorsements," he told me. "It's a fun way to make a statement, what your paper stands for. But the way journalism is evolving, who cares? One journalist's opinion of who to vote for is so meaningless. We're getting to be more important in helping people sift through the information on the Web, less important in terms of trying to convince them to do things. I love that. I have no desire to write an endorsement editorial ever again in my life."[20]

Bass's views may come across as admirably populist. But there can be real value in candidate endorsements, especially at the local level. Readers may not need—or they may even resent—editorials telling them whom to vote for when it comes to major offices such as president, governor, or U.S. senator. But those same readers, excepting those who are unusually active in local affairs, may find themselves wanting intelligent guidance when voting for, say, ward alderman. New Haven's board of aldermen is composed of thirty members, each representing a different geographic slice of the city. The *Independent* covers every aldermanic race in some detail. But for a busy voter who wants to do the right thing, it can still be difficult to know which candidate best stands for her interests and values.

Then, too, even if Bass wanted to endorse, he couldn't. It may seem right and fair that an organization be banned from political advocacy in return for receiving nonprofit, tax-exempt status. In fact, though, the ban sprang forth not from the quill pens of Thomas Jefferson and James Madison but to ensure Lyndon Johnson's reelection to the U.S. Senate in 1954. Johnson inserted the prohibition into a bill in order to silence two tax-exempt organizations that were supporting his opponent back home in Texas.[21] The effect has been to neuter the political voice of nonprofit groups for more than a half-century. The ban on endorsements is an egregious abridgement of the First Amendment guarantee of free speech and freedom of the press.

As the media scholar Robert McChesney and the journalist John Nichols write, "Editorial endorsements—or the denial of them—are among the most powerful tools that newspapers have for holding political figures to account."[22]

There are a few solutions to the no-endorsements rule, some already in practice, some proposed. Perhaps the best known is the hybrid ownership model in place at the *Tampa Bay Times* (formerly and perhaps still better known as the *St. Petersburg Times*), where a for-profit newspaper is owned by a nonprofit educational entity—the Poynter Institute, a journalism training center. Such an arrangement, which is also in effect at the *New London Day* of Connecticut, the *Anniston Star* of Alabama, the *New Hampshire Union Leader,* and the *Christian Science Monitor,* removes the quarterly profit pressures that have harmed many daily papers (though the hybrids still need to operate in the black) and leaves the editorial page's First Amendment rights fully intact.[23]

"What's cool about the Poynter Institute owning the *St. Petersburg Times* is that, because we're concerned about the quality of leadership and the ethics of ownership, we're able to take the long view of success and profitability rather than the short view," Poynter vice president and senior scholar Roy Peter Clark told me. But the hybrid model is unlikely to become widespread, as it requires a newspaper's owner to donate the paper to an educational organization, and because it lacks the tax advantages of a nonprofit—principally, the ability to accept tax-exempt donations.[24]

Another idea, which has not yet gotten off the ground, is to reincorporate a newspaper as a low-profit, limited-liability company. The so-called L3C model combines aspects of for-profit and nonprofit ownership, making it possible for a paper to raise money from donors without having to seek nonprofit status as long as it pursues an educational or other social mission. As of 2012 there were no news organizations that had sought to become L3Cs, and it is not clear whether it would be a workable arrangement or not—though there is a buzz around the idea within journalism circles. An L3C news organization would be free to endorse political candidates.[25]

A more straightforward solution has been proposed by Paul Starr, a prominent sociologist at Princeton University, who has written that Congress should create a new type of nonprofit status for news organizations that would allow them to exercise full editorial freedom. Pointing out that the government has indirectly subsidized journalism from the earliest days of American history through low postal rates for newspapers and magazines, Starr argues that tax-exempt status should similarly come with no strings attached. According to him, news organizations "should not be required to sacrifice any of the rights of a free press—including the freedom to endorse political candidates."[26]

The endorsement conundrum is not even the most daunting of the challenges confronting journalists who wish to start nonprofit news organizations. Given how difficult it has become to pay for journalism, it is crucial that nonprofit funding and the tax benefits that come with it remain a part of the mix. Yet the nonprofit news movement has stalled, and the government itself is at least partly at fault.

When I interviewed Andrew Donohue, the editor of *Voice of San Diego,* in mid-2011, he told me he was struck that the number of prominent nonprofit news organizations had not expanded much beyond the half-dozen or so sites that had been launched a few years earlier. It wasn't for lack of interest. According to Ryan Chittum of the *Columbia Journalism Review,* the Internal Revenue Service had slowed down the approval process for 501(c)(3) status because of the increase in applications and because, historically, the IRS had not approved tax-exempt status for the sort of journalism that was typically produced by for-profit newspapers. The problem is that times have changed. "By stalling approval for new nonprofit news outlets, the IRS is making it harder for them to get past the startup stage and fill the coverage gaps left by weakened for-profit newspapers," Chittum writes.[27] Indeed, as I noted earlier, the Chicago News Cooperative suspended operations in part because its executives could no longer wait for the IRS to rule on its application for nonprofit status.

In 2009, U.S. Senator Benjamin Cardin, a Maryland Democrat, proposed legislation that would specifically recognize newspapers—including, presumably, online news organizations—as engaging in the sort of activity that deserved 501(c)(3) status. Such a bill, were it to become law, could well revitalize the nonprofit news movement. Without something like it, anyone seeking to emulate Paul Bass by launching a *New Haven Independent*-like news site will have a difficult time winning approval from the IRS. Even Cardin, though, would not remove the provision that forbids political endorsements, writing, "Under this arrangement, newspapers would not be allowed to make political endorsements but would be permitted to freely report on all issues, including political campaigns. They would be able to editorialize and take positions on issues affecting their communities."[28]

Oddly absent from these discussions is the notion of simply undoing Lyndon Johnson's handiwork and ending the ban that prevents nonprofit organizations from exercising their full First Amendment rights. There is something unseemly about free speech being held hostage to the corrupt politics of mid-twentieth-century Texas and government officials' laying down the law as to what constitutes acceptable political discourse. Yet these restrictions on speech have powerful supporters—including some liberal groups, such as Americans United for the Separation of Church and State, which fear unleashing conservative religious organizations so that they are free to endorse political candidates.[29]

Nonetheless, as Supreme Court Justice Oliver Wendell Holmes Jr. wrote in *Abrams v. United States* (1919), the Constitution requires that the battle of ideas take place in the "competition of the market" rather than being subjected to governmental regulations and restrictions.[30] The best solution to repairing the law that prevents Paul Bass and other nonprofit journalists from endorsing candidates is to take the First Amendment at face value: "Congress shall make no law . . . abridging the freedom of speech, or of the press."

If there is one person uniquely positioned to judge the influence that the *New Haven Independent* has exerted on city life it is Mayor John DeStefano Jr., who was elected to his first two-year term in 1993. In mid-2011, DeStefano was in the midst of a vigorous reelection campaign against several long-shot challengers who were hoping to take advantage of the city's budgetary problems as well as the sense among some voters that, after eighteen years, it was time for someone new. DeStefano won that November, if not as easily as he had in most of his reelection campaigns.

DeStefano and Paul Bass go back a long way. As I previously mentioned, DeStefano was a city official in the 1980s, working for Mayor Biagio DiLieto, when Bass was editing the original *Independent.* As a columnist and editor at the *New Haven Advocate,* Bass covered the early years of DeStefano's mayoralty. Former *Advocate* publisher Joshua Mamis went so far as to tell me that if Bass had not been so successful in rooting out corruption at city hall and forcing him to clean up his administration, DeStefano might not have emerged as a successful mayor and statewide figure. Indeed, in 2006 DeStefano won the Democratic nomination for governor, though he lost that fall to the Republican incumbent, M. Jodi Rell.[31]

DeStefano is a quintessentially peripatetic urban mayor, turning up at seemingly every event and in the middle of a startlingly high proportion of news stories. I met the then fifty-five-year-old mayor in April 2011 at his expansive city hall office, which overlooked the New Haven Green. It was a disorienting experience. Although I had made an appointment through his office staff, DeStefano seemed not to know why I was there, and he grilled me politely but extensively—while getting me a glass of water—as to who I was and what my intentions were. We sat at one end of a giant conference table, on top of which were several glass jars containing political campaign buttons. He pulled another chair next to him so he could drape his right arm over it and spoke so quietly that I had to keep moving closer, hoping my recorder would pick up the parts that I couldn't hear.

Despite all that, DeStefano proved to be a thoughtful and reflective analyst of the local media. In his view, the *New Haven Register* remained the one news source that reached all of his constituents—or at least enough of them that it could be considered common currency. Others, he said, including the *Independent,* served niche audiences. "The dominant media, to my point of view, is the *New Haven Register.* That said, there are parts of the media that serve different segments of the community," he said. "I think that the *Independent* serves a narrow segment, a segment that likes to be interactive, that enjoys the local coverage that the *Independent* provides. And I think that the *Independent* serves as sort of a content provider for larger media, the daily, and sometimes TV stations."[32] (By "content provider," DeStefano meant that the *Independent* would break stories that the *Register* and local television then follow up on.)

I asked DeStefano for his sense of the typical *Independent* reader. "Those that follow city government and community-based activities," he replied. "And I think those are two distinct things. But I think they tend to be folks who—and I don't know this quantitatively—but my sense of it is that it tends to be populations that care about those two topical areas and who have developed the habit of getting news online."

Other areas of inquiry turned out to be less promising. I asked if the presence of the *Independent* had changed the way he approached his job. Answer: No. Had its coverage of public education been a major factor in how school reform had progressed? Answer: No—other than as another avenue in "delivering information to readers." What did he think of a public forum the *Independent* had organized on school reform that featured, among other things, the mayor as a live blogger? Answer: News organizations have always sponsored happenings such as political events. The only thing different about the school forum was the role played by technology.

Without my bringing it up, DeStefano raised the issue of corruption during the early years of his administration and used it to illustrate what he saw as Bass's changing interests and priorities. "If you ask what's the biggest difference about Paul, it's that I think twenty-five years ago he was really called to write about corruption here or there," the mayor said. "I think we see this in all our own professional lives—that what interested us ten years ago does not interest us today. That's not to say that what interested us ten years ago is no longer important. It's just that we're playing in different things. Paul is playing in a different place that's kind of happening right now."

Innocuous as this sounded, it hinted at a certain lack of self-awareness on DeStefano's part, suggesting that—as with many politicians—his powers of analysis sometimes desert him when he's looking inward. Bass laughed when I told him about it. "Well, he got less corrupt because of the articles," he said. "Seriously, he fired all the corrupt people."[33]

DeStefano had a fund-raiser he needed to get to, but as my half-hour appointment with him was coming to an end, he grew a bit more expansive. He told me he had a son who lived in New York City, and that the one New Haven news source he checked regularly was the *Independent*. "I know why it is," he said. "It's because the content he's interested in is very New Haven–centric. Even though he lives in New York, he wants a fix of New Haven." Thus had the *Independent*'s influence extended to the New Haven diaspora.

Influence cannot be measured. It can be difficult even to define. But it would appear that the *Independent* had succeeded in becoming an influential part of the New Haven media and political environment by reaching a small but diverse audience of active, civically engaged residents and by focusing relentlessly on local issues and the city's neighborhoods. Though it may not have attained as much overall influence as the *Register,* it was taken seriously by the "right people," and was therefore taken seriously by the city's top elected official as well.

As is evident from the *Independent*'s coverage of police and video-recording, at times the news site can drive the agenda, leading to an official response, new policies, and legislation. Through that and other stories, the *Independent* has shown that it can act as a force for civic improvement—a vital function of journalism—despite its relatively small audience in comparison to those of the *Register,* television, and public radio.

CHAPTER EIGHT

The Care and Feeding of the "Former Audience"

ABOUT TWO HUNDRED PEOPLE filed into the auditorium at the Cooperative Arts and Humanities High School in downtown New Haven on the evening of Tuesday, November 30, 2010. They had come to hear Diane Ravitch, an author and expert on public education, talk about the city's nationally recognized effort to reform its schools. As they soon learned, they were also there to take part in an experiment in civic engagement. Using every technological tool at their disposal, Paul Bass and the *New Haven Independent* put together what *Hartford Courant* columnist Rick Green later called "a three-ring 'education summit.' "[1]

Stage right, Ravitch sat with eleven other people—principals, teachers, school officials, a high school student, a board of education member, and the like. Stage left, a half-dozen media folks and elected officials, including Mayor John DeStefano, were live-blogging the event. That morning the forum had been the subject of an hour-long preview on public radio station WNPR. The evening event was webcast by WTNH-TV, New Haven's ABC affiliate, as well as by WNPR, the *Independent,* and the *New Haven Register.* Viewers at home—and, for that matter, those in the auditorium who had laptops—were able to engage in a real-time, online conversation with the live-bloggers. Afterwards, readers posted a total of fifty-three comments to the two stories the *Independent* published.[2] The archived video was posted as well. Finally, in a touch that seemed almost old-fashioned, those who attended were invited to line up at two microphones during an extended question-and-answer period.

What was the impetus for this unusual on- and offline gathering? Bass told me he had read Ravitch's book on education reform, *The Death and Life of the Great American School System: How Testing and Choice Are Undermining Education,* and had recommended it to DeStefano. The mayor, in turn, bought copies of the book for the board of education and suggested that the *Independent* and WTNH bring Ravitch to New Haven.[3] Ravitch was an ideal person to host such a conversation. A former education official in the administration of President George H. W. Bush, she had morphed from advocating to opposing tough reform measures such as charter schools and high-stakes testing, and had emerged as a defender of teachers' unions.[4] New Haven's school-reform program differed from those in some other cities in that union officials and the school administration were working together rather than battling with one another. Ravitch's role was to act as the honest broker. She helped set the tone for the evening— civil and respectful, if occasionally impassioned—as teachers talked about the challenges they faced. And if not much that was said that evening was memorable, well, that wasn't the point.

From my vantage point in the auditorium, I sensed that I was missing half the conversation. I opened my laptop but was unable to get a working WiFi connection, so I couldn't look at the online component of the proceedings until later. In August 2011, though, I got to experience a similar event when the *Independent* and *La Voz* sponsored a mayoral debate between DeStefano and four rivals.[5] This time I stayed home. I found it a bit bewildering—there were two different video feeds, and even after I had picked one it was hard to follow the action taking place in the debate hall and the live-blogging at the same time. Nor did it help that the blogging software, Cover It Live, emitted a clicking-typewriter sound every time someone posted a comment, interfering with the already shaky audio. Still, taken together, Bass and company have come up with some impressively innovative (and award-winning) ways to bring the community together around important public-policy issues—and to get people talking about local news.[6]

There was nothing revolutionary about what I had witnessed. On one level, it is not unusual for a news organization to sponsor a debate or a community forum. As DeStefano told me when I asked him whether he saw anything innovative or unique about the Ravitch event, "News organizations, at least in my experience, have always been part of providing a platform for public discourse."[7] At the same time, though, there has been a debate within journalism circles for several decades over how far a news organization ought to go in helping to shape that conversation. Someone who believes that it should restrict itself to covering, rather than making, the news might have been uncomfortable with the education summit in its totality—not just the forum itself, but the fact that Bass had recommended Ravitch's book to the mayor, that the mayor had then suggested to Bass that he organize a community event, and that the *Independent* and the government both urged residents to read the book.

"It's a legitimate criticism," Bass said when I asked him about it. "I have the luxury in this case of being an agnostic about an answer about education. So I saw this as part of my reporting. Because I really don't know which way's right. I just love the book because it got me thinking. So I think while the question's a good one, I didn't worry that much in this case. Because I felt like this was just journalism. We were interviewing people and we got them talking and we had the readers be part of it."[8]

Now, I realize that people who exist outside the journalism bubble, and who are unfamiliar with the sometimes arcane debates over ethics that take place within that bubble, might be scratching their heads. What I am referring to, and what Bass was responding to, are the traditional rules of objectivity—a word I don't like, but that I think fits well in this context precisely because I don't like it. I am referring to a paradigm, for instance, in which a fine journalist like Leonard Downie Jr. made his refusal to vote an absurd point of pride during his career as executive editor of the *Washington Post,* arguing that taking a position, even in the privacy of the polling place, might compromise his ability to be fair.[9] I think some of the rules are good ones. Folks outside the bubble (and, increasingly, many inside it) question why journalists, even those paid to give their opinions, are generally banned by their employers from contributing money to political candidates, working on their campaigns, or putting bumper stickers on their cars and signs on their lawns. Yet I would argue that such a rule is more a guarantor of independence than of objectivity, and as such it has its place.

But the rules have also created a sense of distance between news organizations and the communities they serve. That distance was unhelpful even when journalism was financially healthy; under the current circumstances it is poisonous. By far the greatest challenge facing journalism is finding ways to bolster civic engagement—that is, to get the public interested in local politics, community events, and other issues from which a mobile, wired generation are disconnected.

Mark Oppenheimer aptly described this when he recalled what it had been like growing up in Springfield, Massachusetts. "My dad and the neighbors would talk about who's running for city council. Not in some hyperintellectualized way, but it was sport," he said. "Were the Irish going to get the seat? Were the Italians going to get the seat? And that just seems to have vanished."[10] That vanishing act has been toxic for the news business. In his now classic book on the decline of civic engagement, *Bowling Alone,* the Harvard University sociologist Robert Putnam found that people who were engaged in civic life—voting in local elections, taking part in volunteer activities, attending religious services, or engaging in any number of other activities—were also more likely to read newspapers. "Newspaper readers," he wrote, "are *machers* and *schmoozers.*"[11]

For the past several decades, few people have thought more deeply about how to turn people into *machers* and *schmoozers*—and, thus, into people who care about journalism—than Jay Rosen, a journalism professor at New York University. Rosen, a founder of the public-journalism movement in the 1980s and 1990s, is today a leading advocate of using technology to help "the former audience" (a term coined by Dan Gillmor in his pioneering 2004 book on citizen journalism, *We the Media*) become active participants in the media ecosystem.[12]

Public journalism, also known as civic journalism, was a movement aimed at helping members of the public shape what journalists ought to cover. An example might involve a newspaper's putting together focus groups and conducting a poll to determine what voters believe are the most important issues in an election campaign and then orienting coverage around those issues. Or organizing a series of public meetings to discuss a contentious local issue and then covering those meetings as a way of giving the public a voice. The idea, Rosen wrote, was to advance the philosopher John Dewey's notion of public policy being shaped by an informed citizenry rather than the journalist Walter Lippmann's darker view that an elite was needed to make decisions in the name of an "inchoate" public. Rosen wrote that "maybe journalism, by doing something to help, could improve itself and regain some of its lost authority."[13]

Public journalism was talked about more than it was practiced. And it fizzled out in the 1990s as prominent critics such as Howell Raines, then the editorial page editor of the *New York Times,* and, yes, Leonard Downie, argued that it amounted to an abandonment of the journalist's traditional status as a disinterested observer.[14] The late Michael Kelly, in a withering article for the *New Yorker,* went so far as to call a public-journalism effort to cover the 1996 U.S. Senate campaign in North Carolina a "fraud," writing, "It is anti-democratic—an attempt to increase the power of a journalistic upper class to dictate what are and are not fit subjects for public debate."[15] There were problems with that particular experiment, as news organizations banded together to exclude any coverage that did not fit their predetermined agenda. Public journalism should be a supplement to traditional coverage, not a substitute for it. But Rosen and other public-journalism advocates were on to something interesting, and it was snuffed out before it got a chance to prove its worth.

Yet even as public journalism was fading away, technology gave the idea a new life. The Internet made it possible to talk back to the media, and for members of the audience—the "former audience"—to talk among themselves. This second wave was far more powerful than the first. Public journalism depended on news organizations that were willing to reach out to their audiences. Citizen journalism enabled the former audience to empower itself. And without getting diverted into a discussion of what citizen journalism means (it has been both oversold by some of its proponents and mischaracterized by its critics), technology enabled the sort of grassroots involvement that media activists like Dan Gillmor and Jay Rosen had been advocating, whether publishers and editors liked the idea or not.

Rosen has long admired Paul Bass and the *New Haven Independent*. He is also a paid adviser at Digital First Media, the umbrella organization for the Journal Register Company and MediaNews Group, which gives him some insight into the thinking of John Paton and the operations of the *New Haven Register*. In an interview conducted by online chat, we talked about New Haven, civic engagement, and two distinct models of local journalism. "What we today call 'engagement' was a central feature of many civic-journalism experiments, but in a way we were working with very crude tools then," Rosen told me. "It was a capital-intensive production process—difficult for users to climb into the position of being producers, huge transaction costs for involving readers (like organizing a meeting). It's almost like we were trying to do civic engagement with heavy machinery instead of the infinitely lighter and cheaper tools we have now."[16]

I pointed out that the Diane Ravitch event involved a lot more than "lighter and cheaper tools"—that there was a considerable amount of heavy machinery involved as well. "Yes, and that is where the sweet spot is," he responded. "Using online tools to organize offline activity, and using offline activity to engage people in the online service."

Rosen recommended an essay by the late University of Massachusetts journalism professor Howard Ziff about the "cosmopolitan" and "provincial" models of journalism. The idea is that large professional news organizations subscribe to a different, but not necessarily better, set of ethics than small, local ones. Traditionally, Ziff wrote, community journalists had been more concerned about the well-being of where they lived than considerations such as covering the news objectively and avoiding conflicts of interest. When the goal of a newspaper is "service to the community and province," Ziff argued, then "our moral obligation is to be subjective and compassionate" rather than to pursue "objectivity and disinterestedness." He also wrote that, as local newspapers fell victim to chain ownership, they adopted a cosmopolitan mindset that benefited neither themselves nor their communities.[17]

Rosen's view was that the *Register,* as the largest of JRC's newspapers, followed the cosmopolitan model, whereas the *Independent* is more provincial. I am not sure it was a perfect analogy—the *Independent*'s journalists believe in ethics that draw as much from the cosmopolitan as the provincial, and some of the staff members will probably move on to other jobs in other cities at some point. But I could detect the cosmopolitan in *Register* managing editor Mark Brackenbury's observation that his paper was "more even-handed" and offered "more balance" than the *Independent*—an observation that, frankly, doesn't make sense if you are scouring the *Independent* for evidence of bias or opinion.[18] Maybe the way to put it, and to reframe Brackenbury's critique, is that the *Independent* is consciously covering the community on behalf of the community, whereas the *Register* (at least before Matt DeRienzo became its editor) was covering the community in service to some ideal notion of objective journalism—the "View from Nowhere," as Rosen has memorably named it.[19] In that respect, applying Ziff's dichotomy to the *Register* and the *Independent* becomes understandable.

Rosen described Bass's achievement on behalf of civic engagement—or on behalf of provincialism, if you like—this way: "Where I think he has begun to succeed is getting readers to care about what happens in the place where they live, which is related to the feeling that if people do care, something can be done about city problems. Correct me if I am overstating it, but the *NHI* actually cares if the problems it reports about are solved. Just creating an atmosphere like that is a huge achievement in itself." And a principal way in which Bass has succeeded in doing that is by encouraging his audience to talk back to the *Independent*—and by listening and acting on what they have to say.

Johnny Cash's voice wafted from an open window as I waited outside a coffee shop on Audubon Street in New Haven's arts district early on a hot, humid morning in July 2010. Not long after I had staked out my position, Jonathan Hopkins pulled up on his bicycle. An architecture student at Roger Williams University in Bristol, Rhode Island, and twenty-one years old when we met, Hopkins and his family lived in the city's Beaver Hills neighborhood, about a ten-minute bike ride away. He was working at an outdoor food cart that summer. He was also something of a celebrity among readers of the *Independent.*

For several years Hopkins had been a prolific commenter, writing under the pseudonym "Norton Street." (He lived on Norton Parkway, near Norton Street.) A staunch advocate of the New Urbanism, he wrote long, at times essay-length, comments on the virtues of density—modest-size developments combining residential and retail uses, and pedestrian- and bicycle-friendly streets and sidewalks—sometimes posting photos, maps, and drawings to bolster his arguments. Then, six months before our interview, Paul Bass coaxed him into revealing his identity and accompanying him on a tour of the city—the " 'Norton Street' Tour," as Bass called it in a subsequent article. Hopkins offered his opinions on a range of new and refurbished buildings, from a rowhouse-style public housing project (thumbs up) to a shopping plaza fronted by a large, mostly empty parking lot (thumbs down; such developments, he said, "sap the life" out of city streets).[20]

Hopkins began posting under his real name after the article appeared. The reason he had started commenting in the first place, he told me, was "because some of the comments on the site were people trying to be factual, and it was obvious that they were just making stuff up. I thought they could easily mislead, perhaps, more impressionable people." He added that, in college, he was surrounded by people from the suburbs, and the *Independent* was a place where he could offer his ideas in a forum read mainly by fellow city-dwellers. "The people who are reading it understand the problems in the cities or issues in cities," he said.[21]

Hopkins is, in some respects, a typical example of how the *Independent* uses comments to conduct a conversation with its audience and build civic engagement. After the " 'Norton Street' Tour" article appeared, he even did some feature writing for the *Independent.* Hopkins is one of a relatively small handful of regular commenters. Though it's hard to say for certain how many commenters post to the site given that Bass allows people to post anonymously and pseudonymously, there are probably a dozen or two dozen people whose names pop up on story after story.[22] Occasionally a story will attract no more than a couple of comments. But oftentimes an article about a political candidate, trouble in the police department, or a controversy in the school system will attract ten, twenty, thirty, or more comments. And though they can be as repetitious and dull as news-site comments anywhere, they are more civil and respectful because they are all prescreened. There's also no telling how many readers who don't comment nevertheless read other people's comments, creating a sense that they are listening in on a community-wide discussion rather than simply reading news stories and moving on.

The *Independent* is not an experiment in citizen journalism. Nor is the *Batavian, Baristanet, Voice of San Diego,* or any of the other digital-journalism projects I have written about. They are professional news organizations run by paid journalists. Nevertheless, built into the DNA of all of them is a fundamentally different relationship with their audiences than you will find at the *New Haven Register,* the *Batavia Daily News,* the *Montclair Times,* the *Newark Star-Ledger,* or *U-T San Diego.* And that relationship is defined in part by how they handle online comments, and how seriously they take them.

A newspaper with a website makes most of its money from its print edition. Although it may no longer be fair to say that newspaper websites are afterthoughts, they rarely receive the same sort of attention as the print product. Before newspapers had websites, they interacted with their audiences primarily through letters to the editor. It was a decidedly one-sided interaction: an editor would choose which letters to run, edit them for space, clarity, and taste, and discard those he thought were uninteresting, off-topic, or potentially libelous. This labor-intensive approach did not carry over to newspaper websites, as many if not most of them allow anonymous comments with no prescreening. Offensive comments are removed, if at all, only when other commenters complain. One reason may be that, under the federal Communications Decency Act of 1996, Internet services, including news sites, cannot be sued for libel on the basis of content posted by third parties, including commenters. This is quite a departure from traditional practice, as print newspapers are fully liable for all their content, including letters to the editor and advertisements.[23]

I have already noted how the lack of screening hurt the *New Haven Register*'s relationship with the African American community, and I shall offer some examples below. But it is hardly unique in this practice. Some large daily newspapers, including the *Boston Globe,* the *San Francisco Chronicle,* and the Gannett papers, have actually outsourced the task of screening and removing offensive posts to a company that does nothing but manage comments. There may be some advantages to such an arrangement in terms of freeing up staff members for other tasks, but building a sense of engagement with their audience is not among them.[24]

By contrast, online news organizations already exist in the same space as their audience. They begin with a more equal relationship—more horizontal, less vertical—and thus they tend to handle comments as content to be taken seriously. Over time, Bass has changed his standards for what should be approved and what should be rejected. In mid-2010, he was starting to reject comments he might have approved earlier. "I'm liking the conversations much better," he said.[25] David Streever, a Web designer, bicycling activist, and minor city official who comments frequently and rather caustically under his real name, agreed, saying that at one time Bass allowed "pretty much everything except the F-word." Streever added: "I think it's a hugely positive thing that he's started curating the comments. It's never really useful to go negative in the commentary, but it's really hard not to go negative if he's allowed three or four really nasty, personal, vindictive comments in a row. I feel like it's a human response. It's very hard to bite your tongue."[26]

A crucial consideration for any news site is whether to require commenters to use their real names. The *Independent* does not, and Bass has told me that he's concerned he would lose too much of the conversation if he didn't allow pseudonyms and anonymity. In particular, he said, city employees and people who do business with the city would not dare to post anything critical. And it is easy to imagine others who would not post if they were required to use their real names—for instance, parents of public school students, residents who want to criticize the police, or just about anyone who has something harsh to say about figures of authority and who fears retaliation.

Danah Boyd (or, as is her preference, danah boyd), a researcher at Microsoft and a fellow at the Berkman Center for Internet and Society, part of Harvard Law School, is withering in her criticism of real-names policies. "The people who most heavily rely on pseudonyms in online spaces are those who are most marginalized by systems of power," she writes. " 'Real names' policies aren't empowering; they're an authoritarian assertion of power over vulnerable people."[27] On the other hand, and of more direct relevance for the *Independent,* Mayor DeStefano criticized Bass's policy of providing cover for nameless commenters. "I'm not a big believer in anonymous behavior. I happen to think that if you go on a website, you should sign your name," he told me. "You ought to create means by which people accept responsibility for their thoughts. I think it'll contribute to a more robust, genuine, and productive discourse."[28] But though I do not doubt DeStefano's sincerity, his observations do nothing to negate the reasons for anonymity cited by Bass and boyd.

A more journalistically substantive argument against news-site anonymity is provided by Howard Owens, who requires commenters to register and use their real names when posting at the *Batavian*. Owens points out that newspaper editors—good ones, anyway—will not allow their reporters to quote anonymous sources except under unusual circumstances and will go to considerable lengths to ensure that folks who submit letters to the editor are who they purport to be. "In most news environments, anonymous comments go live without any verification as to their news value or truthfulness," Owens writes. "No ethical news editor would allow such unfiltered information to flow freely into printed news columns. Why is it OK on the Web?" Nor, he added, should a real-names policy discourage whistleblowers from sending in anonymous tips. Indeed, there's a form prominently placed on the *Batavian* that allows readers to send such tips to Owens directly, privately, and, if they wish, anonymously.[29]

Comments have taken a slightly different direction at the *Independent*'s sister site, the *Valley Independent Sentinel*. Partly it is by design: Jamie Cohen, the head of the Valley Community Foundation, told me he pushed for requiring readers to register before commenting because he was afraid that, without doing so, the "toxic" tone that pervaded some of the local blogs in the Naugatuck Valley would infect the *Valley Indy* as well. The site allows anonymous and pseudonymous comments; but people tend to behave in a more civil manner if they know that someone, at least, knows who they are. Cohen conceded that the *Valley Indy* had probably grown more slowly because of that speed bump. "But," he said, "it built credibility that this was an honest site, that they weren't going to tolerate that kind of garbage."[30]

Another, unexpected development was that some readers started posting comments on the *Valley Indy*'s Facebook page rather than on the site itself. Both the *Valley Indy* and the *New Haven Independent* post links to most of their stories on Facebook. With the *Valley Indy*, though, it is not unusual for a story to have no comments on its actual site and several comments on Facebook. It may be just a function of when the sites began. Facebook was barely on the map in 2005, when the New Haven site launched, but was a phenomenon in 2009, when the *Valley Indy* began publication. Executives at a number of news organizations have discovered that Facebook can facilitate a more respectful conversation, because people are required to register under their real names and are accustomed to sharing photos and other aspects of their personal lives. Thus they are in a friendlier, more community-oriented frame of mind when they use Facebook. "Trolls don't like their friends to know that they're trolls," Jimmy Orr, the online managing editor of the *Los Angeles Times,* told an interviewer. "By using Facebook, it has made a difference."[31]

Valley Indy editor Eugene Driscoll has some additional thoughts on why Facebook sometimes works better than story comments as a tool for community engagement. "I think people have a hesitancy to give their personal information to news organizations," he told me. "They just don't want to do it. But whatever the psychology is, they'll do it on Facebook with no problem. Maybe if New Haven launched today, they would have fewer comments and it would be on their Facebook page. But we just see the interaction is on Facebook. And I don't mind. I encourage it." Added staff reporter Jodie Mozdzer: "Nobody's going to write anything racist. And if they do, their name and face are with it. So we're sort of off the hook. I mean, it's Facebook. You know who wrote it. If you're mad about it, you can complain to that person. I think people get mad and complain to a newspaper because they don't know who wrote these comments."[32]

For a news organization to give control over its comments to a corporate behemoth like Facebook presents its own set of issues. Among other things, Facebook has come under much criticism for frequently changing the ways in which its users can protect their privacy. But for real-names conversations in a civil environment, Facebook has established itself as a worthwhile alternative to the Wild West environment of typical news-site comments.

The best commenting policy I have ever seen—other than Howard Owens's blog post on why he requires real names at the *Batavian*—is the one that appears at the *New Haven Independent.* Here's how it begins:

> Yes we do censor reader comments. We'll continue to.
>
> Want to accuse someone of committing a crime? Make fun of how she looks?
>
> Want to charge that someone had an illicit affair? Want to smear groups of people because of their religion or race?
>
> Post those comments to the ends of stories on the *New Haven Register, Hartford Courant, New Haven Advocate,* and WTNH websites. They don't monitor comments before they go up (although if someone alerts them to problems they sometimes take the comments down later).
>
> We do read comments before we post them. And we remove the ones that violate the rules of the road on the *Independent.*

The policy continues at some length and concludes with a list of dos and (more to the point) don'ts: "no gratuitous swearing," no demeaning comments about ethnicity, religion, or physical appearance, no "personal attacks," and the like.[33]

But even the strongest statement does not mean much if it cannot be enforced. The *New Haven Register* offered some stern words of warning for would-be commenters even under the policy that prevailed before December 2011, when new, stricter rules went into effect. In addition to admonitions such as "be polite" and "don't hate," the site cautioned: "Users who don't play by the rules will be blocked and won't be allowed to participate." By far the most important difference between the *Independent* and the *Register,* though, was that the *Register* did not screen comments. Rather, comments were posted instantly, and readers were encouraged to click on a button that said "Report Abuse" if they found one that was offensive. If you clicked, you were then asked to explain your reasoning and provide your e-mail address.[34]

The result was the sort of negative, pointless discussion that dominates many newspaper comment sections. I don't mean to single out the *Register.* From my observation, the comments at news sites from the *Boston Globe* to the *Guardian* tend to be repetitive, inane, and frequently offensive. In New Haven, though, the *Register*'s comments stood out because there was a better alternative so close at hand.

The most vexing problem the *Register* had was with anonymous commenters who posted racist messages. It is something that African Americans I interviewed brought up repeatedly, from Shafiq Abdussabur, the police officer I quoted in Chapter 7, to Barbara Fair, a community activist and a critic of police brutality. "A lot of racist comments come on their website all the time. *New Haven Independent,* in contrast, will not allow that kind of stuff," she said. "That's why I don't even read the *New Haven Register* anymore. I'm strictly *New Haven Independent.*"[35]

For example, in August 2011 the *Register* published a story about a man who was surrounded by three teenagers and assaulted by one of them. He pulled out a gun and held them at bay until police could arrive and arrest them. The story was accompanied by a photo of the victim, who was white. The race of the three suspects was not reported, but that didn't stop several commenters from assuming they were black. I saved the comments in case the more offensive ones were deleted later. Perhaps the worst one was posted by someone with a real-sounding name, though there was no way of verifying it. He wrote: "Another great description, 3 young men . . . and no names or mugshots of the 19 year olds that were arrested. Typical covering for the coloreds. If I were that guy, I would hang them from a tree and whip them with my belt. It would look like the movie 'Roots.'" Despite the *Register*'s policy of removing offensive comments, when I went back and checked several weeks later, the comment was still there.[36]

If you've seen one racist comment, you've seen them all, so I don't want to get bogged down in quoting too many. But let me offer one other example. In June 2011 the *Register* reported on the murder of two New Haven men, one of them a former high school basketball star. The story did not include the race of either victim, although, again, several commenters assumed that they were African American. Here are some excerpts from the comments: "2 less 'baby makers' and people living off of the taxpayers. Good!"; "When are we going to start sending them back to africa. THey blame it on guns and everything that comes to mind. In africa they kill each other with anything they can get their hands on. SOOO where's the blame? BARBARIANS!!!!!"; "these shootings save the taxpayers millions. YES MILLIONS! not only in welfare costs but in section 8, food stamps, health care. it is time to consider sterilization as an alternative!"; "We should have kept them as pets in cages. They come out of their mothers womb denying they were born. They are incapable of telling the truth. good riddance." When I checked the site two months later, the first and last of those comments were still up, though the other two had been removed.[37]

It is not as though people inside the *Register* were unaware of the problem. I would have asked Jack Kramer, the editor at the time, about the *Register*'s comments if he had not declined to be interviewed. Instead, I asked columnist and reporter Randall Beach, who told me that Kramer and others knew the comments were an issue and had discussed various ways of policing them. "It's discouraging to me that the people I've interviewed may be held up to public ridicule," said Beach, who added that he at least tried to flag offensive comments posted to his own stories. As for screening comments ahead of time, Beach replied, "It's been said that we would have fewer viewers of the website if we did that, and it's all about drawing viewers."[38]

By the end of 2011, all that had changed. As I noted earlier, on August 22 the Journal Register Company removed Kramer from the editor's post and replaced him with Matt DeRienzo, the publisher of the *Torrington Register Citizen*. And the Torrington paper did, in fact, screen comments. Literally on the day that I was writing this section, DeRienzo sent me an e-mail telling me that he had seen a critical post I had written on my blog, *Media Nation,* about the *Register*'s comments. "Expect a big change on the story comment issue that you wrote about," he told me. "What a glaring disconnect to allow that to continue."[39]

In December, the *Register* unveiled a new comments policy warning readers that their words would be screened before posting. "The *Register* will not edit a post, but will delete those that violate these guidelines," the policy said.[40] The move was long overdue, and it showed that the new editor understood the value of keeping offensive comments off the Web in the first place rather than removing them (or not) after they had already been posted. It was, after all, the brand and reputation of his newspapers that were at stake.

I don't mean to suggest that the *Independent*'s comments have been trouble-free. Perhaps the gravest crisis hit in February 2012, when Paul Bass accidentally approved a particularly ugly comment about Mayor DeStefano—part of a rising tide of online negativity that Bass traced back to the previous fall's mayoral campaign. Bass actually suspended comments for about two weeks.[41]

When the commenting system was reinstated, it was with a few changes. The most important: readers would have to register under their real names before commenting, though they could continue to post anonymously and pseudonymously; they would have to click a box certifying that they had read the commenting policy; and no longer would the three journalists most heavily involved in day-to-day coverage—Bass, Melissa Bailey, and Thomas MacMillan—screen comments. Instead, two other journalists would handle the job, the idea being that they could take more time to do it.[42] By spring, the *Independent*'s comments were more or less back to normal.

Such occasional difficulties notwithstanding, what makes the *Independent*'s comments valuable is the type of people who weigh in. Teachers and parents discuss stories about the public schools, police officers offer their expertise on matters involving law enforcement, and elected officials post on all sorts of issues. But is it possible for commenters to do more than that? Can they actually take an issue and run with it, carrying out some of the duties performed by professional journalists?

Joshua Micah Marshall, the editor and publisher of *Talking Points Memo,* won a Polk Award for his site's coverage of a scandal involving the dismissal of U.S. attorneys during the presidency of George W. Bush—coverage that was helped along by reports from his readers, who were monitoring developments in the story by following local news coverage in their communities.[43] *ProPublica* built a broad database of information on the

Obama administration's stimulus spending by drawing on the strength of contributions by users.[44] Such citizen journalism initiatives are sometimes called "crowdsourcing," a term coined by my Northeastern University colleague Jeff Howe in his 2008 book of that name.

At root, crowdsourcing is not what animates the *Independent*. Bass has come to value the conversation, but he sees it as a way to provide perspective and a sense of community involvement rather than as an extension of his journalistic mission. "I think pro-am doesn't work so great," he said. "I think that journalists have to be journalists. Everything has to start with the journalist going out and doing independent, smart, professional work. It all has to start with professional reporting. I've become more and more committed to the central role of the reporters going out and doing stories."[45]

Occasionally, though, the *Independent*'s commenters break through those boundaries. Perhaps the most memorable example involved a would-be mayoral candidate named Andy Ross, who announced his short-lived candidacy in a comment to a story about campaign finance reform that appeared in the *Independent* in early 2007.[46] The crowdsourcing began after publication of a subsequent article in which Bass asked Ross, a real-estate agent who had lived in New Haven for five years, a series of questions, including what he thought was the "best thing about Dixwell and Newhallville," two African American neighborhoods. Ross's response: "I'm not familiar. Is that a neighborhood? I will honestly tell you I don't know anything about them."[47]

The commenters were not amused. One, posting under the pseudonym "Good Luck!," began with this: "Mr. Ross—I believe more people running for public office is great. And your answers even seemed sincere and honest. But New Haven is a city of neighborhoods and if you don't even know where Dixwell and Newhallville are, how do you expect to be mayor? You should really start by getting involved in civic affairs in a more modest way than running for mayor and learn about New Haven first." Another, "That's a Laugh," wrote, "That is offensive, that someone thinks they can be Mayor of a city, and not even know about Dixwell and NewHalville [*sic*]." From "Our Town": "Just a suggestion, before announcing you're a candidate, learn about us." From "Martin": "Does he realize that the heart and soul of any city is its neighborhoods?" On and on it went.

Finally, Ross posted his own comment—to announce the end of his candidacy—saying, in part (typographical errors are his): "I was blinded by the thought that a willingness to want to bring about change and apply grander visions would be enough to convince people that an unknown and admitted inexperinced person of goverment might be able to do the job. Over the last several days however and after many people sharing thier time and knowledge with me has convinced me that it take far more than just passion to effectivly lead a city as diverse and complicated as New Haven."

It was a classy response by Ross, as well as a demonstration of how powerful news-site commenters can be when they are civil and focused on substance. Following his brief candidacy, Ross became an active volunteer in civic affairs, and the *Independent* has published a number of articles and photographs of local events submitted by him.[48]

I began this chapter with something large—the multimedia education-reform event led by Diane Ravitch that Bass put together—and ended with something comparatively small. Each demonstrates the *Independent's* commitment to an ongoing conversation with the city it covers. That conversation enriches its journalism. Rather than the top-down, we-report/ you-read-watch-listen model of traditional journalism, the news site encourages its audience to talk back in a responsible, controlled manner. By defining itself not just as a news organization but as a forum for civic engagement, the *Independent* has succeeded in building an audience for its coverage of local news and public affairs.

I have sometimes heard it said that online comments are a diversion from journalism's mission. Doug Bailey, a media strategist and former business editor at the *Boston Globe,* has gone so far as to write that comments "are insidiously contributing to the devaluation of journalism, blurring the truth, confusing the issues, and diminishing serious discourse beyond even talk radio's worst examples."[49] In fact, comments can be at the heart of a news organization's efforts to engage in a conversation with its community—that is, with the former audience—and to build civic engagement. Just because managing them isn't easy doesn't mean they're not worth doing.

CHAPTER NINE

Race, Diversity, and a Bilingual Future

THE KIDS WERE STARTING to arrive at the Brennan-Rogers School, which serves some of New Haven's most challenging students from kindergarten through eighth grade. It was half past eight on an overcast, late-March morning. Karen Lott, the principal, was patrolling the corridors of the Katherine Brennan building, which houses grades three and up. Lott, forty-five years old and African American, projected a no-nonsense demeanor, wearing a gray business suit and carrying a walkie-talkie.

A tall girl with long braids passed by. Lott joked with her about the earmuffs she was wearing, but at the same time made it clear she wanted them off. The girl replied that no one had told her to remove them. "You have to be told not to wear earmuffs in school?" Lott responded.

Next, Lott sidled up to a boy she had just seen bump into another student. "Ricky, was that really a polite thing to do?" she asked. "What?" "Just walk into him like that?" She gently put her hands on Ricky's shoulders and guided him in the right direction.

Everywhere you looked, there was an inspirational message of one sort or another. Overhead was a big red sign that said "Never Stop Trying." On a wall in the lobby was the "Brennan-Rogers Code of Conduct"—five bullet points that simply read "Unity," "Respect," "Craftsmanship," "Problem Solving," and "Perseverance." On another wall was a large poster labeled

"Celebrate Black History." In the outer office was a sign hand drawn by the school secretary, Celeste Brown, reading "Only the Educated are Free," accompanied by a smiley face.

I had driven to Brennan-Rogers that morning with Melissa Bailey, the managing editor of the *New Haven Independent,* who had been covering the city's nationally recognized education reform effort since its launch in 2009. By the time of our visit in 2011, Bailey had written dozens of stories about school reform. She had also put in many hours at Brennan-Rogers, a so-called turnaround school—an institution for low-achieving students where Lott had been granted authority to lengthen the school day, hire teachers of her choosing, and get rid of those who didn't measure up. I observed as Bailey sat in on a meeting of eighth-grade language-arts teachers who discussed a class project based on the television series *Lost.* We listened as a teacher sought advice on how to help a student with reading problems. The highlight—and what Bailey ultimately chose to write about—was a meeting between Lott and a first-year teacher who was starting to find her footing after a rocky start. We were allowed to observe this formal teacher-evaluation session, or "T-Val," on the condition that we not identify the teacher.[1]

The New Haven education reform story is about many things—whether administrators and union officials can work together to repair a broken school system; whether poor kids, many of them from dysfunctional families, can catch up with their peers rather than being permanently relegated to the underclass; whether Mayor John DeStefano, who had been in office for nearly two decades, could establish a new sense of mission late in his political career. As much as anything, though, it is a story about race. And that is because New Haven itself is a story about race.

A majority of New Haven residents are nonwhite. Many of them are poor, with about a quarter of the city's families living in poverty. According to the U.S. Census Bureau, about 43 percent of the city's 129,779 residents are white, 35 percent are black, and 27 percent are "of Hispanic or Latino origin." The racial tilt is far more pronounced in the city's public schools: only 11 percent of the system's nearly 21,000 students are white, compared to 55 percent African American and 31 percent Hispanic.[2] The city has had just one nonwhite mayor in its history—John Daniels, an African American who served four years in the early 1990s and was succeeded by DeStefano. Yet the school system itself stands almost as an independent political power center, headed by a black superintendent, Reginald Mayo, who was named to the position in 1992, when Daniels was mayor.[3] The city's board of education is appointed rather than elected, which gives the mayor a great deal of say. And though Mayo certainly had his critics, he was considered so valuable to DeStefano as a conduit to the African American community that his position was secure.[4]

"A lot of people would like to see Reggie Mayo go," said Melissa Bailey, who has had her own ups and downs with the superintendent. "But he has a certain amount of credibility—sort of like an ambassador to the black community. People respect him. He is one of the most popular politicians. He acts almost like a cheerleader for the reforms."[5] That is important, because Garth Harries, the assistant superintendent who actually implements the reform program on a daily basis, is a white outsider who was involved in New York City's contentious school-reform effort.[6] Without Mayo, racial resentments could easily come to the fore.

Given that the New Haven school system and the city itself are suffused with undercurrents (and overcurrents) of race and class, the *New Haven Independent,* on the face of it, would not seem to be a promising venue in which to tell those stories. The staff of the *Independent* as of this writing consisted of five full-time journalists, all of them white, all of them college-educated. Yet the *Independent* has succeeded—not perfectly, but well enough that it is perhaps the one news source in New Haven that is read and taken seriously by black, brown, and white readers of all social and economic backgrounds. It accomplishes this in two ways.

First, the *Independent* covers the African American and Latino communities comprehensively and in a way that avoids racial stereotypes— that is, stories frequently highlight nonwhite people and neighborhoods of New Haven, regardless of whether the topic is local politics, development, a neighborhood fair, or a story about a church, an artist, or a gardener. (Among the *Independent*'s recurring features are "From the Pews," about various religious institutions in the city, and, in the summer, "Gardener of the Week.") In particular, African American activists whom I interviewed were virtually unanimous in telling me that the *Independent* was the news source of choice in black New Haven—a choice that had, in effect, been made for them, as there was no strong black media presence in the city.

Second, the *Independent* partners with *La Voz Hispana de Connecticut,* its landlord, to cover news in the city's Spanish-speaking community. Each week, *La Voz* runs a translated article from the *Independent* in its print edition; and the *Independent* runs translated articles from *La Voz.* It is a relationship that Paul Bass and Norma Rodriguez-Reyes, the co-owner of *La Voz,* were hoping to expand.[7]

The *Independent*'s coverage of a poor, diverse community and its public schools is helped by its nonprofit status. It almost goes without saying that such topics are of limited interest to affluent suburban readers and the advertisers who are trying to reach them. Some years ago, a newspaper editor told me with a measure of pride that he insisted on a robust urban education beat even though it was a money loser. And yes, that paper did quite a good job of covering the public schools. But it was significant that the editor saw a conflict between his paper's journalistic mission and its status as a profit-seeking enterprise.

A nonprofit, by contrast, can concentrate on news that is important to readers who are not necessarily from an advertiser-friendly demographic. Some of the foundation money the *Independent* has received has been specifically earmarked for covering New Haven's schools. In one instance, that led to a mini-controversy. The *Independent* reported that a mother from a Latino parents organization broke down and cried after Mayo and his supporters bullied her at a public meeting.[8] Both the *Independent* and the parents group received some of their funding from the local William Graustein Foundation, which led to some caustic online comments from Mayo's defenders and an uncharacteristically hot retort from Paul Bass, who challenged the perception that Graustein funding made the *Independent* any less—well—independent.

"We consider the [Latino parents] group's public actions newsworthy and will not be intimidated into ignoring public events and excluding any voices in the coverage—even when defenders of people in power start getting ugly and bigoted and questioning the motives of those doing their job," Bass wrote. "We don't fear bullies. We don't fear name-callers or mobs." (The next day, Bass told me he thought he'd made a mistake, calling his response "defensive" and "pissy.")[9] Bass has been adamant about the *Independent*'s journalistic integrity, telling me on several occasions that although some of his funders have paid for coverage of certain topics, such as education or nanotechnology, none has a say in how those topics are covered.

Occasional conflicts and perceptions of conflicts aside, the *Independent*'s noncommercial orientation has left it free to pursue stories without regard to commercial interests. That has resulted in a news site that reflects the racial and economic diversity of the city.

The reason why there are so many African Americans in New Haven is because of an occurrence common to many Northern cities—the Great Migration of the twentieth century, a time when several million rural black Southerners moved to metropolises such as Chicago, Detroit, and New York, as well as to smaller cities. The black population of New Haven was small throughout the eighteenth and nineteenth centuries. In 1791, just 207, or 4.5 percent, of the 4,510 residents were black. Of those, 129 were free and seventy-eight were slaves. (Slavery in Connecticut was abolished not long after through a law called the Gradual Emancipation Act—as pernicious as its name implies, given that slavery lingered in the state until 1848.) By 1930, the percentage of New Haven residents who were black had actually fallen, comprising just 5,302 of a total population of 162,655, or 3.3 percent. From that point on, though, the black population of New Haven began to grow substantially. By the early 1990s, there were some 47,000 African Americans living in New Haven even as the total city population had shrunk to about 119,000.[10]

As we saw earlier, in the nineteenth century racial tensions were stirred up in New Haven over plans to establish "a 'college' for Negroes," shamefully demagogued by the press, whereas blacks were seen in a more positive light following the rebellion of would-be African slaves aboard the *Amistad*. Black families lived in neighborhoods dubbed "New Liberia" and "Poverty Hill." Unlike in many Northern cities, the abolitionist movement in New Haven was weak. A number of white Southerners summered in New Haven, and the controversy over slavery threatened the robust trade that had developed between industries in the city and their Southern customers.[11] Overall, the nineteenth century was a time when the city's small, native-born black population presented little challenge to the white majority's way of life. That was to change dramatically in the twentieth century, especially in the 1930s and 1940s.

For New Haven's white elite, the Great Migration disrupted what had been a cozy if unequal relationship between the city's white majority and its small black community. Not only was the number of black residents swelling, but the newcomers were seen as different—coarser, less suited to living in a sophisticated urban environment. A characteristic example of this mentality can be found in a 1940 book titled *New Haven Negroes: A Social History*, written by a white Yale University professor named Robert Austin Warner. No doubt considered a liberal in his day (the book is dedicated to "the Negroes of New Haven"), Warner was nevertheless unable to suppress his revulsion at the background and habits of the black Southerners who had arrived in his city. He wrote of their "slipshod, cotton-raising way of life—loafing half the year and overworking the rest" and their "gregarious, pleasure-loving, possibly courtly, but ill-educated and rustic" nature.[12]

In the 1950s and 1960s, as New Haven was becoming blacker and poorer, city leaders embarked on what became the most ambitious effort at urban renewal in the country. The campaign, led by Mayor Richard Lee, involved buying up strips of properties in poor sections of the city, razing them, and replacing them with larger buildings aimed at attracting more upscale residents—gentrification by fiat, as it were. The Lee administration brought in some $500 million in federal grants. By one estimate, the city received more than $745 per resident from the federal urban-renewal program—more than two and a half times that of the second-place city, Newark, New Jersey, at $277.[13] Although the new construction was aimed in part at providing better housing for families who already lived in those areas, the reality was that many were displaced. As was the case in other cities, the gleaming new projects deteriorated into vacant eyesores within a generation, and urban planners began to rediscover the virtues of old-fashioned, tight-knit neighborhoods. As Mayor DeStefano said at a public event in 2010, "Dick Lee got federal money to build things that I'm now getting federal money to tear down."[14]

During the late 1960s and early 1970s, at a time when Yale and other college campuses across the country were simmering with antiwar activism, the city experienced a widely publicized brush with the Black Panthers, a militantly radical organization that was regarded as a serious threat by the white power structure. New Haven's brief but notorious Black Panther moment is the subject of a book written by Paul Bass and Douglas Rae, a political scientist at Yale, titled *Murder in the Model City.* ("The Model City" was a nickname New Haven had acquired during the urban-renewal years.) Bass and Rae tell the story of Warren Kimbro, a Black Panther who was ordered by higher-ups to execute a suspected police informant, and who, upon his release from prison, transformed himself into a respected educator and social activist. Among other things, Bass and Rae showed how authorities tried to frame the Black Panther leader Bobby Seale for the murder—a tactic that, had it succeeded, could have led to Seale's facing the death penalty.[15]

New Haven was, if anything, on the verge of something even worse than the radicalism of the 1960s and 1970s—namely, the crack-cocaine epidemic of the 1980s and 1990s. In the long first chapter to a horrifying book based on two *New Yorker* articles that were published in 1990, the journalist William Finnegan describes a virtual war zone, with daytime shootings in the downtown district near the New Haven Green and drug-dealing children whose economic prospects were, if anything, even more dismal than those of their dysfunctional parents. Finnegan quotes a nurse at a city hospital, a white woman who lived in the suburbs, as saying that she had not visited the downtown in many years except to drive through it. Her rule on those occasions was to "keep your doors locked and windows rolled up, even in summer. And always look in the backseat of your car before you get in it." Her fears were not exaggerated, although victims of violence were far more likely to be black than white. In 1989, Finnegan writes, there were 320 shootings and thirty-four murders in New Haven— a higher murder rate per capita than was reported in major cities such as New York, Chicago, and Los Angeles. Twenty-nine of those murder victims were black.[16]

Starting in the 1990s, Bass and Rae write, New Haven set out on the long road to revival. For one thing, in 1990 the city appointed a progressive new police chief, Nicholas Pastore, whose emphasis on community policing helped lower the crime rate and improved the relationship between the police department and residents of the city's minority neighborhoods. Community policing has remained the watchword in New Haven, even if it has been practiced effectively at some times more than others. Bass and Rae also wrote that Yale and its president during the Black Panther era, Kingman Brewster, began a deliberate policy of reaching out to the community rather than turning the university's back on its poor neighborhoods, as had been the practice under Brewster's predecessors.[17] Troubled though it remains, New Haven is a more vibrant city today than it was forty years ago, and Yale deserves a good deal of the credit for it. Not only are Yale-affiliated institutions such as Yale–New Haven Hospital major employers, but much of the emotional investment the city has in school reform derives from Yale: under an initiative called the "Yale Promise," the university has pledged to pay for all New Haven public school students to attend a state college or university if they meet certain academic and attendance standards.[18]

New Haven remains a dangerous place. After several years of relative tranquility in the 2000s, the murder rate began to rise. It doubled from twelve in 2009 to twenty-four in 2010. In 2011, the previous year's total was matched by early September.[19] The website *24/7 Wall St.*, citing FBI statistics, reported that New Haven was the fourth most dangerous city in the United States, though the FBI itself cautioned that those statistics were being used in a misleading and simplistic manner.[20] But unlike the war zone described by Finnegan, downtown New Haven in the second decade of the twenty-first century is relatively safe, with people of all races and ethnicities strolling near the New Haven Green and enjoying the city's restaurants, theater, and nightlife. There is nothing new about the reality that most victims of violence are poor people, whether African American or Latino. Today, though, New Haven—as is the case in many cities—feels like a place where mostly white, affluent folks can enjoy the amenities of city life, while mostly black, poor folks live in fear and resentment in neighborhoods such as Dixwell and Newhallville. It is these divisions of class, crime, and neighborhood, for which race is a form of shorthand, that the *New Haven Independent* must negotiate every day.

The Stetson Branch Library is an oasis. Part of a rundown shopping plaza on Dixwell Avenue, the entrance is graced by a mural commemorating black history in the Dixwell neighborhood, the images of well-known local African Americans contained within the outlines of the word "READ."[21] On the day that I visited in the summer of 2010, the walls inside featured spare black-and-white photographs of prominent African Americans taken by Carl Van Vechten, who documented the Harlem Renaissance.[22] Among the most striking was a portrait of the musician Josh White, accompanied by evocative lyrics from the prison work song "Take This Hammer": "I don't want no corn-bread and molasses. I don't want no corn-bread and molasses. I don't want no corn-bread and molasses. It hurts my pride, Lord, hurts my pride."[23]

I met the branch manager, Diane Brown, in her office. Fifty-two at the time of our conversation, a Muslim, she was thin and intense, wearing a colorful loose head covering. Most of the offerings on the shelves seemed geared toward children and young adults, but Brown told me that Stetson was as much a community center as it was a library. Adults would come in to use the computers. There were two adult book clubs. An after-school program was tied in with the local schools so that kids could get help with their homework. Various organizations and black professional groups also met at Stetson. There was a summer camp program for kids. In the past, GED classes had been offered as well. "We have a large mission," she said. "Our mission is to service the community and not sit here behind our walls and feel as though we can dictate their needs."[24]

Brown, who grew up in Dixwell and Newhallville, was on her third career. She became a mother at sixteen and worked as a cosmetologist. Later, she put herself through Southern Connecticut State University and found a job as a city social worker, helping families torn apart by domestic violence, homelessness, and children in crisis. She got the idea of becoming a librarian when she was driving home and saw a billboard touting the Southern Connecticut library science program: "You, Too, Can Be a Librarian." "It just caught my attention," she said. After that, things fell into place quickly. She was accepted into the program. She won a scholarship from the Bill and Melinda Gates Foundation. And she was laid off from her city job, which meant that she could collect unemployment for a year while going to school full-time to earn her master's degree.

Brown told me that she was a regular reader of the *New Haven Independent* and was especially pleased with its responsiveness to her requests for coverage of library events. She also praised the *Independent* for being willing to discuss what she saw as its occasional missteps—such as mentioning a violent crime that had occurred in the neighborhood in a story about something positive taking place at the library, for instance.

"If I feel as though a story was written and there was a wrong slant on it, I will call," Brown said. "My opinion was validated. They listened to me. They said, 'Okay, you're right, maybe we should have looked at it that way.' And I said, 'You know, you have a lot of viewers now. You want to keep that.' So there's an open exchange, and I'm able to share my viewpoints. And I like that. And I like the idea that people can go up and comment. And people have even said things like, 'Oh, boy, Paul or Allan, you didn't do so good on that one.' And I've read some of the comments. It's not that they're disrespectful. But they're honest, and people's opinion was allowed to be not censored—it was put up."

Interestingly, few African Americans I talked with thought the lack of black reporters at the *Independent* was a problem. Brown, though, was an exception, despite her praise for Paul Bass and Allan Appel. "I think there should be some full-time black staff writers," she said. "We have plenty of published, experienced blacks in this Greater New Haven community that are excellent writers that probably need a job. No disrespect to Allan or Paul, but it would be nice sometimes if a black face came out. And there may be a little something that they put in the story because maybe they went to this library as a little child. There's a little bit of something else that they're going to put into it because there's a different viewpoint. I believe that they should have some black people writing for them."

We talked about the ways in which the *Independent* might be able to do a better job of covering the community if it employed a few black journalists. She mentioned youth violence and how someone living in the midst of it would have a different understanding than an outsider. She talked about the difficulty she would have if she were a reporter working in Guilford, a nearby, predominantly white suburb. And she framed that observation in the form of a penetrating piece of media criticism. "It's like you're writing my story right now. It would be better if I wrote my story. That's the best way I can say it," she said. "I think that's where the media gets into trouble a lot, because they're telling somebody else's story. And then you're always putting your own slant on it. And I think that's where people get into trouble at times."

I have thought about Diane Brown's words several times since our meeting. Part of her observation was a typical complaint that the media sometimes twist the facts to make a better story. Not that she was wrong, but I've heard it before. No, what made me pause was the idea that there is something inherently problematic, or inauthentic, about the reality of people's lives being conveyed through the media rather than by the individuals themselves. Those of us who work as journalists will tell you that we offer a bigger platform, or that we are skilled at separating the mundane from the interesting, or that we are somehow uniquely able to sort through masses of conflicting information and find the truth, or a truth. And I would like to believe there is something to all those things. But on the other side of that transaction is an actual person whose truth is being told, well or badly, sincerely or cynically. It's humbling when you think about it, and we need to be reminded of it from time to time.

I learned some years ago that asking readers for their opinion of the local newspaper rarely yields useful insights. They either like it or they don't, and it can be hard for them to say why, especially if they have no specific examples they can cite. And that's unlikely unless they have been the subject of coverage that they can assess as accurate or not, fair or unfair. In the case of African Americans in New Haven, the challenge was compounded by the fact that the person asking the questions—me—was a white outsider who couldn't find his way around their city without a map and a cellphone GPS. In general, the black residents I spoke with, all active in the community, preferred the *New Haven Independent* to the *New Haven Register,* citing the *Independent*'s in-depth coverage of issues in their neighborhoods and its screening of online comments to prevent abusive and racist comments from being posted. Beyond that, specifics were hard to come by, though not entirely lacking.

For instance, there was N'Zinga Shäni, a Jamaican immigrant who hosted a program on local-access cable television and ran a social-advocacy organization called the OneWorld Progressive Institute. "I think Paul understands the issue of race. I think he does. And I think he's awesome," she told me. "I think the *New Haven Register* is more interested in mayhem than in telling people about positive things that might be happening."[25] Yet she also cited an instance in which she thought the *Independent* strayed: a story about an eighteen-year-old female high school student who stole a school bus and backed it into a police cruiser.[26] She attributed the prominent play given the story by the *Independent,* which included several photographs (though there were none of the student, nor was she named), to Bass's need to compete with the *Register* and local television. "But," she added, "I think that he should have taken a stand and not given it so much space."

There was Gary Tinney, president of the New Haven Firebirds, an organization of black firefighters. Tinney and his group supported city hall in its defense of a lawsuit claiming that white firefighters were discriminated against because they were passed over for promotions despite earning higher test scores than their black counterparts. The U.S. Supreme Court ruled in favor of the plaintiffs—nineteen white firefighters and one Latino—in *Ricci v. DeStefano*. The case became briefly famous because one of the lower-court judges who ruled against the white firefighters was Sonia Sotomayor, who had just been nominated to the Supreme Court by President Obama.[27] Tinney said he had been branded as an anti-white racist in some circles and actually moved outside New Haven "just to get away from everything."[28] He praised the *Independent* for reporting on the issue fairly and for covering his organization's events. Yet he also lamented that it had not dug deeply into the underlying issues, such as whether the tests African American firefighters had done poorly on were a valid measurement.

"I wish that they had gone more in-depth as far as the science behind testing, to really reach out to the universities, and to these industrial psychologists who filed the briefs on the case," Tinney said. "I think if they were able to do that, then they would really have a better understanding of where I was coming from and my point of view." It was a valid observation, but it might more properly be directed at community journalism in general than at the *Independent* specifically. The *Independent* does manage to offer more depth than some community newspapers, both through relatively long story lengths and repeated coverage of certain issues. But breaking news is at the heart of community journalism.

And there was Clifton Graves, chair of the New Haven NAACP political-action committee. Graves is a courtly lawyer who was mocked by Glenn Beck after a video surfaced on YouTube of his leading middle-school boys in a Jesse Jackson–style inspirational chant that ended with them saying in unison, "For I am an Obama scholar." "Dictatorship," "fascism," and "communism," Beck proclaimed.[29] I met Graves a year before he waged an unsuccessful 2011 campaign for mayor, but he spoke with a politician's diplomacy, being careful to say nice things about both the *Independent* and the *Register*. "In some circles I know, the *Independent* has more credibility than the *Register* because of Paul's journalistic skills and journalistic approach," Graves said. "The *Register* obviously has a different mission than the *Independent.* They're advertisement-based and have to do what they have to do. So I think for the most part the *Register* could do a better job. But they *have* done better, quite frankly. Over the years there has been an improvement in the coverage, and I think there's a commitment to be fair and balanced and to address the larger community. I think there's been a concerted effort to do that."[30]

Of course, it's one thing to meet people for polite conversations in coffee shops and libraries. It's another to understand the realities of daily life and to convey those realities accurately and fully. I cannot say I've accomplished that here. What I can say is that important people in New Haven's black community believe the *Independent* is doing a reasonably good job of covering their issues and their neighborhoods.

But there is another side to this, and it is one Thomas MacMillan got at when we talked over breakfast in the spring of 2010. He was a bit bleary; he and I had attended a political debate moderated by N'Zinga Shäni the night before, and afterward he'd gone out to cover a late-night shooting. Thirty years old, an outsider from Northampton, Massachusetts, who had been in New Haven for only three years, MacMillan admitted that it could sometimes be difficult for a white journalist to cover a largely minority community. "Sometimes I feel that there are parts of New Haven that I know really well, where I'm comfortable when news breaks and I can figure it out. Like downtown, or even parts of Fair Haven or East Rock, definitely," he said. (East Rock is a white neighborhood, and Fair Haven is largely Latino.) "But then Newhallville, Dixwell, I don't know as well, and it's a little harder to navigate."

Often, he said, he would find himself in black neighborhoods when there had been a shooting, a controlled situation in which police officers were in charge, and he would interview black residents who had come out to see what was going on. "People humor me," he said. "But going there when there's not a shooting, when the police aren't there, when it's not a big scene, it's much harder to get people to talk to you. Sometimes I get greeted with suspicion. 'Are you the police? What are you doing?' I do think that is a challenge." Adding to the challenge, he said, was that residents of black neighborhoods were less likely to be *Independent* readers than those who lived in white sections.[31]

I pressed him. Did he ever feel unsafe? He thought about it for a moment. "Not really," he replied. "I know there have been times when I've been slightly nervous, but never really fearful for my safety." He told me about the previous night's shooting, which had taken place around half past ten. "As I was walking back to my car, this carful of black teenagers yelled at me, 'You're in the wrong neighborhood, boy,' or something like that," he said. "I was walking on Whalley Avenue, which is a very busy street, obviously. So I didn't feel unsafe. I just felt like, 'That's kind of annoying.' They're just trying to get a rise out of me or something. It didn't make me feel nervous." It didn't make him nervous, but it did underscore his status as an outsider—an outsider who, as Diane Brown might put it, spent his days and nights telling someone else's story.

The first time Norma Rodriguez-Reyes met Paul Bass, in March 2000, she was yelling at him. She and about a hundred other Latinos were protesting an article he had written for the *New Haven Advocate.* Demonstrators waved American and Puerto Rican flags and complained that Bass had shown disrespect for the community by claiming the city's Latino community suffered from "a lack of effective advocates." One woman—not Rodriguez-Reyes—tore up a copy of the *Advocate* in front of Bass and said she wanted to hit him with a baseball bat. (They reportedly shook hands afterward.)[32] Today, Rodriguez-Reyes is the co-owner of *La Voz Hispana de Connecticut.* In effect, she is the *Independent's* landlady. And she is the board chair of the Online Journalism Project, the nonprofit organization Bass established to act the *Independent's* publisher of record.

Their friendship began on the day of the protest. Rodriguez-Reyes told me she thought things were getting out of hand, and she arranged for a security guard to call Bass inside to take a phone call. In fact, there was no phone call. Later, she said, Bass helped her get some advice from the *Advocate's* then owners on how to run a newspaper, as she had come into the business almost by accident after a career as the director of a center for senior citizens. "When I bought the newspaper, the owner leaves," she said. "So now I get stuck with a product that I know absolutely nothing about. I used to cry. I didn't know where to start."[33]

The *Independent* does not reach Spanish-speaking New Haveners except through the one story a week that *La Voz* translates and publishes. Yet it is through its partnership with *La Voz* that the *Independent* stands the best chance of becoming a truly diverse news organization. It is a partnership that has already had significant benefits for the *Independent* as well as for the Latino community. In 2009, Thomas MacMillan wrote a series of articles about a New Haven priest who was arrested for video-recording police harassment of Latino business owners in the bordering city of East Haven.[34] MacMillan speaks some Spanish, and he told me he put it to good use when reporting those stories. The articles, for which MacMillan won a national award for coverage of Latino issues (beating out CNN), ran in *La Voz* as well.[35] Rodriguez-Reyes also told me about an e-mail she received about another case of police brutality that she passed along to Bass, which led to another *Independent* exclusive.[36] "When I see stories that are of interest, I let them know what's going on," she said.

Bass and I have talked several times about the *Independent*'s all-white staff and whether he could have—or will—add minority reporters at some point. His answer is that the *Independent*'s staff grew organically—that he has never advertised for a reporter, and that he has simply hired people he knew were good and who sought him out. He does use a few black freelancers and has had black interns. But since it struck him in 2011 as unlikely that his full-time staff would grow any larger, it could be some time before he has a chance to hire an African American journalist.

Bass has a disarming way of defusing uncomfortable issues by agreeing with the person raising those issues. "You're right. Yeah, definitely a failure," he told me on one occasion when I asked him about the *Independent*'s lack of black reporters. "We've done a bad job of that." But he was excited about his partnership with *La Voz,* and said that it represented the best chance for the *Independent* to address its lack of diversity. He and Rodriguez-Reyes were pursuing grant money with the idea of merging the *Independent* and *La Voz* into one bilingual newsroom. "We're trying very hard to get the money to be one organization with *La Voz,*" he said. "I mean, we work together now, but we really want their reporters and our reporters be one team. We're united now in that we plan some stuff together, but to really have it be every day we want it so we're planning our stories together, we're editing them together."[37]

Rodriguez-Reyes said a closer partnership with the *Independent* also appealed to her because English-speaking Latinos were not interested in reading *La Voz*. "A lot of the younger crowd will not be looking into *La Voz,*" she said. Although Rodriguez-Reyes was middle-aged, she was actually a good example of that herself—she moved to New Haven from Puerto Rico when she was five and was more fluent in English than in Spanish. It was Latino readers like herself, she told me, who wanted an English-language news source that would cover their community.

It was a little before 10 a.m. at the Brennan-Rogers School, and a group of young children had lined up for a bus ride. Along with kids from other schools, they were going to perform at a "Spring Sing." One of the students, a girl, was in tears. There had been a mix-up, and she was afraid that her mother wouldn't know where she was. An administrator assured her that she didn't have to go—she could stay at the school instead. A bit later, Melissa Bailey and I were in the outer office, waiting to meet Karen Lott for the T-Val to which we'd been invited. A mother came in looking for her daughter. Bailey spoke to her in a combination of English and Spanish, and showed her a map on her smartphone of where the Spring Sing was taking place.

After the T-Val, Bailey peppered Lott with questions, asking about the evaluation process, about class sizes, about the possibility that first-year teachers Lott had recruited would be laid off due to their lack of seniority. The following year, Brennan-Rogers was slated to become a magnet school with a focus on media. Lott asked: Would the *Independent* help? Bailey replied that she'd check with Bass. Bailey then asked Lott if she could meet the family of a fifth-grader we had heard about who had recently come back after moving away after the third grade—a time before school reform, when "everyone was running amok," as one teacher put it. Lott said she'd see what we could do.

On the way back to the *Independent,* Bailey asked me to make a stop in a black neighborhood along Whalley Avenue, where a former Shaw's supermarket was being fixed up to reopen as a Stop & Shop. She took some pictures of the outdoor sign being swung into place by a crane. She interviewed a former Shaw's employee, a young African American, who had landed a job with the new owner. "I'm excited. I live close, and I'm one of the experienced grocery workers here," he said.[38]

A white reporter had spent her morning meeting black and white educators and talking with a Spanish-speaking parent. She had also stopped in a black neighborhood to cover a story about economic development.

Perhaps what was most remarkable about all this was that it was so unremarkable. As I have argued throughout this book, the *New Haven Independent's* journalism and its commitment to civic engagement are inextricable. Its coverage of a racially diverse community advances civic engagement by encouraging people from different backgrounds to talk across ethnic and neighborhood borders. What the *Independent* staff lacks in diversity it makes up for in the diversity of the people on whom it reports.

Diversity is also a theme that pulls together the various threads that have allowed the *Independent* to succeed. It matters that the *Independent* is an online publication, because it allows for a low-budget operation, a necessity given that it serves a poor community. It matters that the *Independent* takes interacting with its readers seriously, because that fosters the conversation that makes civic engagement possible, and in turn sparks an interest in the stories it covers. And it matters that the *Independent* is a nonprofit organization, because it allows Bass and his reporters to cover stories that well-heeled advertisers don't care about but are important to their readers.

Journalism's nostalgists yearn for a past that never was. Though the financial woes that have befallen the newspaper industry have surely resulted in less coverage of local news than was the case a decade ago, the quality of that coverage was always uneven. In an ideal world, every community would have a *New Haven Independent*—or a *Batavian,* a *Baristanet,* or a *Voice of San Diego.* But the reality is that, even when owning a newspaper was a license to print money, there were good papers and bad. Indeed, New Haven itself was not especially well covered in the days when the *Register* was solidly profitable. In fact, the current "Digital First" leadership seems more committed to serving the community than has been the case at any time since the late 1980s, when Ralph Ingersoll II was amassing newspapers and Tom Geyer was telling Paul Bass how wrong it was that the *Register* was not running wedding announcements about black couples.

In that context, the *Independent* should not be seen as *the* model for journalism's future. Rather, it is one model—parts of which might be (and have been) adapted to other cities, parts of which are utterly unique. What matters is that the *Independent* exists, it is thriving, and it is likely to continue to do so for at least the next several years. As we grope our way into the post-newspaper age, that's going to have to be good enough.

EPILOGUE

The Shape of
News to Come

ONE DAY in late May 2012, I was paging through Jim Romenesko's media-news website when I came across a picture titled "*Times-Picayune* Photo Says It All."[1] The photograph had been taken at a meeting where employees of the *New Orleans Times-Picayune* were formally told that the print edition of their paper was being cut from seven days a week to three, that salaries were being slashed, and that a substantial number of jobs would be eliminated as well.[2] The photographer was Ted Jackson, who, along with the rest of the *Times-Picayune* staff, had been hailed nearly seven years earlier for his courageous coverage of Hurricane Katrina and its aftermath.[3]

I looked at the picture more closely. An anguished man sat with his head in his hand. A middle-aged woman, downcast, wrapped her arm around the back of her neck. And off to the right, holding a coffee cup and staring blankly, was a familiar face. It was a former student of mine, Richard Thompson. I reached out to him.

Like everyone else at the *T-P*, Thompson said he learned about the cuts not from management, but from a blog post in the *New York Times*. "There was a feeling of shock and a feeling of total disrespect among the people who were there," he told me.[4] Two weeks later it was déjà vu all over again, as not a single representative of the paper's New York–based corporate owner, Advance Publications, bothered to show up for meetings at which individual employees learned who would be laid off and who'd be able to keep their jobs.[5]

Thompson, twenty-six when we talked, had started freelancing for the *Times-Picayune* in the fall of 2009, and was hired the following March as a business reporter. He covered the oil and gas industries, electric utilities, and pension funds, among other things. Even before the devastating cuts of 2012, the paper had shrunk considerably. The business staff, Thompson said, comprised three reporters and an editor, down from eleven reporters and two editors before Katrina. But he had figured the downsizing was more or less over.

"I was surprised," he said. "I mean, we were getting doomsday reports about where the business was going for a while now. But our sense was that New Orleans was a unique place where we were continuing to turn a profit. My head's not in the sand. I understand what's going on. But this seems like kind of an outlier—a strange place to do it and a strange way to go about it."

A week after our conversation, Thompson and the rest of the staff learned what the bad news would mean to them. Management announced that 201 people would lose their jobs, including eighty-four of 173 newsroom employees. (Another 400 people would be laid off at three sister papers in Alabama.)[6] Thompson was among those who were let go. According to the *Gambit*, New Orleans's alternative weekly, Thompson brought a bottle of Crown Royal to work and split it with the business editor, Kim Quillen, who also lost her job. They and others were invited to apply for new positions that were being created later in the year. Thompson told me he hoped to have another job by then, but by late summer he had returned to the paper.[7]

I began researching this book because of a crisis that had befallen the newspaper industry—a crisis that hit its worst moments in 2009. My hope was to show that nonprofit and, to a lesser extent, for-profit community news sites could provide at least some of the journalism that we used to rely on from newspapers, with the *New Haven Independent* as my leading example. As the worst of the Great Recession eased, so did the newspaper crisis. But as the meltdown in New Orleans demonstrated, the problems facing journalism have not been solved. Indeed, the years immediately following 2009 represented not a reversal of misfortune so much as they did a mere slowdown in the rate of deterioration.

Newspaper advertising revenue in 2011—both print and online—totaled a little less than $24 million, a decrease of 7.3 percent over the previous year.[8] Given that newspaper executives such as John Paton of "Digital First" renown are staking the future on Internet advertising, developments on that front were even more depressing. In the first quarter of 2012, newspapers reported that digital advertising revenue was up just 1 percent—the fifth consecutive quarter in which growth had slowed, even as online advertising at non-news sites remained strong.[9]

The challenges are real enough, and as the fate of the *Times-Picayune* showed, they are often compounded by pernicious ownership. Though the paper's Sunday circulation had fallen from 285,000 to 150,000 between 2005 and 2012, mainly because so many people had left the city after Hurricane Katrina, the *T-P* also had some real advantages—such as a 65 percent market-penetration rate, among the highest in the country. The paper was profitable enough to pay bonuses to its employees at the end of both 2010 and 2011. And though cutting down on the frequency of the print edition was not necessarily a bad idea in the abstract, the reality was rather different. Just 36 percent of the population had Internet access; the reduction in the print schedule was compounded by deep cuts in the reporting staff; and the *T-P*'s website was already thin and unattractive.[10]

The pillaging of the *Times-Picayune,* among other developments, led the media critic Jack Shafer to wonder whether "the great liquidation" was under way. Shafer was referring to a 2004 book by the journalist turned media scholar Philip Meyer titled *The Vanishing Newspaper,* in which Meyer predicted that newspaper owners would slowly liquidate their properties by selling off their "goodwill"—that is, by shrinking their staffs and reducing their coverage in order to earn as much money as possible before they turned the lights out for once and for all.[11]

Meyer's book was an argument for quality. Newspapers that maintained their standards, he wrote, also reported fewer losses in terms of circulation and advertising revenue. Among other things, he presented data that demonstrated a positive correlation between measurements of a newspaper's credibility and advertising rates.[12] Unfortunately, with few exceptions, corporate newspaper owners in the years that followed publication of Meyer's book were clearly more interested in cashing out than they were in investing in an uncertain future.

Ownership matters. Ownership has always mattered. And in the post-newspaper age, it matters more than ever. For every community served by a nonprofit news site such as the *New Haven Independent* or *Voice of San Diego,* or by a scrappy for-profit such as the *Batavian* or *Baristanet,* there are dozens, if not hundreds, of communities that are so unserved or underserved that their residents lack the basic information they need to govern themselves and participate in civic life.

You might call such communities "news deserts." That's the term used by Tom Stites, a longtime editor who is the founder of an initiative called the Banyan Project. Stites consciously adopted "news deserts" from "food deserts," a term used to describe lower-income urban neighborhoods where grocery stores are scarce and fast-food restaurants proliferate. Significantly, the boundaries of news deserts and food deserts tend to overlap, as the folks who run supermarkets and commercial media have little interest in serving those who are not part of a high-spending demographic group. A lack of fresh, relevant news can be as harmful to civic health as a lack of fresh, nutritious food can be to personal health.[13]

Stites's idea is a bold one: to launch cooperatively owned news sites in news deserts across the country. These co-ops, similar to credit unions and food co-ops, would be owned by their members, who would pay annual fees or earn membership by working for the site. Someone who writes a neighborhood blog for the site might be awarded with a membership, for example. The members would elect a board of trustees, which in turn would hire the editor. Stites hopes the membership fees make it easier to sustain a news co-op than a nonprofit—although, as with a nonprofit, individual co-op sites would also seek advertising and grant money.

It's a small world. I had known Stites for many years before I interviewed him about Banyan in June 2012, as I had written several articles for him when he was editor of the Unitarian Universalist Association's denominational magazine, the *UU World.* (Stites has a long and distinguished career in journalism, having worked at a number of newspapers, including the *New York Times.*) More small world: Stites is a former editor and friend of Dan Gillmor, who is a Banyan adviser and who provided me with much-appreciated guidance at several stages of researching this book. And finally: When Stites and I met, he was planning to launch a pilot site in the small Massachusetts city of Haverhill. Joining us was a local activist, Mike La-Bonte, whom I had known for several years, and who had helped run several workshops for my students using *NewsTrust,* a social-media tool used to assess journalism for qualities such as accuracy, fairness, and thoroughness.

I interviewed Stites and LaBonte several months before they planned to hold their coming-out party in the form of a community-wide meeting. If they detected enough interest, they hoped to launch their site, *Haverhill Matters,* in the first half of 2013.

Stites's membership goals for *Haverhill Matters* were ambitious. He told me he thought the site could break even if 1,200 people signed up at about $36 a year, which would bring in a little more than $43,000. By way of contrast, Paul Bass estimated that the *New Haven Independent* made about $13,000 a year from roughly 100 voluntary subscribers. Both Haverhill and New Haven are less-than-affluent cities, but Haverhill, with a population of about 60,000, is only half the size.[14] On the other hand, Stites planned to push the idea of paid membership harder than Bass had. Perhaps most important, although content at *Haverhill Matters* would be free for anyone to read, those who wished to take advantage of the interactive tools that would be available to communicate with the editor and with other users would be asked to become paid members—a request that, after a few months, would become a requirement.

"This is different from a hyperlocal news site," Stites said. "This is a community institution owned by a widely distributed, large number of community members. It has to be owned by members of the community, and they've got to support it or it doesn't happen."

Now, $36 a year—about a dime a day—is a pittance for "journalism that's actually relevant to your life," as Stites puts it. And if he succeeds, then there's no question he will have shown the way for a model that could be more easily replicated in other communities than the classic nonprofit, since it would be considerably less dependent on foundation grants. Nevertheless, it struck me that he was depending on an extraordinary number of people to become paid members at a time when we've been conditioned to believe that news should be free. Maybe that culture will change, but it's going to take time.

Stites was planning to launch *Haverhill Matters* with two paid staff members: a full-time, professional editor with roots in the city and a "general manager" whose job would be to build a community around the site and to write. Beyond that, his ideas for covering the news were evolving. Journalism students from a local community college would be involved. High school interns might be put to work assembling a community calendar. Neighborhood bloggers would appear on the site as well. In our conversation, all of it came across as amorphous but potentially interesting— well worth watching, but with compelling, useful journalism by no means assured. Haverhill may be a news desert, but it is not entirely without moisture. The *Eagle-Tribune,* a chain daily based in nearby North Andover, publishes a Haverhill edition. The same chain also publishes a weekly paper called the *Haverhill Gazette.* But LaBonte, one of a number of local advisers to Stites, told me that coverage was a far cry from the days when the *Gazette* was an independently owned daily. He cited extensive coverage the *Gazette* gave to the founding of a farmers market in 1971—coverage that he came across while doing research in the local library. By comparison, he said, the paper provided minimal coverage when he was involved in an effort to revitalize the market some forty or so years later.

"That was a thriving daily at one point," LaBonte said. "What I'm hearing from an awful lot of new people is, how do I find out what is going on in Haverhill?"

Local journalism that people can act on is crucial to making smaller cities such as Haverhill livable. And such cities, abandoned and neglected for the past several decades, may be on the rise, according to Catherine Tumber, the author of *Small, Gritty, and Green.* Tumber writes that the post-industrial cities of the Northeast and the Rust Belt are in the midst of a revival that will accelerate as environmental pressures and diminishing resources make suburban sprawl economically unsustainable.[15] (Tumber is also a friend who provided some valuable editing suggestions for this book.) And though she does not specifically write about Haverhill, she told me it fits the model of a once-thriving smaller city that may soon be thriving again. Quality journalism, she said, is crucial to that revival.

"I think that one of the things that is so important to these places is to restore not just a sense of place but to restore community engagement with place," Tumber said. "And having a fully engaged newspaper culture is an indispensable part of that. Reinventing journalism requires relearning how to be invested in the community again. It's one facet of that larger project that's going on in these places. How you do that is another question. People have to learn how to care again about the world they're living in and have a sense of their own agency in recreating it."[16]

Fostering civic engagement, providing a sense of place, helping people learn how to care about their community in the context of the world around them—at root, the themes Tumber brought up are essential qualities of local journalism. Unfortunately, they are qualities that, in all too many instances, were shunted aside as newspapers devolved from independently owned community institutions to profit-driven links in the corporate chain to, finally, hollowed-out, debt-ridden shells. The sites launched by the Banyan Project may help fill that void. And those values are at the heart of what Paul Bass has been trying to accomplish with the *New Haven Independent* since 2005.

My final in-person interview with Bass took place in the spring of 2012. I met him at *La Voz,* and we walked over to Brū Café, just as we had almost exactly three years earlier. I can't say I learned much new; over the course of numerous conversations and e-mail exchanges, we had exhausted pretty much every topic. When I asked Bass what he had learned during the previous seven years, he talked mainly about his surprise at the growth of the *Independent*—he had originally envisioned it as a solo project—and more mundane matters about such things as the role of opinion and video on a community news site.

But then he moved on to a topic of greater significance—about how unlikely it had been seven years earlier that both the *Independent* and the *New Haven Register,* for different reasons, would be looked to as models for how to reinvent local journalism in the post-newspaper age. In 2005, Bass was a well-regarded journalist little known outside the New Haven area. He was seeking to carve out a niche in the shadow of a moribund daily owned by a corporation that would soon go bankrupt. Outside of New Haven, virtually no one cared about the *Independent* or the *Register.* By 2012, all that had changed.

"I didn't expect when we started that New Haven was going to have two of the most closely watched new-media models in the country," he said. "I didn't expect that one of the most interesting experiments in how to do for-profit local journalism and one of the most closely watched experiments in how to do not-for-profit local news would both be in the same city, that we'd both be helping each other while competing, and that we would be so completely different still."[17]

The road ahead is murky. A startling example of how murky unfolded in September 2012, when John Paton announced that he was taking the Journal Register Company back into bankruptcy. Paton described the move as a strategy to get out from under long-term obligations that a shrinking industry could not afford: debt; leases on buildings that weren't being used; and future pension costs. It was an unexpected development, and though Paton predicted the company would reemerge in a stronger position in a matter of months, his only assurance to worried employees was that their pensions were guaranteed by the federal government. Paton said the bankruptcy was necessary to fulfill his vision of restoring the newspaper business to profitability. The media analyst Michael Wolff, though, mocked Paton's admirers and wrote, "It was a classic disparity between the way journalists wishfully see their business and the way the people they work for see it."[18]

The Journal Register bankruptcy also illustrates the perils of trying to write a book like this without being overtaken by events. I completed my research and writing in September 2011. Through September 2012, I continued to do some updating where appropriate, but there's only so much an author can do with a moving target. As of September 2012, for instance, the staffing and budget of the *Independent* were not precisely as I describe them in the preceding pages, and no doubt they will have changed again by the time this book is published. Thus *The Wired City* should be regarded as a series of snapshots taken between March 2009 and September 2012. The story I have attempted to tell is one that continues to unfold every day.

Bankruptcy has complicated the already uncertain matter of whether the *Register*'s "Digital First" model will transform what we used to call newspapers into profitable businesses that provide communities with the journalism they need. It's impossible to say whether the *Independent* will be around five or ten years from now, whether the Banyan Project will find a way forward, or whether any of the numerous other projects now up and running will be able to make enough advertising money, line up enough nonprofit funding, or hit upon some new way of doing business. Ideas will come and go. Promising, well-funded enterprises will fail. Obscure sites will unexpectedly catch fire.

"In America," de Tocqueville wrote more than a century and a half ago, "there is scarcely a hamlet which has not its own newspaper."[19] That is no longer the case, and in the years to come, we can expect an increasing number of newspapers to go out of business. But as Clay Shirky has said, we don't need newspapers; we need journalism. The *Independent* and many other innovative projects give us reason to hope that out of the destruction now taking place, journalism will survive and thrive—even if it looks very different from the newspapers of decades past, less arrogant, more willing to listen and take part in a conversation with their communities, more willing to *be* part of their communities.

It's easy to focus on what's been lost, and what we continue to lose every day. Too often, discussions about how to save journalism revolve around preserving an industry rather than identifying what is great about that industry and reimagining it for a new technological and cultural era. Fortunately, the transformation will take place—is taking place—at ground level, as entrepreneurial journalists like Paul Bass, Christine Stuart, Howard Owens, Debbie Galant, Jim Cutie, Andrew Donohue, Tom Stites, and a host of others work to bring the future into being.

The next few decades are likely to be as exciting a time for journalism as the mid-nineteenth century, when a revolution in printing technology brought newspapers to the masses, or the mid-twentieth century, when television brought national and world events into our homes. What we are living through now is not the death of journalism but, rather, the uncertain and sometimes painful early stages of rebirth. We may not know what local journalism will look like in the mid-twenty-first century. But it will survive. And it just may be better than what appears in the newspapers whose demise we are lamenting today.

NOTES

Introduction: Apocalypse or Something Like It

1. Job figures: Joe Strupp, "My Top 10 Newspaper Biz Stories 2009," *Editor & Publisher*, December 23, 2009, editorandpublisher.com (no longer available); circulation figures: "Total Paid Circulation," Newspaper Association of America, naa.org/TrendsandNumbers /Total-Paid-Circulation.aspx; print and online advertising revenue: "Advertising Expenditures," Newspaper Association of America, naa.org/TrendsandNumbers/Advertising-Expenditures.aspx. On the closing of daily and weekly papers, see Alan D. Mutter, "Presses Stopped Forever at 140+ Papers in 2009," *Reflections of a Newsosaur*, December 21, 2009, newsosaur.blogspot.com/2009/12/presses-stopped-forever-at-140-papers.html; and on the *Seattle Post-Intelligencer*'s move to online publication, see "The Inheritance of Loss," *On the Media*, National Public Radio, May 29, 2009, onthemedia.org/transcripts/2009/05/29/05.

2. The phrase was used by Stewart Brand, the founder of the *Whole Earth Catalog*, in 1984. The full quotation: "On the one hand, information wants to be expensive, because it's so valuable. The right information in the right place just changes your life. On the other hand, information wants to be free, because the cost of getting it out is getting lower and lower all the time. So you have these two fighting against each other." Richard Siklos, "Information Wants to Be Free . . . and Expensive," *CNN Money*, July 20, 2009, tech.fortune .cnn.com/2009/07/20/information-wants-to-be-free-and-expensive/.

3. Mark Brackenbury, interview by author, June 8, 2009.

4. Richard Pérez-Peña, "*Boston Globe* Union Rejects Deal on Pay Cuts," *New York Times*, June 8, 2009.

5. Colin Poitras, interview by author, March 4, 2009.

6. Richard Prince, "*Star-Ledger* to Lose 40% of Newsroom," *Journal-isms*, October 28, 2008, mije.org/richardprince/star-ledger-lose-40-newsroom.

7. Tom Turnbull, interview by author, June 30, 2009.

8. Alex S. Jones, *Losing the News: The Future of the News That Feeds Democracy* (New York: Oxford University Press, 2009), 3–4.

9. Clay Shirky, "Newspapers and Thinking the Unthinkable," *Shirky.com*, March 13, 2009, shirky.com / weblog / 2009 / 03/newspapers-and-thinking-the-unthinkable/; remarks by Clay Shirky at the Joan Shorenstein Center for the Press, Politics, and Public Policy, September 22, 2009, transcribed by the Nieman Journalism Lab, niemanlab.org/2009/09 /clay-shirky-let-a-thousand-flowers-bloom-to-replace-newspapers-dont-build-a-paywall-around-a-public-good/.

10. Dan Kennedy, "*Global Voices*' Man in Kazakhstan," *Media Nation*, April 29, 2009, dankennedy.net/2009/04/29/conversation-with-adil-nurmakov/.

11. Paul Bass and Thomas MacMillan, "As Crime Ranking Rises, Cops Rev Up Hogs," *New Haven Independent,* May 26, 2011, available at newhavenindependent.org.

12. Adam Liptak, "Supreme Court Finds Bias against White Firefighters," *New York Times,* June 29, 2009.

Chapter 1: Annie Le Is Missing

1. Paul Bass, interview by author, October 14, 2009.

2. Paul Bass, "Help Find Annie Le," *New Haven Independent,* September 9, 2009. All news articles from the online *Independent* cited in this chapter are available at newhavenindependent.org.

3. Annie Le, "Crime and Safety in New Haven," *B Magazine,* February 2009, bbs.yale .edu (no longer available).

4. Paul Bass, "City Cops Join Search for Annie Le; $10,000 Reward Posted," *New Haven Independent,* September 11, 2009. The story originally, and incorrectly, stated that Le was a medical student. The quotation is from the revised version.

5. Paul Bass, "'Serious' Suspect in Annie Le Case," *New Haven Independent,* September 14, 2009.

6. Paul Bass, e-mail message to author, March 1, 2010.

7. "Advertising Expenditures," Newspaper Association of America, naa.org /TrendsandNumbers/Advertising-Expenditures.aspx.

8. Joshua Benton, "Clay Shirky: Let a Thousand Flowers Bloom to Replace Newspapers; Don't Build a Paywall around a Public Good," *Nieman Journalism Lab,* September 23, 2009, niemanlab.org/2009/09/clay-shirky-let-a-thousand-flowers-bloom-to-replace -newspapers-dont-build-a-paywall-around-a-public-good/.

9. Jeff Sonderman, "Paywalled *BostonGlobe.com* Launches, While *Boston.com* Remains Free," *Poynter.org,* September 14, 2011, poynter.org/latest-news/top-stories/145687 /subscription-only-bostonglobe-com-launches-with-boston-com-free/.

10. Andrew Donohue, interview by author, July 6, 2011.

11. Paul Bass, interview by author, June 8, 2009.

12. Paul Bass, "Liberation! Guest Writer Paul Bass on Creating the *New Haven Independent,*" *PressThink,* August 8, 2006, journalism.nyu.edu/pubzone/weblogs/pressthink /2006/08/08/pl_bass.html.

13. Paul Bass, "Here's What $150,000 Got Us," *New Haven Independent,* September 6, 2005; Paul Bass, "From the NFL to Wooster Square," ibid, August 9, 2005.

14. Ibid.

15. I sat in on this staff meeting of the *New Haven Independent* on October 14, 2009.

16. Allen Appel, "He Found a Church—& 'Radical Inclusivity,'" *New Haven Independent,* October 12, 2009.

17. Melissa Bailey, interview by author, June 8, 2009.

18. Melissa Bailey, "Mom's Not Saying," *New Haven Independent,* October 16, 2009.

19. "Upset in the Heights," *New Haven Independent,* November 3, 2009.

20. Thomas MacMillan, "Finance Co. OKs Mayor's Budget Cuts," *New Haven Independent,* May 18, 2010.

21. Thomas MacMillan, interview by author, June 4, 2010.

22. Allan Appel, "Thousands Seek Bargains, Jobs," *New Haven Independent,* October 15, 2009.

23. Allan Appel, interview by author, October 14, 2009.

24. Gwyneth Shaw, interview by author, May 19, 2011.

25. MacMillan interview.

26. Kyle Summer, interview by author, February 24, 2011; smartphone findings: Aaron Smith, "Mobile Access 2010," Pew Internet & American Life Project, pewinternet.org

/~/media//Files/Reports/2010/PIP_Mobile_Access_2010.pdf; broadband findings: Gretchen Livingston, "Latinos and Digital Technology, 2010," Pew Hispanic Center, pewhispanic.org/files/reports/134.pdf.

27. David Mizner, "The Facebook Conundrum: The *New Haven Independent* and the Annie Le Murder," Knight Case Studies Initiative, Graduate School of Journalism, Columbia University, May 2010, 5, casestudies.jrn.columbia.edu/casestudy/files/global/53/New%20Haven%20Independent%20Text.pdf.

28. Paul Bass, "Focus in Annie Le Probe Less on 'State Lines,'" *New Haven Independent,* September 12, 2009.

29. Christine Stuart and Paul Bass, "Annie Le Hunt Extends to Hartford," *New Haven Independent,* September 13, 2009.

30. Paul Bass and Melissa Bailey, "Remains of Annie Le Believed Found; 'A Time for Compassion,' Levin Says," *New Haven Independent,* September 13, 2009.

31. Bass, "'Serious' Suspect in Annie Le Case."

32. William Kaempffer, "Police Sources: Lab Worker Possible Suspect in Yale Student's Death," *New Haven Register,* September 14, 2009. All *Register* articles cited in this chapter are available at nhregister.com.

33. "New Haven Police Department News Release," *New Haven Register,* September 15, 2009.

34. William Kaempffer and Mary O'Leary, "Cops Seek DNA Link—Police Pick Up Yale Animal Tech in Le Slaying—Branford High Grad Is 'Person of Interest,'" *New Haven Register,* September 16, 2009.

35. Melissa Bailey, "Cops Take DNA from Annie Le Target," *New Haven Independent,* September 15, 2009.

36. Paul Bass, "Arrest Imminent in Annie Le Murder," *New Haven Independent,* September 17, 2009.

37. Paul Bass, Melissa Bailey, and Thomas MacMillan, "Cops Arrest Lab Tech in Annie Le Murder," *New Haven Independent,* September 17, 2009.

38. Mizner, "The Facebook Conundrum," 5.

39. Melissa Bailey, "Suspect in Annie Le Case Has Fiancée," *New Haven Independent,* September 15, 2009.

40. Bass interview, October 14, 2009.

41. Bailey, "Suspect in Annie Le Case Has Fiancée."

42. Bass interview, October 14, 2009.

43. Mizner, "The Facebook Conundrum," 1.

44. Marcia Chambers and Melissa Bailey, "Ex-Girlfriend 'Shocked' about Annie Le Target," *New Haven Independent,* September 16, 2009.

45. Mizner, "The Facebook Conundrum," 9.

46. Melissa Bailey, "The Girlfriends of Raymond Clark," *DoubleX,* September 23, 2009, doublex.com/section/news-politics/girlfriends-raymond-clark.

47. Bass interview, October 14, 2009.

Chapter 2: The Outsider

1. I attended the party, which was held on September 15, 2010, and my account is based on my notes and audio recordings.

2. Quotations in this and the next several paragraphs are from Paul Bass, interviews by author, June 8, 2009, and May 18, 2011, and e-mails to author on May 18, May 25, and May 31, 2011.

3. Carole Bass, interview by author, May 18, 2011; Paul Bass, e-mail message to author, May 31, 2011.

4. Bruce Shapiro, telephone interview by author, July 1, 2011.

5. "A Community Newspaper," *New Haven Independent,* September 11, 1986.

6. Nancy K. Polk, "Not Bombing in New Haven," *Columbia Journalism Review,* November/December 1988, 4–5, quotation on 4.

7. Ibid., 5.

8. Carol A. Leonetti, "A 'Fair' Voice for People Is Stilled," *New Haven Register,* March 4, 1990.

9. "Morton Downey Jr. Dies at Age 67," Associated Press Online, March 13, 2001.

10. Margaret Spillane, "Downey Storms the Palace," *New Haven Independent,* August 18, 1988.

11. Ibid.

12. Quoted in Jim Puzzanghera, "The Morning After," *New Haven Register,* August 16, 1988.

13. Randall Beach, "If Mort Represents Civilization, We're in Trouble," *New Haven Register,* August 16, 1988; Nick Povinelli, "Prosecutor KOs Downey Court Bout," *New Haven Register,* August 26, 1988.

14. Paul Bass, "No Regrets," and Carole Bass, "A Different Vision," *New Haven Independent,* June 29, 1989.

15. Quoted in Randall Beach, "Editor Bass Sad Paper No Longer 'Independent,'" *New Haven Register,* June 27, 1989.

16. "*Independent*'s Editor Out; Paper to Continue," *New Haven Register,* October 19, 1989; "Dispute at *Independent* Ends in Arrest," *New Haven Register,* October 18, 1989; Shapiro interview; Terry Sacks, "Gutsy Paper Folds after Huge Losses," *New Haven Register,* February 28, 1990.

17. Paul Bass, e-mail message to author, June 1, 2011.

18. Shapiro interview.

19. Bass e-mail, June 1, 2011.

20. Paul Bass interview, May 18, 2011, and e-mail message to author, May 23, 2011.

21. "More *Advocate* Layoffs," *New Haven Independent,* July 8, 2011, available at newhavenindependent.org.

22. Joshua Mamis, interview by author, October 28, 2009.

23. Paul Bass, "The Cop & the 'Killer,'" *New Haven Advocate,* September 17, 1998; Michelle Tuccitto, "DNA Tests Don't Help 2 Men in Prison," *New Haven Register,* August 6, 2005.

24. Paul Bass, "Who's Afraid of Raymond," *New Haven Advocate,* December 4, 2003.

25. Paul Bass, "A $2M Divorce," *New Haven Advocate,* October 1, 1992.

26. Mark Oppenheimer, interview by author, March 4, 2011.

27. Paul Bass, interview by author, October 28, 2009.

28. Richard L. Madden, "Connecticut Journal: Khomeini No. 1 . . . Rte. 15 Amended," *New York Times,* October 12, 1980.

29. Tom Scott, interview by author, March 30, 2011.

30. Paul Bass interview, May 18, 2011.

31. Scott interview.

32. Dan Kennedy, "Chomp, Chomp," *Boston Phoenix,* May 6, 1999, bostonphoenix.com/archive/features/99/05/06/DON_T_QUOTE_ME.html.

33. "Tribune Buys Times Mirror," *Online NewsHour,* March 21, 2000, pbs.org/newshour/bb/media/jan-june00/tribune_3-21.html.

34. Kennedy, "Chomp, Chomp."

35. Paul Bass interview, June 8, 2009.

36. Ibid.

37. For instance, see Jay Rosen, "The View from Nowhere: Questions and Answers," *PressThink,* November 10, 2010, pressthink.org/2010/11/the-view-from-nowhere-questions

-and-answers/. The term "viewlessness" comes from an e-mail message from Rosen to author, June 2, 2011.

38. Mark Oppenheimer, *Thirteen and a Day: The Bar and Bas Mitzvah across America* (New York: Farrar, Straus & Giroux, 2005), 54.

39. Carole Bass interview.

40. Oppenheimer, *Thirteen and a Day,* 76.

41. Paul Bass interview, May 18, 2011.

42. Oppenheimer interview.

Chapter 3: Rebooting the *Register*

1. Robert Waters, "Jackson Family's Newspaper Dynasty Ends after 91 Years," *Hartford Courant,* May 22, 1986.

2. Randall Beach, interview by author, March 30, 2011.

3. Lauren Kirchner, "John Paton's Big Bet," *Columbia Journalism Review,* July/August 2011, cjr.org/feature/john_patons_big_bet.php.

4. "1755—*Connecticut Gazette,*" Society of Colonial Wars in the State of Connecticut, colonialwarsct.org/1755.htm; Rollin G. Osterweis, *Three Centuries of New Haven, 1638–1938* (New Haven: Yale University Press, 1953), 235.

5. Robert Austin Warner, *New Haven's Negroes: A Social History* (New Haven: Yale University Press, 1940), 53–59.

6. Warner, *New Haven's Negroes,* 66–68; Osterweis, *Three Centuries of New Haven,* 297–301.

7. For instance, the Connecticut Freedom Trail has posted a map with information on twenty-one *Amistad*-related memorials and historical sites; see ctfreedomtrail.org/trail/amistad/.

8. Carole Bass, "Why Luis *Can* Read," *New Haven Advocate,* April 8, 2004, carolebass.com/samples/Why_Luis_Can_Read.pdf.

9. Osterweis, *Three Centuries of New Haven,* 398 and 304–5.

10. Ibid., 398; Eric Pace, "Lionel Jackson Sr., 84, Publisher of New Haven Papers until '82," *New York Times,* September 6, 1999.

11. Waters, "Jackson Family's Newspaper Dynasty Ends."

12. "L. S. Jackson Sr., Ex-Publisher, Dies," *New Haven Register,* September 3, 1999.

13. Ibid.; Waters, "Jackson Family's Newspaper Dynasty Ends"; Andrew Houlding, "Daddy Dearest," *Connecticut Law Tribune,* February 18, 1991.

14. Pace, "Lionel Jackson Sr., 84."

15. Beth Healy, "2 Bidders Invited in for Tour of *Globe,*" *Boston Globe,* August 21, 2009; Dan Kennedy, "Goodbye to All That," *Boston Phoenix,* July 19, 2001, bostonphoenix.com/boston/news_features/top/features/documents/01721875.htm.

16. Casey Ross, "Businessman Prepares Bid to Buy *Globe,*" *Boston Globe,* April 29, 2011.

17. Paul Bass, "The Man behind the *Register* Shake-Up," *New Haven Independent,* November 20, 1986.

18. Eric Boehlert, "Nightmare in Elm City," *Inside Media,* November 21, 1990.

19. Bass, "The Man behind the *Register* Shake-Up."

20. Boehlert, "Nightmare in Elm City"; Paul Bass, "A $2M Divorce," *New Haven Advocate,* October 1, 1992.

21. Phyllis Berman, "A Quixotic Father's Acquisitive Son," *Forbes,* October 20, 1986, 105–8, background on *PM* on 106.

22. Paul Bass, interview by author, April 30, 2012.

23. Berman, "A Quixotic Father's Acquisitive Son," 105.

24. Ibid., 108.

25. Kathleen Morris, "The Reincarnation of Mike Milken," *Businessweek,* May 10, 1999, businessweek.com/1999/99_19/b3628001.htm.

26. Patrick M. Reilly, "Deadline Squeeze," *Wall Street Journal,* March 26, 1990.

27. Bill Carter, "Mark Goodson, Game-Show Inventor, Dies at 77," *New York Times,* December 19, 1992.

28. Boehlert, "Nightmare in Elm City"; Reilly, "Deadline Squeeze."

29. Boehlert, "Nightmare in Elm City."

30. Bass, "A $2M Divorce."

31. Mary Walton, "The State of the American Newspaper: The Selling of Small-Town America," *American Journalism Review,* May 1999, ajr.org/Article.asp?id=3245.

32. Jeffrey Benzing, "On the Front Lines," *American Journalism Review,* April 27, 2011, ajr.org/article.asp?id=5079.

33. Alan D. Mutter, "What Went Wrong at JRC," *Reflections of a Newsosaur,* April 13, 2008, newsosaur.blogspot.com/2008/04/what-went-wrong-at-jrc.html; "Journal Register Seeks Bankruptcy," Associated Press, February 22, 2009.

34. Chris Nolter, "Publishers Look for Answers in Chapter 11," *Daily Deal,* August 14, 2009.

35. Jeff Jarvis, "John Paton on Newspapers' Future," *BuzzMachine,* January 11, 2010, buzzmachine.com/2010/01/11/john-paton-on-newspapers-future/.

36. Board of advisers: Megan Garber, "Journal Register's Open Advisory Meeting: Bell, Jarvis, and Rosen Put Those New Media Maxims to the Test," *Nieman Journalism Lab,* March 25, 2011, niemanlab.org/2011/03/journal-registers-open-advisory-meeting-bell-jarvis-and-rosen-put-those-new-media-maxims-to-the-test/; Newspaper Café: Peter Applebome, "Walk in, Grab a Muffin and Watch a Newspaper Reinvent Itself," *New York Times,* December 15, 2010; profitability: Benzing, "On the Front Lines"; Paton quotation: James Rainey, "News Exec John Paton Is Out to Stop the Presses," *Los Angeles Times,* January 15, 2012.

37. Kirchner, "John Paton's Big Bet."

38. Press releases announcing the Brady and Buttry appointments are from the Journal Register Company, journalregister.com.

39. Martin Langeveld, "Alden Global Capital Drops a Shoe: Is the Journal Register Acquisition Prelude to More Consolidation?" *Nieman Journalism Lab,* July 18, 2011, niemanlab .org/2011/07/alden-global-capital-drops-a-shoe-is-the-journal-register-acquisition-prelude -to-more-consolidation/.

40. Staci D. Kramer, "New Company Led by John Paton Will Manage Journal Register, Media News," *paidContent.org,* September 7, 2011, paidcontent.org/article/419-new -company-led-by-john-paton-will-manage-journal-register-media-news/. Information on MediaNews Group's holdings is from the company's website, medianewsgroup.com.

41. Press release announcing the DeRienzo promotion is from the Journal Register Company, journalregister.com.

42. Jack Kramer, telephone interview by author, May 16, 2011.

43. Dan Kennedy, "How to Handle Comments—and How Not To," *Media Nation,* July 18, 2011, dankennedy.net/2011/07/18/how-to-handle-comments-%e2%80%94-and -how-not-to/.

44. Matt DeRienzo, interview by author, August 30, 2011.

45. Paul Bass, "*Register* Plans 105 Layoffs," *New Haven Independent,* January 10, 2012. All news articles from the online *Independent* cited in this chapter are available at newhavenindependent.org.

46. "2 More *Register* Layoffs," *New Haven Independent,* August 23, 2011.

47. Paul Bass, e-mail message to author, September 7, 2011.

48. Dan Kennedy, "What Does 'Digital First' Really Mean?" *Media Nation,* September 10, 2011, dankennedy.net/2011/09/10/what-does-digital-first-really-mean/.

49. Paton's tweet can be found at twitter.com/#!/jxpaton/status/112629140934492160.

50. "Limon-Fair-Antunes: Uncut! at Brü," *New Haven Independent,* February 22, 2011.

51. I had already formed that view based on listening to WNPR during my numerous trips to New Haven. My opinion was solidified during an interview with Mark Oppenheimer on March 4, 2011.

52. Paul Bass, "Vinnie Penn, Act II," *New Haven Independent,* January 15, 2010.

53. WELI website, 960weli.com.

54. Paul Bass, interview by author, April 30, 2012.

55. Beach interview.

56. Christopher Keating and Jon Lender, "Greg Hladky Laid Off by *New Haven Register;* One of Best-Known Capitol Reporters of the Past 25 Years," *Capitol Watch* (blog), *Hartford Courant,* blogs.courant.com/capitol_watch/2008/03/greg-hladky-laid-off-by-new-ha .html.

Chapter 4: A Hotbed of Experimentation

1. John H. Lieland, "The Paige Compositor," *Engines of Our Ingenuity,* University of Houston College of Engineering, uh.edu/engines/epi50.htm. The article is the transcript of a radio program.

2. Jennifer Dorroh, "Statehouse Exodus," *American Journalism Review,* April/May 2009, ajr.org/article.asp?id=4721.

3. "What We Found," *American Journalism Review,* April/May 2009, ajr.org/images /statehouse.pdf.

4. James Cutie, chief executive officer and publisher of the *Connecticut Mirror,* interview by author, March 28, 2011.

5. Christine Stuart, interview by author, March 4, 2009.

6. Christine Stuart, "National Domestic Violence Study Released," March 5, 2009, *CT News Junkie,* ctnewsjunkie.com/ctnj.php/archives/entry/national_domestic_violence _study_released/.

7. Gerald Fox and Colin Poitras, interviews by author, March 4, 2009.

8. David Downs, "The *Connecticut Mirror:* Former *Courant* Staffers Step Up to Fill the State's Hard News Gap," *Columbia Journalism Review,* May 25, 2011, cjr.org/the _news_frontier_database/2011/05/the-connecticut-mirror.php; "Staff," *Connecticut Mirror,* ctmirror.org/page/about/staff.

9. "Funders," *Connecticut Mirror,* ctmirror.org/page/about/funders; Cutie interview.

10. Cutie interview.

11. Lucas Graves, John Kelly, and Marissa Gluck, "Confusion Online: Faulty Metrics and the Future of Digital Journalism," Tow Center for Digital Journalism, Columbia University Graduate School of Journalism, September 2010, journalism.columbia.edu/page/633/437.

12. The *Hartford Courant*'s paid weekday circulation was about 135,000, and Sunday circulation was about 197,000. Audit Bureau of Circulations report for six-month period ending on March 31, 2011, accessabc.com.

13. "Board and Friends," *Connecticut Mirror,* ctmirror.org/about-us/board.

14. Bill Mitchell, "Nonprofit *Connecticut Mirror* Targets Gaps in Political Coverage and Data," *Poynter.org,* January 23, 2010 (updated March 4, 2011), poynter.org/latest-news /business-news/newspay/100377/nonprofit-connecticut-mirror-targets-gaps-in-political -coverage-and-data/.

15. Daniel E. Slotnick, "News Sites Dabble with a Web Tool for Nudging Local Officials," *New York Times,* January 3, 2010.

16. Ben Berkowitz, interview by author, May 18, 2010.

17. "Mark the Potholes," *Boston.com,* boston.com/news/local/massachusetts/specials /013009_pothole/.

18. Ben Berkowitz, e-mail message to author, June 22, 2011.

19. Berkowitz interview.

20. Melissa Bailey, "Downtowners Hung Up on AT&T Facade," *New Haven Independent,* January 25, 2010, available at newhavenindependent.org.

21. Anya Kamenetz, "How an Army of Techies Is Taking on City Hall," *Fast Company,* November 29, 2010, fastcompany.com/magazine/151/icitizen-bonus.html.

22. Patrick Sanders, "George Gombossy, *Hartford Courant* Consumer Columnist, Cries Foul over Departure," Associated Press, August 18, 2009; George Gombossy, "Watchdog Sues Tribune: Accuses *Courant* of Violating Its Written News Mission, by Pressure to Be Nice to Major Advertisers," *CT Watchdog,* September 29, 2009, ctwatchdog.com/2009 /09/29/watchdog-tribune-accuses-courant-of-violating-its-written-news-mission; "Gombossy's Suit Quietly Withdrawn," *Hartford Courant Alumni Association and Refugee Camp,* February 16, 2012, courantalumni.org/2012/02/16/gombossys-suit-quietly-withdrawn/; George Gombossy, "*CT Watchdog* and *Courant* Resolve Wrongful Termination Suit," *CT Watchdog,* March 16, 2012, ctwatchdog.com/business/ctwatchdog-and-courant-resolve -wrongful-permination-suit.

23. George Gombossy, e-mail message to author, June 23, 2011.

24. "About Us," *Connecticut Health I-Team,* newhavenindependent.org/index.php /health/page/about_c_hit/.

25. Lynne DeLucia, e-mail message to author, June 28, 2011.

26. Financing: DeLucia e-mail; media partners: "Our Media Partners," *Connecticut Health I-Team,* c-hit.newhavenindependent.org/health/page/our_media_partners/.

27. DeLucia e-mail.

28. The original article is Mark Pazniokas, "AFSCME Unit Rejects Concessions, Making Ratification Unlikely," *Connecticut Mirror,* June 23, 2011, ctmirror.org/story/13028/afscme -unit-rejects-concessions-making-ratification-unlikely.

29. Shelly Banjo, "'Connecticut's Paperboy,' on the Web," *Wall Street Journal,* May 18, 2011.

30. Sarah Darer Littman, "Op-Ed: Does Tone Influence Debate?" *CT News Junkie,* June 3, 2011, ctnewsjunkie.com/ctnj.php/archives/entry/op-ed_does_tone_influence_debate/.

31. Dan Kennedy, "Watertown's Net Gain," *CommonWealth,* Winter 2006, 33–38.

32. Population figures are from "State & County QuickFacts," U.S. Census Bureau, quickfacts.census.gov.

33. Christine Stuart and Doug Hardy, interview by author, May 18, 2011.

34. Doug Hardy, e-mail message to author, May 17, 2012.

35. Hugh McQuaid and Christine Stuart, "Death Penalty Repeal in Doubt; Prague Has Her Own Ideas of Justice," *CT News Junkie,* May 11, 2011, ctnewsjunkie.com/ctnj.php /archives/entry/sen._prague_has_her_own_ideas_of_justice/; Christine Stuart and Hugh McQuaid, "There's a Tentative Labor Deal," *CT News Junkie,* May 13, 2011, ctnewsjunkie .com/ctnj.php/archives/entry/breaking_theres_a_labor_deal/.

36. Stuart interview, March 4, 2009.

37. Leonard Downie Jr. and Michael Schudson, "The Reconstruction of American Journalism," *Columbia Journalism Review,* October 19, 2009, cjr.org/reconstruction/the _reconstruction_of_american.php.

38. Hardy e-mail, May 17, 2012.

39. Web-traffic figures: Christine Stuart, e-mail message to author, June 21, 2011; Doug Hardy, e-mail message to author, July 1, 2011; state-budget articles: Christine Stuart, "AFSCME Pulls Plug on Deal; Rejection Leaves Leaders Struggling for Answers," *CT News Junkie,* June 24, 2011, ctnewsjunkie.com/ctnj.php/archives/entry/struggling_for_answers _in_the_face_of_defeat/; Christine Stuart, "Clarified Agreement Reached; Will the Second Time Be the Charm?" *CT News Junkie,* July 23, 2011, ctnewsjunkie.com/ctnj.php/archives /entry/clarified_agreement_reached/.

Chapter 5: Print Dollars and Digital Pennies

1. Paul Bass, "Liberation! Guest Writer Paul Bass on Creating the *New Haven Independent," PressThink,* August 8, 2006, journalism.nyu.edu/pubzone/weblogs/pressthink /2006/08/08/pl_bass.html.

2. Paul Bass, interview by author, June 8, 2009.

3. Steven Waldman and the Working Group on Information Needs of Communities, *The Information Needs of Communities: The Changing Media Landscape in a Broadband Age,* Federal Communications Commission, June 2011, 17, transition.fcc.gov/osp/inc-report /The_Information_Needs_of_Communities.pdf.

4. Ibid., 39.

5. "Become a 'Friend,'" *New Haven Independent,* newhavenindependent.org/index.php /donate/support_NHI/.

6. Dan Kennedy, "Will *BostonGlobe.com* Give Papers a Blueprint to Avoid Apple's 30% Cut?" *Nieman Journalism Lab,* September 12, 2011, niemanlab.org/2011/09/will-boston -globe-com-give-papers-a-blueprint-to-avoid-apples-30-cut/.

7. Howard Owens, interview by author, June 29, 2009.

8. Genesee County population: "State & County QuickFacts," U.S. Census Bureau, quickfacts.census.gov; Batavia population: "Batavia, New York," *City-Data.com,* city-data .com.

9. Howard Owens, telephone interview by author, June 30, 2011.

10. For more on GateHouse Media and its debt woes, see Dan Kennedy, "Local Ink," *CommonWealth,* Fall 2008, 37–42.

11. Bill Kauffman, *Dispatches from the* Muckdog Gazette*: A Mostly Affectionate Account of a Small Town's Fight to Survive* (New York: Picador, 2002), 16.

12. Owens interview, June 29, 2009; "About the *Batavian," Batavian,* thebatavian .com/1917/about-batavian.

13. In addition to my conversations with Owens, I relied on Bill Grueskin, Ava Seave, and Lucas Graves, *The Story So Far: What We Know about the Business of Digital Journalism,* Tow Center for Digital Journalism, Columbia University Graduate School of Journalism, May 10, 2011, 46–48, cjrarchive.org/img/posts/report/The_Story_So_Far.pdf.

14. Dan Fischer, interview by author, June 29, 2009.

15. Howard Owens, "Elba Robbery Defendant Reportedly Sterling Citizen Prior to Alleged Crime," *Batavian,* July 1, 2009, thebatavian.com/blogs/howard-owens/elba-robbery -defendant-reportedly-sterling-citizen-prior-alleged-crime/7373.

16. The *Daily News* is not tracked by the Audit Bureau of Circulations. Turnbull's circulation figures come from a comment he posted to Adolfo Mendez, "Howard Owens Shares His Thoughts on *Patch,* Newspapers," *Inlander,* January 5, 2011, inlandpress.org /articles/2011/01/06/knowledge/current_stories/doc4d23601e083f1832442622.txt.

17. "State & County QuickFacts," U.S. Census Bureau, quickfacts.census.gov.

18. Tom Turnbull and Mark Graczyk, interview by author, June 30, 2009.

19. Mendez, "Howard Owens Shares His Thoughts."

20. Owens telephone interview, June 30, 2011.

21. The interviews took place on June 30 and July 1, 2009.

22. Howard Owens, "Newspapers Started Small, Cheap, and with Different Standards," *HowardOwens.com,* June 24, 2009, howardowens.com/node/7347.

23. Howard M. Ziff, "Practicing Responsible Journalism: Cosmopolitan versus Provincial Models," in *Responsible Journalism,* ed. Deni Elliott (Beverly Hills, Calif.: Sage, 1986), 165.

24. Andrew Zajac, "*Sidewalk* Scares Newspapers," *San Francisco Chronicle,* October 12, 1997.

25. Mark Potts, "*Backfence:* Lessons Learned," *Recovering Journalist,* July 15, 2007, recoveringjournalist.typepad.com/recovering_journalist/2007/07/backfence-lesso.html;

Michael Schaffer, "*TBD*'s Night of the Long Knives," *CityDesk* (blog), *Washington City-Paper,* February 23, 2011, washingtoncitypaper.com/blogs/citydesk/2011/02/23/tbds-night-of-the-long-knives/.

26. Ken Auletta, "You've Got News: Can Tim Armstrong Save AOL?" *New Yorker,* January 24, 2011, 32–38; hiring and salary information at 32–33.

27. Dan Kennedy, "Hard Times Working the *Patch,*" *Media Nation,* August 5, 2010, dankennedy.net/2010/08/05/hard-times-working-the-patch/.

28. James Rainey, "On the Media: Trying to Patch into the Hyper-Local News Market," *Los Angeles Times,* April 24, 2010.

29. Jeremy W. Peters and Verne G. Kopytoff, "Betting on News, AOL Is Buying the *Huffington Post,*" *New York Times,* February 7, 2010.

30. Jeff Bercovici, "The Case against AOL, in Numbers," *Forbes.com,* May 24, 2012, forbes.com/sites/jeffbercovici/2012/05/24/the-case-against-aol-in-numbers/.

31. "Authentically Local Campaign Reclaims the Word 'Local,'" *AuthenticallyLocal.com,* May 12, 2011, authenticallylocal.com/news.

32. Auletta, "You've Got News," 33.

33. Debbie Galant, interview by author, June 11, 2009; Debbie Galant, e-mail message to author, July 21, 2011.

34. "Do the Ill Usually Get Punished at Montclair High School?" *Baristanet,* June 9, 2009, baristanet.com/2009/06/do-the-ill-usually-get-punished-at-montclair-high-school/.

35. Mark Porter, interview by author, June 11, 2009.

36. Tracie Powell, "Hyperlocal Sites Mature as Founders of *Baristanet, Dallas South News* Move On," *Poynter Online,* July 10, 2012, poynter.org/latest-news/top-stories/180489/hyperlocal-news-sites-mature-as-founders-of-baristanet-dallas-south-move-on/.

Chapter 6: From Here to Sustainability

1. "2009–2010 Report," Community Foundation for Greater New Haven, cfgnh.org/AboutUs/20092010Report/Grants/FoundationGrants/tabid/447/Default.aspx.

2. Paul Bass, e-mail message to author, July 27, 2011.

3. Ginsberg's biography is online at the Community Foundation for Greater Haven's website, cfgnh.org/Portals/0/Uploads/Documents/Public/Bios/Will_Ginsberg_Bio.pdf.

4. William Ginsberg, "Yes, We Have a Policy," *New Haven Independent,* October 30, 1986.

5. William Ginsberg, interview by author, October 29, 2009.

6. William Ginsberg, e-mail message to author, June 25, 2012. Ginsberg's comment in full was: "My sense of the *Register* is that it is definitely moving in a different and very promising direction. As a daily reader of the print edition, I cannot say that this new direction is yet manifested in a dramatically different reading experience, but I do think the *Register* management understands very well the challenges and opportunities of serving this kind of community in the Internet age and is willing to make bold changes to act on those understandings. They deserve real kudos for this, in my judgment."

7. "Knight Foundation Fact Sheet," knight.box.net/shared/f9qtbcefrx.

8. Gloria Rubio-Cortés, "An Interview with Alberto Ibargüen," *National Civic Review,* Spring 2011, 57–61; quotation at 57–58.

9. Steven Waldman and the Working Group on Information Needs of Communities, *The Information Needs of Communities: The Changing Media Landscape in a Broadband Age,* Federal Communications Commission, June 2011, 10, 16, 34, and 124, transition.fcc.gov/osp/inc-report/The_Information_Needs_of_Communities.pdf.

10. James Cohen, interview by author, July 29, 2010.

11. Population figures from City-Data.com, city-data.com.

12. Google Analytics numbers are from Paul Bass, e-mail message to author, July 29, 2011.

13. Jodie Mozdzer left the *Valley Independent* in mid-2012 to accept a position at Southern Connecticut State University; see Jodie Mozdzer, "Leaving the *Valley Indy*," *Mozactly*, July 26, 2012, mozactly.wordpress.com/2012/07/26/leaving-the-valley-indy/.

14. Eugene Driscoll and Jodie Mozdzer, interview by author, July 8, 2010.

15. *Valley Independent Sentinel* articles: Jodie Mozdzer, "Update: Suspect in Shelton Standoff Appears in Court," August 19, 2009; "Menchetti Wins Again!" February 16, 2010; Eugene Driscoll, "That Storm Was Insane," August 2, 2011. All are available at valley.newhavenindependent.org.

16. Christopher Sopher, rapporteur, *Seeking Sustainability: A Nonprofit News Roundtable: Summary & Report*, John S. and James L. Knight Foundation, April 26, 2010, 4 and 12, npjhub.org/wp-content/uploads/2010/07/seeking-sustainability-061110.pdf.

17. Ibid., 14–15.

18. Staci D. Kramer, "*Bay Citizen, Texas Tribune* to Split $975,000 Knight Tech Grant," *paidContent*, March 11, 2011, paidcontent.org/article/419-bay-citizen-texas-tribune-to-split-975000-knight-tech-grant/.

19. Public radio information: "Public Radio Finances," *NPR.org*, npr.org/about/aboutnpr/publicradiofinances.html; *Texas Tribune* demographics: Jake Batsell, "Lone Star Trailblazer," *Columbia Journalism Review*, July–August 2010, cjr.org/feature/lone_star_trailblazer.php; New Haven data: "State & County QuickFacts," U.S. Census Bureau, quickfacts.census.gov.

20. "State & County QuickFacts," U.S. Census Bureau, quickfacts.census.gov.

21. Andrew Donohue, interview by author, July 6, 2011. In September 2012, Donohue stepped down as editor to accept a John S. Knight Journalism Fellowship at Stanford.

22. Randy Dotinga, "After Six Decades, *Union-Tribune* Shutters D.C. Bureau," *Voice of San Diego*, September 17, 2008. News articles from the *Voice of San Diego* cited in this chapter are available at voiceofsandiego.org.

23. Thomas Kupper, *Union-Tribune* Sold to Platinum Equity, *Sign on San Diego*, March 18, 2009, signonsandiego.com/news/2009/mar/18/bn18sale105226/.

24. "About Us," *Voice of San Diego*, voiceofsandiego.org/support_us/about_us/; donor information is from the site's Form 990 federal tax return, which is linked from the "About Us" page. Information about the La Jolla Community Foundation is available on the San Diego Foundation's website at sdfoundation.org/CommunityFoundations/LaJollaCommunityFoundation/BoardandMembers.aspx.

25. Jim Barnett, "Comcast's Christmas Present to Nonprofits," *Nonprofit Road*, January 5, 2011, journalismnonprofit.blogspot.com/2011/01/comcasts-christmas-present-to.html.

26. "We Have 1,351 Members. Are You One of Them?" *Voice of San Diego*, voiceofsandiego.org/support_us/; "Be Seen. Be Heard. Be a Leader," *Voice of San Diego*, voiceofsandiego.org/support_us/site_sponsorship/.

27. David Rolland and David Maas, interview by author, July 6, 2011.

28. Scott Lewis and Andrew Donohue, "Changes at *VOSD*," *Voice of San Diego*, December 9, 2011.

29. Rob Davis, "A Newsmaker Buys the Local Newspaper," *Voice of San Diego*, November 17, 2011.

30. David Carr, "Newspaper as Business Pulpit," *New York Times*, June 10, 2012.

31. Paul Bass has discussed finances and sustainability with me on a number of occasions, in person and via e-mail, most prominently on July 8, 2010, and May 18, 2011.

32. Michael Miner, "Why CNC Is Closing," *The Bleader* (blog), *Chicago Reader*, February 18, 2012, chicagoreader.com/Bleader/archives/2012/02/18/why-cnc-is-closing; Tanzina Vega, "*Bay Citizen* Ends Publishing Relationship with the *Times*," *Media Decoder* (blog), *New York Times*, April 11, 2012, mediadecoder.blogs.nytimes.com/2012/04/11/bay-citizen-ends-publishing-relationship-with-times/.

33. Paul Bass, interview by author, April 30, 2012.

34. Paul Bass, interview by author, May 31, 2012.

35. William Ginsberg, e-mail message to author, July 29, 2011.

36. A particularly useful explanation of journalism as a public good appears in Robert W. McChesney and John Nichols, *The Death and Life of American Journalism: The Media Revolution That Will Begin the World Again* (New York: Nation Books, 2010), 101–2.

Chapter 7: How to Win Readers and Influence Government

1. My account of the events of March 3, 2011, is based on firsthand observations.

2. The online story posted by the *New Haven Register* that upset Paul Bass was updated following a news conference by New Haven police chief Frank Limon and is no longer available in any recognizable form. The *Independent*'s first story on the raid at the Yale party is Paul Bass, "Mayor on Cop Videos: 'This Is America,'" *New Haven Independent,* October 4, 2010. Both the *Independent* and the *Register* credit the *Yale Daily News* for breaking the story on October 2. The first story on the sidewalk arrest is Thomas MacMillan, "Top Cop: You're Arrested for Videotaping Us," *New Haven Independent,* November 11, 2010. All news articles from the online *Independent* cited in this chapter are available at newhavenindependent.org.

3. Paul Bass, interview by author, April 30, 2012.

4. Paul Bass and Thomas MacMillan, "Officers Cleared, Dept. Faulted in Elevate Raid," *New Haven Independent,* March 3, 2011; Paul Bass and Thomas MacMillan, "IA: Top Cop Trampled Citizen's Rights," *New Haven Independent,* March 3, 2011; William Kaempffer, "Updated: New Haven Police Cleared of Most Misconduct in Raid at Yale Party, but Officers Must Undergo Training," *New Haven Register,* March 3, 2011, available at nhregister.com; Paul Bass, "Cops Roll Out Citizen Video Order," *New Haven Independent,* March 4, 2011.

5. Paul Bass, "Amid Probes, #2 Cop Bails—with $124K Annual Pension," *New Haven Independent,* January 6, 2011.

6. Thomas MacMillan, "Looney Backs Citizen Cop-Photogs," *New Haven Independent,* February 28, 2011; Martin Looney, interview by author, March 28, 2011.

7. Michael Morand, interview by author, October 28, 2009.

8. Lucas Graves, John Kelly, and Marissa Gluck (contributor), *Confusion Online: Faulty Metrics and the Future of Digital Journalism,* Tow Center for Digital Journalism, Columbia University Graduate School of Journalism, September 2010, 20 and 24, journalism.columbia.edu/page/633-confusion-online-faulty-metrics-the-future-of-digital-journalism/437.

9. "Where Does Compete's Data Come From?" Compete.com, compete.com/resources/methodology/.

10. My summary of the problems with measuring online audiences is based not just on the Columbia study by Graves et al. but also on conversations with a number of Web experts over a period of years.

11. Howard Owens, e-mail message to author, August 3, 2011.

12. "Facts and Figures," National Newspaper Association, nna.org/eweb/DynamicPage.aspx?Site=nna_eweb&WebKey=37b9b1ee-9894-402a-b2cb-934939697678.

13. Audit Bureau of Circulations, accessabc.com.

14. Melissa Bailey, e-mail message to author, July 13, 2011.

15. Mark Oppenheimer, "It's a Wonderful Block," *New York Times Magazine,* October 5, 2008.

16. Mark Oppenheimer, interview by author, March 4, 2011.

17. Paul Bass, "Man of the Year," *New Haven Independent,* December 21, 2006.

18. Shafiq Abdussabur, interview by author, July 28, 2010.

19. Paul Bass, interview by author, June 8, 2009; Paul Bass, "Hill-Trey Truce Struck," *New Haven Independent,* July 10, 2008.

20. Paul Bass, interview by author, October 14, 2009.

21. Mary C. Segers, "Political Endorsements by Churches," in *Church–State Issues in America Today: Vol. 1, Religion and Government,* ed. Ann W. Duncan and Steven L. Jones (Westport, Conn.: Praeger, 2008), 197.

22. Robert W. McChesney and John Nichols, *The Death and Life of American Journalism: The Media Revolution That Will Begin the World Again* (New York: Nation Books, 2010), 181.

23. Douglas McCollam, "Somewhere East of Eden: Why the *St. Pete Times* Model Can't Save Newspapers," *Columbia Journalism Review,* March/April 2008, cjr.org/essay /somewhere_east_of_eden.php.

24. Dan Kennedy, "Disappearing Ink," *CommonWealth,* April 26, 2007, 37–43, quotation on 40.

25. Bill Mitchell, "L3Cs a 'Low-Profit' Business Model for News," *Poynter.org,* February 28, 2009 (updated March 4, 2011), poynter.org/latest-news/business-news /newspay/94390/l3cs-a-low-profit-business-model-for-news/.

26. Paul Starr, "First Read: Journalism Minus Its Old Public," *Columbia Journalism Review,* October 19, 2009, cjr.org/reconstruction/journalism_minus_its_old_publi.php.

27. Ryan Chittum, "Nonprofit News and the Tax Man," *Columbia Journalism Review,* November 17, 2011, cjr.org/the_audit/nonprofit_news_and_the_tax_man.php.

28. Benjamin L. Cardin, "A Plan to Save Our Free Press," *Washington Post,* April 3, 2009.

29. "Religion, Partisan Politics, and Tax Exemption: What Federal Law Requires and Why," Americans United for the Separation of Church and States, au.org/resources /brochures/religion-partisan-politics-and-tax-exemption/.

30. *Abrams v. United States,* 250 U.S. 616 (1919).

31. Joshua Mamis, interview by author, October 28, 2009.

32. John DeStefano Jr., interview by author, April 20, 2011.

33. Paul Bass, interview by author, May 18, 2011.

Chapter 8: The Care and Feeding of the "Former Audience"

1. Rick Green, "New Haven a Leader on Schools," *Hartford Courant,* December 3, 2010.

2. Staff, "Ravitch Sparks Digital Debate," *New Haven Independent,* December 1, 2010; Paul Bass, "Where the Schools Debate Heads Next," *New Haven Independent,* December 1, 2010. All news articles from the online *Independent* cited in this chapter are available at newhavenindependent.org.

3. Paul Bass, interview by author, November 30, 2010.

4. Diane Ravitch, *The Death and Life of the Great American School System: How Testing and Choice Are Undermining Education* (New York: Basic Books, 2010).

5. Dan Kennedy, "Bringing the Public into the Conversation," *Media Nation,* August 12, 2011, dankennedy.net/2011/08/12/bringing-the-public-into-the-conversation/; "Note-Reading, Clemente Deal Spark Debate," *New Haven Independent,* August 12, 2011.

6. The Ravitch forum and several webcast collaborations the *Independent* has done with NBC Connecticut received an honorable mention for community engagement from the Knight-Batten Awards in 2011; j-lab.org/about/press-releases/storify-wins-10000-knight -batten-award/.

7. John DeStefano, interview by author, April 20, 2011.

8. Bass interview, November 30, 2010.

9. Jim Romenesko, "Will Downie Register and Vote When He Retires as *WP* Editor?" *Poynter.org,* June 25, 2008 (updated on March 3, 2011), poynter.org/latest-news /romenesko/89709/will-downie-register-and-vote-when-he-retires-as-wp-editor/.

10. Mark Oppenheimer, interview by author, March 4, 2011.

11. Robert D. Putnam, *Bowling Alone: The Collapse and Revival of American Community* (New York: Simon & Schuster, 2000), 218.

12. Jay Rosen, "The People Formerly Known as the Audience," *Press Think,* June 26, 2006, archive.pressthink.org/2006/06/27/ppl_frmr.html.

13. Jay Rosen, *What Are Journalists For?* (New Haven: Yale University Press, 1994), 64–67, 5.

14. Dan Kennedy, "Thinking Big: Two Very Different Books Share One Vision: The Renewal of Civic Life through a Genuinely Democratic Media," *Boston Phoenix,* September 30, 1999, bostonphoenix.com/archive/features/99/09/30/don_t_quote_me.html.

15. Michael Kelly, "Media Culpa: What Happened When the Press Tried to Get High-Minded? It Fudged the Most Clear-Cut Race in the Country," *New Yorker,* November 4, 1996, 45–49, quotation on 49.

16. Jay Rosen, interview by author, June 29, 2011.

17. Howard Ziff, "Practicing Responsible Journalism: Cosmopolitan versus Provincial Models," in *Responsible Journalism,* ed. Deni Elliott (Beverly Hills, Calif.: Sage, 1986), 161–62.

18. Mark Brackenbury, interview by author, June 8, 2009.

19. Jay Rosen, "The View from Nowhere: Questions and Answers," *Press Think,* November 10, 2010, pressthink.org/2010/11/the-view-from-nowhere-questions-and-answers/.

20. Paul Bass, "New Haven's New Face: The 'Norton Street' Tour," *New Haven Independent,* January 26, 2010.

21. Jonathan Hopkins, interview by author, July 9, 2010.

22. Nearly 7,000 people registered as *Independent* users between 2005 and June 2012. Registration became a requirement for posting only in February 2012. It is Paul Bass's sense that the number of people who have actually commented on the site over the years may be several thousand. Paul Bass, online text message to author, June 7, 2012.

23. Jeffrey D. Neuburger, "CDA Protects Newspapers from Liability for Libelous Comments," *MediaShift,* May 12, 2010, pbs.org/mediashift/2010/05/cda-protects-newspapers-from-liability-for-libelous-comments132.html.

24. Dan Kennedy, "*Globe* Outsources Online-Comment Screening," *Media Nation,* April 12, 2011, dankennedy.net/2011/04/12/globe-outsources-online-comment-screening/.

25. Paul Bass, interview by author, July 8, 2010.

26. David Streever, interview by author, February 24, 2011.

27. danah boyd, "'Real Names' Policies Are an Abuse of Power," *Apophenia,* August 4, 2011, zephoria.org/thoughts/archives/2011/08/04/real-names.html.

28. DeStefano interview.

29. Howard Owens, "The Why and How of a Real Names Policy on Comments," *HowardOwens.com,* April 2, 2010, howardowens.com/2010/04/02/7349/.

30. James Cohen, interview by author, July 29, 2010.

31. Jeff Sonderman, "News Sites Using Facebook Comments See Higher Quality Discussion, More Referrals," *Poynter.org,* August 19, 2011, poynter.org/latest-news/media-lab/social-media/143192/news-sites-using-facebook-comments-see-higher-quality-discussion-more-referrals/.

32. Eugene Driscoll and Jodie Mozdzer, interview by author, July 8, 2010.

33. "Rules of the Road," *New Haven Independent,* newhavenindependent.org/index.php/site_policies/.

34. The wording of the *New Haven Register*'s commenting policy changed after new rules went into effect in December 2011.

35. Barbara Fair, interview by author, February 24, 2011.

36. William Kaempffer, "Man Holds Would-Be New Haven Robbers at Gunpoint until Cops Arrive," *New Haven Register,* August 2, 2011. Although the publication date is listed as August 2, the offensive comment is dated August 1, indicating that August 2 was the date of print publication. The comment was still online on August 26. All news articles from the *Register* cited in this chapter are available at nhregister.com.

37. Jim Shelton, "Police: New Haven Basketball Player's Homicide Was Linked to Domestic Dispute; Latest Homicide Victim Identified," *New Haven Register,* June 26, 2011. Comments were checked again on August 26, 2011.

38. Randall Beach, interview by author, March 30, 2011.

39. Kramer's dismissal: Paul Bass, "*Reg* Replaces Kramer," *New Haven Independent,* August 22, 2011; comments policy: Matt DeRienzo, "Sound Off, Story Comments and Our School Superintendent," *Torrington Register Citizen,* June 23, 2011, registercitizen.com /articles/2011/06/23/opinion/doc4e033c1f95474869823232.txt; Kennedy blog post: Dan Kennedy, "How to Handle Comments—and How Not To," *Media Nation,* July 18, 2011, dankennedy.net/2011/07/18/how-to-handle-comments-%e2%80%94-and-how-not-to/; DeRienzo response: Matt DeRienzo, e-mail message to author, August 26, 2011.

40. "*New Haven Register* Online Comments Policy," *New Haven Register,* December 12, 2011.

41. Dan Kennedy, "In New Haven, a Crisis of Confidence over User Comments," *Nieman Journalism Lab,* February 15, 2012, niemanlab.org/2012/02/in-new-haven-a-crisis-of -confidence-over-user-comments/.

42. Dan Kennedy, "The *New Haven Independent* Reboots Its Comments Engine," *Nieman Journalism Lab,* February 20, 2012, niemanlab.org/2012/02/the-new-haven -independent-reboots-its-comments-engine/.

43. Noam Cohen, "Blogger, Sans Pajamas, Rakes Muck and a Prize," *New York Times,* February 25, 2008.

44. Megan Garber, "*ProPublica* Goes Pro-Am," *Columbia Journalism Review,* March 5, 2009, cjr.org/behind_the_news/propublica_goes_proam.php.

45. Paul Bass, interview by author, May 31, 2012.

46. Melissa Bailey, "Campaign $$ Limit Upped," *New Haven Independent,* February 13, 2007. Ross posted his comment on March 5.

47. Paul Bass, "Ross on the Record," *New Haven Independent,* March 7, 2011.

48. Paul Bass, e-mail message to author, August 24, 2011.

49. Doug Bailey, "Got a Comment? Keep It to Yourself," *Boston Globe,* July 15, 2009.

Chapter 9: Race, Diversity, and a Bilingual Future

1. Melissa Bailey, "The Evaluation: Episode Two," *New Haven Independent,* April 1, 2011. All news articles from the online *Independent* cited in this chapter are available at newhavenindependent.org.

2. "State & County QuickFacts," U.S. Census Bureau, quickfacts.census.gov; "Demographics," New Haven Public Schools, nhps.net/nhpsdemographics.

3. "Reginald Mayo, Superintendent of Schools," New Haven Public Schools, nhps.net /sites/default/files/BIO_-_DR._MAYO.pdf.

4. I made several unsuccessful attempts through Mayo's office to schedule an interview.

5. Melissa Bailey, interview by author, November 30, 2010.

6. "New Haven Confirms New Assistant Superintendent," New Haven Public Schools, June 8, 2009, nhps.net/node/568.

7. Paul Bass, interview by author, May 18, 2011; Norma Rodriguez-Reyes, interview by author, March 2, 2011.

8. Thomas MacMillan, "School Board Makes Mom Cry," *New Haven Independent,* October 27, 2009.

9. Paul Bass, interview by author, October 28, 2009.

10. Black population through 1930: Robert Austin Warner, *New Haven Negroes: A Social History* (New Haven: Yale University Press, 1940), 301; Gradual Emancipation Act: Warner, *New Haven Negroes,* 7; black population in early 1990s: William Finnegan, *Cold New World: Growing Up in a Harder Country* (New York: Random House, 1998), 4.

11. Warner, *New Haven Negroes,* 28–31, 106–7.

12. Ibid., 159.

13. Paul Bass and Douglas W. Rae, *Murder in the Model City: The Black Panthers, Yale, and the Redemption of a Killer* (New York: Basic Books, 2006), 46–47.

14. John DeStefano made that statement at a public event on education reform sponsored by the *New Haven Independent* on November 30, 2010.

15. Bass and Rae, *Murder in the Model City.*

16. Finnegan, *Cold New World,* 17.

17. Bass and Rae, *Murder in the Model City,* 251.

18. Melissa Bailey, "Public School Kids Get a College 'Promise,'" *New Haven Independent,* November 9, 2010.

19. Paul Bass, "24 Murdered. None White," *New Haven Independent,* January 12, 2010; Melissa Bailey, "Basketball Star Killed," *New Haven Independent,* September 3, 2011.

20. Douglas A. McIntyre, Michael B. Sauter, and Charles B. Stockdale, "The Most Dangerous Cities In America," *24/7 Wall St.,* May 24, 2011, 247wallst.com/2011/05/24/the -most-dangerous-cities-in-america/; Paul Bass and Thomas MacMillan, "As Crime Ranking Rises, Cops Rev Up Hogs," *New Haven Independent,* May 26, 2011.

21. Allan Appel, "Dixwell Mural Celebrates Living History," *New Haven Independent,* August 17, 2009.

22. "Portraits by Carl Van Vechten," Library of Congress, memory.loc.gov/ammem /collections/vanvechten/index.html.

23. Robert B. Waltz and David G. Engle, eds., "The Traditional Ballad Index," Columbia State University, Fresno, Calif., csufresno.edu/folklore/BalladIndexDocs.html.

24. Diane Brown, interview by author, July 29, 2010.

25. N'Zinga Shäni, interview by author, June 3, 2010.

26. Thomas MacMillan, "Police: Girl Stole School Bus, Hit Cop Car," *New Haven Independent,* May 3, 2010.

27. Adam Liptak, "Supreme Court Finds Bias against White Firefighters," *New York Times,* June 29, 2009.

28. Gary Tinney, interview by author, July 29, 2010.

29. Dan Kennedy, "Glenn Beck's War on the Obama Initiative," *Guardian,* August 3, 2010, guardian.co.uk/commentisfree/cifamerica/2010/aug/03/glenn-beck-obama-initiative.

30. Clifton Graves, interview by author, July 30, 2010.

31. Thomas MacMillan, interview by author, June 4, 2010.

32. JoAnne Viviano and Susan A. Zavadsky, "Crowd Assails *Advocate* Reporter," *New Haven Register,* March 28, 2000.

33. Norma Rodriguez-Reyes, interview by author, March 2, 2011.

34. The first of those stories was Thomas MacMillan, "Cross-Border Cops Arrest Father Jim," *New Haven Independent,* March 3, 2009.

35. "MacMillan Wins National Award," *New Haven Independent,* May 14, 2010.

36. Melinda Tuhus and Thomas MacMillan, "Cop Accused of Brutality—a 9th Time," *New Haven Independent,* January 17, 2011.

37. Bass interview, May 18, 2011; as of June 2012, when research for this book ended, Bass had not yet succeeded in securing the grant money he sought.

38. Melissa Bailey, "Stop & Shop Hires 150 Workers—All from City," *New Haven Independent,* March 31, 2011.

Epilogue: The Shape of News to Come

1. "*Times-Picayune* Photo Says It All," *JimRomensko.com,* May 25, 2012, jimromenesko .com/2012/05/25/times-picayune-photo-says-it-all/.

2. David Carr, "*Times-Picayune* Confirms Staff Cuts and 3-Day-a-Week Print Sched-

ule," *Media Decoder* (blog), *New York Times,* May 24, 2012, mediadecoder.blogs.nytimes .com/2012/05/24/new-orleans-times-picayune-to-cut-staff-and-cease-daily-newspaper/.

3. Beverly Spicer, "The Ordeal of Ted Jackson and the *New Orleans Times-Picayune,*" *Digital Journalist,* December 2005, digitaljournalist.org/issue0512/jackson_intro.html.

4. Richard Thompson, telephone interview by author, June 7, 2012.

5. Kevin Allman, "After the Cuts at the *Times-Picayune,*" *The Media's Lovely Corpse* (blog), *Gambit,* June 13, 2012, bestofneworleans.com/blogofneworleans/archives/2012/06/13 /after-the-cuts-at-the-times-picayune.

6. Steve Myers, "Advance Publications Lays Off 600 People at *Times-Picayune,* Alabama Papers," *Poynter.org,* June 12, 2012, poynter.org/latest-news/mediawire/176888/employee -meetings-scheduled-today-at-advance-papers-in-new-orleans-alabama-times-picayune -birmingham-news-mobile-press-register-huntsville-times/.

7. Richard Thompson, e-mail message to author, June 12, 2012.

8. "Trends & Numbers," Newspaper Association of America, naa.org/Trends-and -Numbers/Advertising-Expenditures/Annual-All-Categories.aspx.

9. Jennifer Saba, "Analysis: In Scare for Newspapers, Digital Ad Growth Stalls," Reuters, June 7, 2012, reuters.com/article/2012/06/07/us-newspaper-digital-ads -idUSBRE85605E20120607.

10. Jason Berry, "Rolling the Dice at the *Times-Picayune,*" *Nation,* June 11, 2012, thenation.com/article/168330/rolling-dice-times-picayune.

11. Jack Shafer, "The Great Newspaper Liquidation," Reuters, June 5, 2012, blogs.reuters .com/jackshafer/2012/06/05/the-great-newspaper-liquidation/.

12. Philip Meyer, *The Vanishing Newspaper: Saving Journalism in the Information Age* (Columbia: University of Missouri Press, 2004), 54.

13. Much of the information about the Banyan Project is taken from its website, ban-yanproject.com. The rest is from an interview the author conducted with Tom Stites and Mike LaBonte on June 7, 2012.

14. "State & County QuickFacts," U.S. Census Bureau, quickfacts.census.gov. Haverhill is not nearly as poor as New Haven, as per capita and median family income are only slightly below the average for Massachusetts as a whole.

15. Catherine Tumber, *Small, Gritty, and Green: The Promise of America's Smaller Industrial Cities in a Low-Carbon World* (Cambridge: MIT Press, 2011).

16. Catherine Tumber, interview by author, June 8, 2012.

17. Paul Bass, interview by author, May 31, 2012.

18. Joshua Benton, "Journal Register Co. Declares Bankruptcy . . . Again: Is This the Industry's First Real Reboot?" *Nieman Journalism Lab,* September 5, 2012, niemanlab .org/2012/09/journal-register-co-declares-bankruptcy-again-is-this-the-industrys-first-real -reboot/; Christine Haughney, "For Paton, Bankruptcy for Journal Register Is 'Embarrassing' but Necessary," *Media Decoder* (blog), *New York Times,* September 11, 2012, mediadecoder .blogs.nytimes.com/2012/09/11/for-paton-bankruptcy-for-journal-register-is -embarrassing-but-necessary/; Michael Wolff, "The Journal Register Debacle: Why Chapter 11 Comes Before 'Digital First,'" *Guardian,* September 10, 2012, guardian.co.uk/commentisfree /2012/sep/10/journal-register-chapter-11-digital-first.

19. Alexis de Tocqueville, *Democracy in America,* vol. 1 (1835), part 2, chap. 3.

ACKNOWLEDGMENTS

In the fall of 2009 I feared that my book project had gone off the rails. I had spent the previous six months investigating various online news sites for what I hoped would become a survey of the burgeoning world of digital journalism. But I was dispirited at the prospect of writing a book that skipped from topic to topic without saying all that much about any one of them.

My mind kept wandering back to New Haven where, several months earlier, I had met Paul Bass, the editor and founder of the *New Haven Independent,* a nonprofit online news site. Bass and his staff practiced the sort of in-depth community journalism that appealed to me. New Haven seemed like an interesting place, and it was just a few hours' drive from my home on Boston's North Shore.

With the encouragement of my Northeastern University colleagues Stephen Burgard, the director of our School of Journalism, and Alan Schroeder, a professor of journalism, I discarded my original idea in favor of a comprehensive examination of the *Independent,* supplemented by several other projects that I believed were serious and substantial enough to warrant inclusion—especially the *Batavian, CT News Junkie,* the *Connecticut Mirror, Voice of San Diego,* and *Baristanet.* Steve and Alan deserve my thanks for trusting my instinct to go narrow and deep rather than wide and shallow. Another Northeastern journalism professor, my old friend Bill Kirtz, provided invaluable help with proofreading. All of my colleagues in the School of Journalism have been wonderfully supportive of my work, and the university itself was generous with course releases and funding for travel expenses.

Journalists should never take for granted the willingness of people to share their stories. It is a privilege, and we honor that privilege by telling their stories honestly and fairly. Everyone who is quoted in this book, as well as those who were interviewed but not quoted, have my thanks and appreciation. In particular, for three years Paul and Carole Bass opened their home, their files, and their lives to me. Reporters are taught not to get too close to their subjects. But now that this project is behind me, I hope I can say that I consider the Basses to be friends.

In 1993, when I was working as an editor at the *Boston Phoenix,* I asked the top editor, Peter Kadzis, if he would consider me for the political columnist's job, which had just opened up. He wanted to hire someone else. A year later the media columnist's position became available, and Peter offered it to me. I took it. Of such random occurrences are careers sometimes made. I have spent the past two decades reporting on and commenting about the news media, both at the *Phoenix* and in various other capacities, and have had a lot of fun along the way. Peter and the *Phoenix*'s founder and publisher, Stephen Mindich, were great bosses, tough but supportive and loyal, and I value their friendship to this day.

Two other friends from my years at the *Phoenix* played an important role in bringing this book to fruition. Susan Ryan-Vollmar, a communications consultant and the principal of Influence Consulting, edited the entire manuscript, making a number of valuable suggestions for improving it. Catherine Tumber, the author of *Small, Gritty, and Green: The Promise of America's Smaller Industrial Cities in a Low-Carbon World* (2011), reviewed and edited the first several chapters. It was a privilege to be able to engage editors as accomplished as Susan and Cathy, and *The Wired City* is a much better book for their efforts.

I was also fortunate to enter into a relationship with University of Massachusetts Press. Brian Halley, the editor who acquired the project, guided me through the sometimes arcane world of academic publishing and coached me through the process of proposals and approvals. Managing editor Carol Betsch and her colleague Mary Bellino were friendly and helpful in response to my e-mails. Barbara Folsom expertly copyedited my manuscript. No doubt she is still vacuuming deleted hyphens out of her carpet. Production manager Jack Harrison came up with the book's striking design, and promotion manager Karen Fisk diligently pursued publicity opportunities. Steven Moore did a fine job compiling the index.

As is customary in academic publishing, my first draft was reviewed by outside readers. Usually those readers choose to remain anonymous. One, though, did not: William Densmore, the director and editor of the Media Giraffe Project at the University of Massachusetts Amherst. I had known Bill for several years, and respected and admired his tireless advocacy of new forms of journalism to replace those that were passing from the scene.

Bill's review took the form of a long, detailed memo with numerous suggestions for follow-up. Densmore is also an adviser to the Banyan Project, and it was his memo that convinced me to build my Epilogue around that nascent idea.

Another adviser to the Banyan Project who provided me with wise counsel on several occasions was Dan Gillmor, who is among the most respected thinkers in the fields of online journalism, citizen media, and news ethics. Dan's books, *We the Media: Grassroots Journalism by the People, for the People* (2004) and *Mediactive* (2010), are foundational documents of the post-newspaper age.

Finally, I could not have written this book with the support of my family. It was during this period that our children, Tim and Becky, grew from teenagers to young adults on the verge of independence. They are smart, funny, responsible, and caring, yet in other ways they are so different that it is sometimes hard to believe they grew up in the same house. It is my privilege to be their father.

My wife, Barbara Kennedy, is my source of love, support, and friendship, as well as my favorite editor. I cannot imagine taking on a project of any significance without her. She is not just my wife and best friend. She is someone I look up to.

INDEX

Dan Kennedy is an assistant professor of journalism at Northeastern University and an award-winning media analyst who has written for the *Guardian, Nieman Reports* and the *Nieman Journalism Lab,* the *Huffington Post, Slate, Salon,* the *New Republic, CommonWealth* magazine, the *Boston Globe,* and other publications. He is a regular panelist on *Beat the Press,* a weekly program on WGBH-TV in Boston that covers media issues. His first book, *Little People: Seeing the World through My Daughter's Eyes* (Rodale, 2003), a memoir about raising a daughter with dwarfism, received critical praise from the *Wall Street Journal,* the *Boston Globe,* and the *Providence Journal.* From 1994 to 2005 he was the media columnist for the *Boston Phoenix,* where he is still a contributor. He and his wife, Barbara Kennedy, a library teacher, live on Boston's North Shore and are the parents of two adult children. For more information, visit Kennedy's blog, Media Nation, at www.dankennedy.net.